EXPLORING THE ESSENCE & MEANING FROM THE SOUND OF EXPERIENCES

Qualitative Research

By

Prof. Resty Samosa

COPYRIGHT © EXPLORING THE ESSENCE & MEANING FROM THE SOUND OF EXPERIENCES:
Qualitative Research
By Prof. Resty Samosa

Edited by Marie Ezekiel

ISBN:
Softbound/Paperback-978-621-470-106-3
Hardbound-978-621-470-107-0
Mobile/Kindle-978-621-470-108-7

Published by:
Poetry Planet Book Publishing House
Rosario, Pozorrubio, Pangasinan, Philippines
Contact No.: 09554960044
Email: maritesritumalta@gmail.com

PREFACE

Nowadays, qualitative research is a major branch of inquiry in the social sciences, encompassing a wide range of phenomena. Qualitative studies share a naturalistic and situated concern as the basis of their inquiry: they seek to study phenomena through a person's perspective, paying attention to the context where they emerge.

Considering this aim, experience and meaning appear as crucial concepts for reaching a deeper understanding of a participant's perspective, thus improving the qualitative comprehension of the social and psychological phenomena studied. Moreover, Qualitative research involves asking participants about their experiences of things that happen in their lives. It enables researchers to obtain insights into what it feels like to be another person and to understand the world as another experiences it.

Despite the relevance of these concepts—for methodological design, data production strategy, information analysis, and results from presentation, it is rather unusual to find any academic references on what these concepts mean for qualitative researchers. This, regrettably, reflects the scholarly neglect of the study of what is involved in capturing human phenomena through the experiences and meanings of participants. For the author, the aim of this book is to contribute to the growing body of academic references in qualitative research is still considered a "minority" type of research compared to quantitative research.

This book was written for the purpose of teaching the rudiments of qualitative research design in the simplest and most practical way. Each module begins with a tough discussion of qualitative research concepts, illustrative examples of research parts and ends with assessment tasks. It is followed by performance tasks geared to equip the students with the skills in developing competencies in qualitative research writing.

The book is divided into the following modules:

Module 1: Nature of Inquiry and Research;

Module 2: Qualitative Research and Its Importance in Daily Life;

Module 3: Identifying the Inquiry and Stating the Problem;

Module 4: Learning from Others and Reviewing the Literature;

Module 5: Understanding Data and Ways To Systematically Collect Data;

Module 6: Finding Answers through Data Collection

Module 7: Analyzing the Meaning of the Data and Drawing Conclusions;

Module 8: Reporting and Sharing the Findings.

The students using this book would easily and readily comprehend and absorb its content and the teachers will also find the discussion very practical, relevant, and easier to disseminate.

It is hoped that with this simplified textbook in qualitative research, the student- beginners in qualitative research will gain an adequate orientation on the subject of qualitative research.

Prof. Resty C. Samosa

TABLE OF CONTENTS

MODULE 1:

NATURE OF INQUIRY & RESEARCH

LEARNING OUTCOMES
At the end of this module, students should be able to:

1. shares research experiences and knowledge

2. explains the importance of research in daily life

3. describes characteristics, processes, and ethics of research

4. differentiates quantitative from qualitative research

5. provide examples of research in areas of interest (arts, humanities, sports, science, business, agriculture and fisheries, information and communication technology, and social inquiry)

What is Research?

Let's begin finding an answer to this question by examining the definition of research according to many experts. Different perspectives on the subjects have been adopted that resulted in the following definitions:

Research derives new knowledge, generally involving studious inquiry and a search for new theories in order to contribute to an existing academic wealth of Knowledge (Oldfield, 2015).

Research is the scientific investigation of phenomena that includes collection, presentation, analysis, and interpretation of facts that line an individual's speculation with reality (Serrano, 2016).

Research is a systematic inquiry that explains or describes a phenomenon, predicts an outcome, and poses questions for further studies (Barrot, 2018).

Research is a scholarly activity (that means, an activity related to your education or academic journey) that consists of addressing a specific problem through the collection, analysis, and interpretation of data (Wa-Mbaleka & Gladstone, 2018).

Research is a systematic process of gathering, interpreting, and analyzing information that may lead to the development of generalizations, principles, or theories resulting in a prediction that describe, explain, predict, control, and resolve the specific problem encountered and observable phenomenon

Research involves inductive and deductive methods. Research is done in Inductive methods if *"works from the bottom-up, using the participants' views to build broader themes and generate a theory interconnecting the themes"*, it means to analyze the observed phenomenon and identify the general principles, structures, or processes underlying the phenomenon observed; while, deductive methods *"work from the 'top-down, from a theory to hypotheses to data to add to or contradict the theory"* which mean to verify the hypothesized principles through observations. The purposes are different: one is to develop explanations (inductive - qualitative research), and the other is to test the validity of the explanations (deductive - quantitative research). Whichever your method is, you should produce a research paper as the final output of your academic investigation.

Aims of Research

Research is conducted to attain one or more of the following major aims (Gregorio, 2000).

1. To serve as a tool in the continued search for more knowledge to advance the frontier of science, and satisfy curiosity inherent to inquisitive minds. Research leads to discoveries, inventions, and more exploration of the universe.

2. To enhance a greater understanding of human behavior, environment, and their relationships and interactions.

3. To generate and develop more efficient technologies and innovations essential for socio-economic development and improvement.

4. To test, verify, modify, or evaluate new and existing technologies and innovation in the fields of agriculture, fishery, and other sciences and industries.

5. To test known theories and hypotheses for their validity.

Characteristics of Research

As already pointed out, research as a process has distinguishing characteristics, which differentiates it from other methods of gaining knowledge or solving problems. Let us go over some of these characteristics of research (Garcia, 2003).

1. **Systematic**. It is systematic as there are interrelated steps or procedures a researcher has to observe in solving the problem.

2. **Objective**. It is not based on guesswork. This is because empirical data have to be gathered by the researcher before making any conclusion or proposing any solution to an identified difficulty or problem.

3. **Comprehensive**. If a researcher is serious about understanding a phenomenon, he has to examine and analyze all its aspects or angles before making a generalization or conclusion.

4. **Critical**. This means that procedures employed by the researcher must be able to withstand critical scrutiny by other researchers.

5. **Rigorous**. It is rigorous as procedures to be followed in solving a problem should be

relevant, appropriate, justified, and strictly observed.

6. **Valid**. Whenever a researcher formulates conclusions, these are based on actual findings.

7. **Verified**. Research is said to be verified as other researchers can check on the correctness of its results by replicating the study, based on the methods and procedures employed by the researcher.

8. **Empirical.** Research is empirical as generalization drawn by a researcher is rotted upon hard evidence gathered from information collected from real-life experiences or observations.

Ten Qualities of a Good Researcher

With the abovementioned characteristics of good research, it follows that the researcher should develop the following qualities (Toledo-Pereyra, 2012).

1. **Interest.** It is obvious that without interest, desire, or disposition toward research, we

cannot even start thinking about developing some kind of research. This kind of research is not as important as attempting to get involved in some aspect of research, from thinking of the idea to the different steps involved in completing the process. The ideal circumstance would be that the possible trainee has a question that he/she wants to answer and, therefore, research is the conduit for reaching the sought-out level of understanding or offering a well-analyzed response to the question. It is suggested would be to get interested in research and you will find a universe of worthwhile considerations that satisfy your desire for having appropriate and rational responses.

2. **Motivation.** Even though this quality is very close to the previous one of having interest/desire/disposition toward research, it is somewhat different in that motivation takes us one step further to the initial interest reflected toward the research field. The dictionary gives an accurate characterization of motivation as

"providing for a reason to act in a certain way," the equivalent of "inducement, cause, impetus". In this way, motivation provides the reasoning behind the initial interest in research. It gives the impetus for advancing the initial desire expressed toward the research process. It gives us the inducement for continuing our path of research interest.

3. **Inquisitiveness.** This quality is not difficult to introduce since an inquisitive mind is almost a requirement for a good research experience. Without inquisitiveness, it would be in many ways impossible to advance the research enterprise. It is suggested to the newly initiated in research is to find the ways in which you can advance your questioning one step beyond your current understanding of facts. Being inquisitive is being curious or, as many dictionaries would describe it, being "unduly curious". Asking frequent questions and showing eagerness for knowledge completes the sphere of the inquisitive mind or the inquisitive individual. In research, this is a

fundamental quality that accompanies the initial interest and motivation expressed for research matters.

4. **Commitment.** The development of a good research plan or strategy needs commitment to move forward in the completion of the research project. The perseverant hand of the researcher—from the conception of the idea through the required regulatory items and the collection and analysis of the data—is fundamental in the completion of the research study. Remaining committed to the research project is an essential quality in the development and execution of the study. Commitment takes the researcher to the end of the planned experiment but at the same time permits the advance of plans for possible publication in a referred journal and/or presentation at a recognized venue.

5. **Sacrifice**. The researcher is not only interested, motivated, inquisitive, and committed to do research, but is also ready to sacrifice time and efforts in other areas to

apply to his/her research plans and ideas. With some personal sacrifice, it is possible to create an atmosphere of progress and advancement for the studies being carried out. And this will be indispensable in the research work. Sacrifice becomes an intricate part of the researcher's strategy since it is necessary when using a commitment to complete the research operation.

6. **Excellence.** When doing research, the researcher should be ready to excel in developing the research idea, the research hypothesis, the experimental design, and the appropriate collection of data. Taking into consideration these various stages of research is fundamental in the completion of the research protocol. Excelling or excellence also applies to the analysis and interpretation of the data, including the writing of the study and its presentation, which will culminate the long hours of dedication to the research.

7. **Knowledge.** It is evident that knowledge is a quality that the researcher cannot do without,

since the whole research project depends on it. Knowledge equals advancement, which at the same time equals innovation and discovery. In order for the research idea to progress, one needs knowledge to support it and eventually move it forward. Knowledge is behind any substantive progress in research. Acquiring knowledge becomes then the main foundation on which research will stand.

8. **Recognition.** The recognition quality more generally refers to being aware of the research project and how to carry it out and evaluate it. Recognition is needed when the researcher is attempting to maintain a good evaluation path for acquired data and its subsequent assessment. Recognizing the research process, how it is evolving, and whether any important developments might be occurring is critical to the research evaluation. Recognition then will be helpful to the researcher who wants to excel in his/her study.

9. **Scholarly Approach.** Once the research project is fully completed, the next step is to

assemble it for presentation at a local, regional or national meeting, and eventually to submit it for publication in a peer-reviewed journal of repute. To do this, the researcher needs to carefully review his/her data, analyze the literature, and begin the process of writing the manuscript for publication. If the goal is to submit for presentation first, an abstract will have to be elaborated in a manner that includes: introduction, rationale, hypothesis, material and methods, results, discussion, and conclusion. All these elements help secure its acceptance. The scholarly approach represents, then, the best manner in which a researcher prepares himself/herself to publish or present the data collected and analyzed.

10. **Integration**. The integration of all the previous qualities of a good researcher is needed when developing a good research project. A researcher must utilize the various characteristics already mentioned when proceeding to do the best research project possible. Integration of the research process or

study is of great magnitude when advancing successfully along the path of research. In this area, collaboration with other researchers or a group of researchers has to be successfully integrated when obtaining results that will be meaningful in clinical or experimental medicine. Integration can work by helping the researcher to accumulate information obtained from all research stages or by clarifying all aspects of the research. In this way, the researcher will have the best result possible.

Research Processes

The research process consists of six principal stages: problem identification, hypothesis formulation, research design, measurement and collection, data analysis, and generalization.

The research process was also summarized by Dr. Willie Depositario (1990) of UPLB as cited by Alicay (2014). His idea, called Depositario's F-F Theory, consists of Four Fs which can be used as a mnemonic device for the research processes. This concept about the research processes emphasizes the importance of facts in science. According to him, the research process can be summarized with the following four stages or steps:

1. **F**ocus Facts. In this stage, the researchers have to identify what specific questions need to be answered. He formulates the research objectives or statement of the problem. He specifies what variables are involved and what data need to be collected.

2. **F**ind Facts. This stage consists of selections and construction of measuring tools and collections of needed data. In historical research and descriptive researches, the researcher constructs interview guides, observation guides, questionnaires, scales, or tests and collects the needed data by using the instruments. In experimental research, the researchers conduct the experiment and collect the needed data.

3. **F**ilters Facts. In this stage, the researcher organizes and analyzes the collected data with the use of appropriate statistical tools to come up with answers to his research questions. He records his findings based on the analysis.

4. Finalize Facts. This is the last stage of the research process where the researcher draws conclusions and answers the research problem based on the outcomes of his data analysis.

A simplified illustrates chart of the research processes is shown in Figure 1.

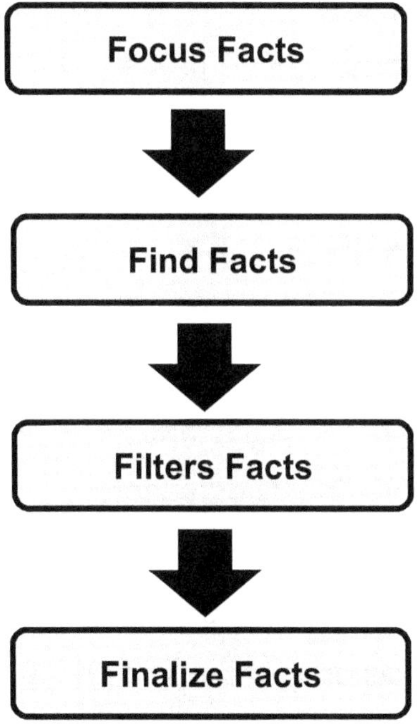

Figure 1: Schematic Diagram of the Research Process through Depositario's F-F Theory

Ethics of Research

Research ethics provides guidelines for the responsible conduct of research. In addition, it educates and monitors researchers researching to ensure a high ethical standard. The following is a general summary of some ethical principles (City University of Hong Kong, 2021):

1. **Honesty**. Honestly report data, results, methods and procedures, and publication status. Do not fabricate, falsify, or misrepresent data.

2. **Objectivity**. Strive to avoid bias in experimental design, data analysis, data interpretation, peer review, personnel decisions, grant writing, expert testimony, and other aspects of research.

3. **Integrity.** Keep your promises and agreements; act with sincerity; strive for consistency of thought and action.

4. **Carefulness.** Avoid careless errors and negligence; carefully and critically examine your own work and the work of your peers. Keep good records of research activities.

5. **Openness.** Share data, results, ideas, tools, resources. Be open to criticism and new ideas.

6. **Respect for Intellectual Property**. Honor patents, copyrights, and other forms of intellectual property. Do not use unpublished data, methods, or results without permission. Give credit where credit is due. Never plagiarize.

7. **Confidentiality.** Protect confidential communications, such as papers or grants submitted for publication, personnel records, trade or military secrets, and patient records.

8. **Responsible Publication.** Publish in order to advance research and scholarship, not to advance just your own career. Avoid wasteful and duplicative publication.

9. **Responsible Mentoring.** Help to educate, mentor, and advise students. Promote their welfare and allow them to make their own decisions.

10. **Respect for Colleagues.** Respect your colleagues and treat them fairly.

11. **Social Responsibility.** Strive to promote

social good and prevent or mitigate social harms through research, public education, and advocacy.

12. **Non-Discrimination.** Avoid discrimination against colleagues or students based on sex, race, ethnicity, or other factors that are not related to their scientific competence and integrity.

13. **Competence**. Maintain and improve your professional competence and expertise through lifelong education and learning; take steps to promote competence in science as a whole.

14. **Legality.** Know and obey relevant laws and institutional and governmental policies.

15. **Animal Care.** Show proper respect and care for animals when using them in research. Do not conduct unnecessary or poorly designed animal experiments.

16. **Human Subjects Protection.** When researching human subjects, minimize harms and risks and maximize benefits; respect human dignity, privacy, and autonomy.

What are research misconducts?

    a. **Fabrication.** making up data or results and recording or reporting them.

    b. **Falsification.** manipulating research materials, or changing or omitting data or results such that the research is not accurately represented in the research record.

    c. **Plagiarism.** the appropriation of another person's ideas, processes, results, or words without giving appropriate credit.

    d. Research misconduct does not include honest errors or differences of opinion.

Rights of Research Participants (Smith, 2003; & Polit, et al., 2006).

    1. **Voluntary participation.** Any person needs to be coerced to participate in any research undertaking.

    2. **Informed consent.** Prospective research participants must be fully informed about the procedures and risks involved in research. Their consent to participate must be secured.

    3. **Risk of harm.** The harm that is either physical, financial, or psychological must be experienced

by the participants. The principle of non – maleficence states that the researcher must avoid, prevent, or minimize harm to participants.

4. **Confidentially.** Participants must be assured that identifying information will not be made available to anyone who is not directly involved in the study (Smith, 2003).

5. **Anonymity.** It means that the participants will remain anonymous throughout the study, sometimes even to the researchers themselves.

Kinds of Research

Calmorin (2016) enumerated the three kinds of research namely:

1. **Basic or Pure Research** aims to discover basic truths or principles. It is intended to add to the body of scientific knowledge by exploring the unknown to extend the boundaries of knowledge as well as to discover new facts and learn more accurately the characteristics of known facts without any particular thought of

immediate practicality. In other words, the results of basic research are theoretical knowledge. It has no immediate usefulness or value to man.

2. **Applied Research** is seeking new application of scientific knowledge of developing a new system or procedure, a new device, and a new method, in order to solve problems. In this type of research, the problem is identified and a new system or new method is applied in order to solve the problem. In other words, applied research produces knowledge of practical use to man.

3. **Developmental Research** is decision-oriented involving the application of scientific methods in response to an immediate need to improve existing practices. This process involves the study. In other words, if the researcher finds practical applications of the theoretical knowledge and uses this to produce useful products.

Classification of Research

Calmorin and Calmorin (2007) classified research into:

1. **Library Research.** This is done in the library where the answer to specific questions or problems of the study is available. Historical research lends itself to library research because the study is focused on the past and much of the secondary sources are found in the library. Some historical evidence may be from archeological findings. Field and laboratory researches also make use of the library researches but answers to certain problems are not available in the library. The data are gathered through surveys or experimentation.

2. **Field Research.** Here, research is conducted in a natural setting. No changes in the environment are made. Field research is both applicable to descriptive surveys and experimental methods.

3. **Laboratory Research.** The research is

conducted in artificial or controlled conditions by isolating the study in a thoroughly specified and equipped area. The purposes are: (a) to test hypothesis derived from theory, (b) to control variance under research conditions, and (c) to discover the relations between the dependent and independent variables. Laboratory research applies to experimental, descriptive, and case study methods.

Research Approaches

The concepts of the types of research are synonymous with the concepts of the approaches to research. Traditionally, there are only there approaches or methods of research, which are qualitative research, quantitative research, and mixed methods.

Qualitative Research

Qualitative research is a means for exploring and understanding the meaning individuals or groups ascribe to a social or human problem. The process of research involves emerging questions and procedures, data typically collected in the participant's setting, data analysis inductively building from particulars to general themes, and the researcher making interpretations of the meaning of the data. The final written report has a flexible structure. Those who engage in this form of inquiry support a way of looking at research that honors an inductive style, a focus on individual meaning, and the importance of rendering the complexity of a situation (Creswell, 2007).

Quantitative Research

Quantitative research is a means for testing objective theories by examining the relationship among variables. These variables, in turn, can be measured, typically on instruments, so that numbered data can be analyzed using statistical procedures. The final written report has a set structure consisting of introduction, literature, and theory, methods, results, and discussion (Creswell, 2008). Like qualitative researchers, those who engage in this form of inquiry have assumptions about testing theories deductively, building in protections against bias, controlling for alternative explanations, and being able to generalize and replicate the findings.

Mixed Research Design

Mixed methods research is an approach to inquiry that combines or associates both qualitative and quantitative forms. It involves philosophical assumptions, the use of qualitative and quantitative approaches, and the mixing of both approaches in a study. Thus, it is more than simply collecting and analyzing both kinds of data; it also involves the use of both approaches in tandem so that the overall strength of a study is greater than either qualitative or quantitative research (Creswell & Plano Clark, 2007).

Table 1: Overview of Fundamental Differences Between Qualitative Research and Quantitative Research Methods

Research Process	Qualitative Research	Quantitative Research
Focus	Understanding or interpretation of a phenomenon, experience	Causal explanation, establishing the extent

Research design	Flexible, open, case study	Linear, pre-established experimental
Data Collection techniques	Interviews, focused group discussions (FGDs), field observation, survey.	Mathematical models, measurements, surveys.
Sampling	Purposeful, non-probabilistic	Statistical, probabilistic
Data Analysis	Inductive, theory generation, depth of critique or interpretation	Deductive, generalizability, theory -testing.

Adapted to Abila & Fernandez (2020)

Table 1 presents an overview of the differences between Quantitative and qualitative researches. It does this by focusing on key parts or elements of the research processes (research focus, research design, data collection techniques, sampling, and data analysis) and highlighting the differences between the two types of research. First, qualitative and Quantitative researchers differ from each other in the focus of the study – the quality or the nature of the knowledge being examined. Whereas quantitative research focuses on cause-effect explanations while qualitative research fundamentally seeks an in-depth and critical understanding of the phenomenon under study.

Secondly, the two types of research differ in their understanding of research design that includes the data collections tools, sampling, and sampling strategy. Quantitative research designs are typically statistical and probabilistic in nature. In practice, this means that testing a theory consists of using measurable variables that are analyzed using statistics to determine if the theory explains or predicts the phenomena of interest. The broad aim of this type of calculative research is to determine the generalizability (i.e extent) of the results to other but similar phenomenon. Quantitative Research attempts to determine whether sample-based results could be extended to a greater population. To achieve this, a research design, therefore, has to use mathematical models or statistical tools as well as determine the appropriate population (i.e sample population) that could yield statistical correct data.

Qualitative research is inductive and interpretive because it aims to gain a critical understanding of the phenomenon or experience that it examines. Thus, in terms of research design, it is flexible and open to potential changes in the actual field when collecting data. Qualitative research design thrives in-depth interviewing and/or time–consuming field observations. The reason for this is there are aspects of the real environment of the phenomenon or people under study that cannot be captured by the traditional Quantitative data collection tools and measurement but rather require the interpretation and/or in-depth understanding of a researcher by being exposed to the natural environment of the phenomenon or people under study.

Quantitative and qualitative researches differ in the analysis of their research findings or results because the former aims for its results and conclusion to be generalizable, whilst the latter tend to aim for a more in-depth understanding in the analysis of findings.

Research Across the Fields

Research is not only a process that is limited to the field of science. It can, as well, cater to people and scholars from artistic, historic, or any other field where an individual is willing to do extensive study to get relevant information. Research can be creative, exploring, or just reassuring in nature. Each one of them does some or the other research in his life for sure. Research can affect a subject both positively and negatively and can be constructive or destructive in nature. However, everyone needs to understand that it's not the results from research that determine its use; it's the people who handle the results.

Approaches to research depend on epistemology, which varies considerably both within and between humanities and sciences. There are several forms of research: scientific, humanities, artistic, economic, social, business, marketing, practitioners research, and so on.

Arts Research

These disciplines consist of different fields of fine arts and liberal arts including painting, music, film, classic literature, and music among the most popular ones on which research is conducted. The researcher can use an empirical approach to conduct surveys of public opinion. Conversely, he can use the non – empirical approach to perform analysis on the application and theory of literature, music, and other related topics.

In addition, art research topics may come in the form of art history, architecture, artist, theater, and plays and works of art topics. Some topics could be the following:

1. Analyze one work of art.
2. Compare two art critics.
3. Compare and contrast works from one period or movement.
4. Investigate the iconography in the work of one artist.
5. Write a screenplay to narrate an artist's life.
6. Review an exhibition in a local museum.
7. Visit an auction house and describe the experience.
8. Investigate an artist's technique and media.
9. Discuss art in one ethnicity, religion, or nationality.
10. Challenge one's comfort zone.

Humanities Research

Research in the humanities involves different methods such as hermeneutics and semiotics, and a different, more relativist epistemology. Humanities scholars usually do not search for the ultimate correct answer to the question, but instead, explore the issues and details that surround it. Context is always important, and context can be social, historical, political, cultural, or ethnic. An example of research in the humanities is historical research, which is embodied in historical method. Historian uses primary sources and other evidence to systematically investigate a topic, and then to write histories in the form of accounts of the past.

The study of humanities might start with researching in the library, but its practical applications are not limited to it. A researcher has the opportunity to go out in the field and observe the different cultures and societies, interview people and compile case studies from real-life experiences.

Here are some suggested topics for research in the field of humanities:

1. **Religion.** The development of religions and the way these affected modern society is a very intriguing topic. In many countries, the social atmosphere is still dictated by religious

aspects. Also, it is very common to notice how two countries that share a border are completely different because they do not share the same religion. A close look over the Middle East and Asia will bring plenty of examples to work with.

2. **History of Law.** There are few things that can influence society more than the laws of a country. Starting from a very rudimentary system of law and finishing with complicated underlines for every law article, there was an interesting journey influenced by politics, religion, or social and economic factors.

3. **Literature.** This is one of the most diverse topics one can choose. In the last century, literature was not only an art but also a manifestation of social problems, a manifest against corrupted regimes or a form of protest against religious restrictions. A researcher can choose any book that he likes and present the historical context of that time.

4. **History of visual arts.** From ancient times, there was always a certain mystery in the way

artists represent the limitations of society through art. Even if one talks about the ancient Greek statues that evolved around the human shape on the paintings from the Italian Renaissance, he can discover how a simple object can speak about hundreds of years of history.

5. **Music.** One will not find a topic more pleasant than music. It has been a form of art present in society since the beginning of time. Even if a person listens to Beethoven or he prefers modern music, this topic will allow him to express his opinion and preferences and may even discover new artists.

Sports Research

Sports can be a very interesting topic for a research paper. There is plenty of information out there to use as research evidence for a sports topic such as the following:

1. **Drugs and steroids**. The use of drugs and steroids can give a lot of the use of drugs or famous athletes that have used them.

a. Researchers can write on is how many athletes get caught.

b. Researchers can also write about the negative consequences that this has on their careers.

c. Writers can discuss the negative effects dugs have in the sporting world.

d. Long–term ramifications and health problems can also be discussed.

e. The effects of long–term use along with the disadvantage can be another discussion point.

2. **Sport injury recovery.** Another great sports-related topic is the recovery from a sports injury. This is a good topic to choose because there are plenty of different ideas that can be discussed. A researcher can write about preventing injuries or training after experiencing an injury.

a. Famous athletes can be cited who have had particularly damaging injuries.

b. How certain injuries are specific to particular sports.

   c. The writer may have had a personal experience in sports where they fell victim to an injury.

3. **Sport as a career.** Still another intriguing sports research topic is about sport as career choice. There are lots that can be said on the subject of sport as a career.

   a. A researcher may find it interesting to research the amount of money that athletes are paid.

   b. He may wish to write on the average length of a sports career and how a person can make it.

   c. He may wish to take is to research how to become a professional athlete and some of the challenges that people face.

4. Women in sports. A good sport research topic also that is unique is the comparison between men and women who play sports.

   a. Research may want to research some famous female athletes

   b. Make a comparison to their male counterparts.

5. Sport and employment. Employment in sport can provide more inspiration for academic research papers. Many viewpoints and discussions can be looked at.

   a. What options are available for successful athletes in sports?

   b. What are the options for athletes who may not hold the same celebrity status as others?

   c. The writer will be able to research high school athletes and look at sports scholarships.

6. The history of the sport. History and sport can go in hand in hand when it comes to writing a research paper. Whether researchers are looking at the history of the sport itself or famous sporting events, they can be sure that there is more than enough information to produce some fantastic work.

   a. Writers could look at females entering a male-dominated sport and how this changed the way athletes were viewed.

   b. A writer can also research famous sporting

events and discuss why they are memorable.

7. How media affect sports. The media are well suited to many sports, whereas others do not seem to garner the same attention. Topics can include how different sports attract different age ranges and sexes.

   a. Writers can discuss how athletes are portrayed as potential role models for today's youth.

   b. Why are some sport more worthy of being televised than others?

   c. How the advertising industry performs during sporting events.

Science Research

Most science researchers need to present a current problem (or even a future problem) and discuss how science can help solve it. A researcher might find that the problem is so new that no one has come up with a theory.

The scientific disciplines of medicine, mechanics, physics, and cell biology are just a few sciences on which researchers use the empirical modes to perform first-hand research both in the field as well as in the laboratory. The applications of these areas of sciences are endless and apt for students who prefer to spend time in laboratories.

These are a few topics for different science subjects.

1. **Chemistry**
   a. Creating an affordable alternative to petroleum
   b. Mercury in our food (especially fish)
   c. Polymers and 3D printing
   d. Chemistry and terrorism
   e. Bioluminescence
   f. pH and human diets
2. **Earth and Physical Science**
   a. Tampering with weather systems
   b. The role of the storm chaser
   c. Elastic – rebound theory
   d. Protecting groundwater
   e. The role of government regarding invasive species, like Asian carp.
   f. Engineering and geography
   g. Protecting habitats.

3. **Physiology**

   a. Aging and plastic surgery

   b. Artificial body replacement

   c. Medication and the brain

   d. Physical effects of food allergies

   e. Hearing and the earbuds

4. **Ecology**

   a. Carbon credits

   b. Status of the ozone

   c. Oceans and pollution

   d. Digging for gold and the effects on the environment

   e. Fluoride in water systems

   f. Turning cities into urban farms

5. **Genetics**

   a. Overpopulation

   b. Gene mapping

   c. Choosing genetics

   d. Genetically engineered food

   e. Disappearing foods

Business Research

Business Research is a field of practical study in which a company obtained data and analyzes it in order to better manage the company. Business Research can include financial data, consumer feedback, product research, and competitive analysis. Executives and managers who use business research methods are able to better understand their company, the position it holds in the market, and how to improve that position.

1. **Financial Data**. Financial data takes qualitative information such as sales, reports, revenues, and cost reports to see what areas make money and what costs money. By reviewing data, managers can find products, staff, and departments that are most efficient and determine areas of unnecessary costs.

2. **Consumer Feedback.** Understanding what the public says about the products and services a company provides is essential to making sure the company is meeting consumer needs. Customer feedback includes case studies, focus groups, customer surveys, and questionnaires.

3. **Product Research**. Product research seeks to improve the product to meet the needs of

consumers. This may include technological advancement, improved customer service, or access to the product through a variety of distribution channels.

4. **Competitive Analysis.** Competitive analysis is when one company compares its products and services to those of another company. This can be done to improve the product, create a niche or determine a more attractive price to lure customers.

5. **Industry Data.** Using research tools such as the information compiled by Dun and Bradstreet can help a company to understand how the industry as a whole is doing. This can help executives make decisions based on economic factors affecting their industry that are not limited to their own products.

Agriculture and Fisheries Research

Agriculture is the art and science of growing plants and other crops and the raising of animals for food, other human needs, or economic gain. It has two main division: plant or crop production and animal or livestock production. Its ultimate purposes are for production, other human needs such as clothing, medicines, tools, artistic display, and dwelling, or for economic gain or profit. While fishery is the industry or occupation devoted to the catching, processing, or selling of fish, shellfish, or other aquatic animals. Ideally, the following are suggested topics for research.

1. What organisms are cultivated for human use or consumption.

2. The consequences farming fish has on the environment.

3. Find out if the breeding process is constantly changing to make sure that the fish has more favorable characteristics and those unfavorable characteristics.

4. Differences between the standards of farmed fish and naturally caught fish and investigate why there are differences if the standards are different.

5. Possible use of the steroid or antibiotics to create bigger or certain quality fish for consumption.

Information and Communication Technology Research

Information and Communication Technology (ICT) is an umbrella term that includes any communication device application, encompassing radio, television, cellular phones, computer and network hardware and software, satellite system, and so on, as well as the various services and applications. Here are some suggested topics for research in this field:

1. Overview. Developing regional communities with ICT.
2. Community informatics and regional development.
3. Community Technology: Policy, partnership, and practice.
4. Enhancing information access and e-commerce opportunities.
5. Information access in regional communities: Bridging the digital divide.
6. Effective use of ICT: Digital Inclusion.

Social Research

Social Research is the scientific study of society. More specifically, social research examines a society's attitudes, assumptions, beliefs, trends, stratifications, and rules. The scope of social research can be small or large, ranging from the self or a single individual to spanning an entire race or country.

Social research determines the relationship between one or more variables. For example, sex and income level are variables. Social scientists will look for underlying concepts and cause–and–effect relationships of a social issue. Before even beginning research, scientists must formulate a research question. For example, a researcher might ask if men have higher incomes than women. Are women most likely to be poor?

Popular topics of social research are:

1. Criminal behavior
2. Race, nationality, and ethnicity
3. Mass media
4. Sociology of food
5. Youth cultures
6. Sociology of gender and sexuality

7. Social movements

8. Cults, clans, and communities

9. Class conflict and inequalities

10. Spirituality, superstition, and legends

11. Consumerism

12. The family

Philosophy Research

The discipline of philosophy does not have much application in the practical field, yet a researcher can create a theoretical study based on analytical thinking, metaphysical interpretation, and several hours of readings.

1. **The philosophy behind body image**. This is one of the timeliest topics, especially as so many people on social media and the world of celebrities are trying to change the popular ideas of the perfect body. From fat-shaming to eating, disorders, body image is truly a hot topic that could become a fascinating research paper for a philosophy class.

2. **The philosophy of discrimination**. If you have watched the news lately, you know that

discrimination has not left our world. From schools and police departments, movie castings, and professional athletics, racial discrimination and gender discrimination continues to live on today.

3. **Abuse of animals vs. abuse of children**. These are both horrible things and they both can be looked at through a variety of different philosophical lenses. You can investigate the different opinions and theories behind abusing weaker beings and why it is so prevalent in a modernized world.

4. **Philosophy behind offering aid**. Whenever a major disaster occurs, like a famine, weather-related disaster, or earthquake, some people are ready, willing, and able to drop everything to help those who are in need. Often, these people do not know anyone who was affected, but they still go to help. Look at the philosophy behind helping those who are unable to help themselves in the time of great need.

5. **Why do people do evil things**. All too often, people see horrible, evil events unfolding on

evening news channels? People do not neglect children, or terrorize innocent people, how can people commit these horrible acts? What do they use as justification? Why commit these horrible acts? What do they use as justification? Why is it so hard for people to understand?

History Research

The opportunities for a research in this subject are spread far and wide. A student can create research through the theoretical approach of compiling data from archives, public courthouses, and from societies of history. For a more practical approach, a researcher can participate in archaeological expeditions or interview participants of past battles. The possibilities for this area in research writing are endless.

ASSESSMENT TASKS

I.   **Direction.** Why is research important to our daily life? Cite five reasons?

1.   _______________________________

____

2.   _______________________________

____

3.   _______________________________

____

4.   _______________________________

____

5.   _______________________________

____

II. **This is a fact:** That many students enrolled in a program that requires a thesis are not able to graduate in due time. This has been attributed to the fact that they have not developed the qualities needed by a researcher. Below write a letter advising them on what to do in order to be able to successfully finish their research. Be sure to include the characteristics of a researcher, good research, and the research process.

III.

IV. **Direction:** Identify the characteristics of research being described in each of the situations.

1. Rhed Simon identifies a problem for his research. After gathering for the first problem, he found out and identified another problem that arose from his previous problem. He suggested that other researchers continue to research on the newly found problem.

2. Maxene Joy uses the scientific method in doing her research procedures. She ensures that all the instruments and procedures used are valid before proceeding to the next step to assure that the final outcome and conclusion are also valid.

3. Alexandra Natalia has finished conducting research in her field of expertise. She wants to submit it to examine the validity of the results of Alexandra Natalia's paper. The committee decided to include Alexandra Natalia's paper since the results from the experiment of the committee are the same as the results reported by Alexandra Natalia on

her paper.

4. Aze Christof is interested to conduct research about the factors affecting the growth of fish in saltwater. He chose this topic because he lives in an area near the seashore. He always walks near the shore during his free time. Because of this, it will be easy for him to conduct observations and gather the data he needs regarding his chosen topic.

5. After finishing her data analysis, Agatha Cyrine continues to examine the result of the data analysis, before she supports or rejects her hypothesis, she makes sure that she has established a high level of confidence in her data analysis. She is confident and precise in her interpretations whether the results are significant or not.

Direction: Identify which quality of a good researcher is demonstrated in each of the following situations.

1. Ms. Jessalyn Tampipi is curious about many things around her. She seeks to find out the causes of the different phenomena she

experiences daily. She goes to the library to search for answers to her inquiries. She regularly attends research forums and never lets herself be outdated to the new and current trends in research.

2. Ms. Jane Pagulayan, a research teacher, is an organized person. She strictly follows a certain process in all of her investigations. She makes sure she follows the proper process of inquiry, especially the scientific method. She also applies this method in her everyday endeavors. Because of this, all of her inquiries are solved with ease.

3. Mr. Patrick Carl Gilok was investigating about the effect of a certain antimicrobial substance on a certain type of bacteria. He was expecting that the substance will prevent the growth of the population of the bacteria. After his experiment, he found out the bacteria still grew its population. Although he was not expecting this result, Mr. Patrick Carl Gilok still reported his finding in his paper.

4. Ms. Jerimay Novido was planning to conduct

an experiment. Before she could start her experiment, she needed to measure the area of the field where the experiment will be conducted. She planned to use a tape measure to be used for measuring. However, when she went to the stock room, she did not find any tape measure available. There were only three meter sticks present there. She just used the available meterstick in measuring the area of the field.

5. Mr. Robert Jonnydel Rayo wants to make sure that every material needed in his experiment will be used wisely. He makes sure that he will buy sufficient materials enough for the needs of the experiment. He does not want that his budget to be wasted in buying unnecessary or excess materials.

V.   **Direction:** Choose the letter of the correct answer.

1. Research that seeks new applications of scientific knowledge to solve problems (e.g development of a new system or procedure, a new device, or new method).

    A. Basic research

    B. Field research

    C. Applied research

    D. Developmental research

2. Otherwise known as pure research.

    A. Field research

    B. Basic research

    C. Developmental research

    D. Applied research

3. **Which of the following does not belong to the group?**

    A. Pure research

    B. Applied research

    C. Developmental research

    D. Field research

4. Classification of research that is conducted in a natural environment wherein no changes are made.

    A. Library research

    B. Laboratory research

    C. Basic research

    D. Field research

5. Classification of research that is conducted in

artificial and controlled conditions by isolating or separating the study in a specified and thoroughly operationalized area.

A. Laboratory research

B. Library research

C. Field research

D. Basic research

6. Under what kind of research does the Archimedes principles fall?

   A. Library research

   B. Laboratory research

   C. Basic research

   D. Field research

7. Utilization and Commercialization of Milkfish Bones into Sausage is an example of:

   A. Field research

   B. Laboratory research

   C. Library research

   D. Basic research

8. "Culturing of Mussel (*Mytillus edulis*) in Brackish Water of Dipolog City in Staking Method and Hanging Method" is kind of:

    A. Laboratory research

    B. Basic research

    C. Field research

    D. Library research

9. Newton's Law Motion is an example of:

    A. Library research

    B. Laboratory research

    C. Field research

    D. Basic research

10. "History on the implementation of K to 12 Curriculum of the Department of Education in the Philippines" is a kind of:

    A. Library research

    B. Laboratory research

    C. Basic research

    D. Field research

VI. **Direction:** Read the following statements carefully, and decide if they are ethical or not. Write **E** if the statement is ethical and **U** if it is otherwise.

1. Copying and using an explanation of a concept without referring to the source.

2. Copying the text word for word but

paraphrase it. You decide to use it in your own work without citing the source as it has been paraphrased.

3. Submitting all parts of the work in two separate versions.

4. Copying a statement verbatim from a printed book and enclosing it with quotation marks without citing the source.

5. Using many words from the original text and citing the source in another work.

6. Lifting a diagram or a data table to your own work with the source information underneath.

7. Using a photo from any website and slightly modifying the color without indicating the source.

8. Turning in an assignment output of your classmate and claiming it your own.

9. Using common knowledge without citing the source.

10. Changing some parts of the original text and integrating them into your work without citing the source.

VII.   **Direction:** Below are some ethical dilemmas. Answer the questions for each situation to solve the problem.

1. You conduct a phenomenological study of teenage from a public school system. You conduct an in-depth interview with a teenager to whom you have promised confidentiality. She started to tell you about how her stepfather was getting too friendly with her and had touched her in those "special places." She tells you she is depressed and plans to commit suicide. You believe she means it. Can you break your promise? If so, who do you tell?

2. You conduct a case study on a small school in a rural location. When you write up the results, it is almost impossible to disguise the school, yet you promised you would treat the data anonymously. How should you deal with this?

3. You conduct an ethnographic study of a young adult over a long period. Your field work takes you to his home, his school, the

bars he frequents, his church, and so on. Over time, you become very attached to him. You find your friendship leads to feelings toward him that you cannot control. You know that getting too close is inappropriate, but you find it difficult to control your feelings. What should you do?

4. Your plan is to study educational practice among a particular tribe of the Philippines. You approach the leader of the school on the reservation. He attempts to get the participation of these groups, no one is willing to sign your permission form. They are willing to talk to you, but they do not trust what you might do with the form. Even though you assure them that you will keep the information private, they see you as someone who represents the leadership and thus are mistrustful. What should you do? How do you convince them that they need to sign the form for you to continue?

5. You interview senior high school students about life on campus. One student tells you

that his roommate seems seriously depressed and spends much on the internet looking at sites for making bombs. Do you tell someone?

VIII. **Direction:** Complete this table by providing the similarities and dissimilarities of the two research approaches.

Specific to Quantitative Research	Common between the two	Specific to qualitative Research

IX. **Direction:** Think of a least two qualitative research topics relevant to pressing issues in each of the following fields.

Areas of Interest	Research Topics
Arts and Humanities	
Sports	
Science	
Business	

Agriculture & Fisheries	
ICT	
Social Inquiry	

PERFORMANCE TASK

Visit any internet sources or online research journal. Based on your field of expertise or strand examine five of these research studies. Based on what you have learned about research, make a report on these containing information or description about the aspects of the study: topic, approach, importance, and type based on different methods of classifying research. Share your report about these research studies with your teacher and classmates by giving them a copy of your report.

Cited References and Suggested Readings

Abila, S. & Fernandez, C. J. (2020). *Practical Research 1: Introduction to Qualitative Research for Senior High School.* Anvil Publishing House.

Alicay, C. B. (2014). *Research Methods and Techniques.* Great Books Publishing.

Barrot, J. S. (2017). *Practical Research 1 for Senior High School*. C & E Publishing, Inc.

Calmorin, L. P. (2016). *Research and Thesis Writing with Statistics Computer Application*. Rex Book Store, Inc.

Calmorin, L. P. & Calmorin, M. A. (2007). *Research Methods and Thesis Writing (2nd Edition)*. Rex Book Store, Inc.

Creswell, J. W. (2007). *Qualitative Inquiry and Research Design: Choosing Among Five Approaches (2nd Edition)*. SAGE Publications.

Creswell, J., & Plano Clark, V. (2007). *Designing and Conducting Mixed Methods Research*. SAGE Publications.

Creswell, J. W. (2008). *Educational research: Planning, conducting, and evaluating quantitative and qualitative research (3rd Edition)*. Pearson Education, Inc.

City University of Hong Kong. (2021). *What is Research Ethics and Research Misconducts?* https://libguides.library.cityu.edu.hk/researchmethods.

Garcia, C. D. (2003). *Fundamentals of Research and Research Designing*. Katha Publishing Co., Inc.

Gregorio, G. L. (2000). *Research Methods and Technical Writing in Agriculture*. Rex Book Store, Inc.

Oldfield, C. (2015). *Another look at the research*. Teaching Public Administration, 34 (1), pp. 40-53, http://doi.10.1177/0144739415597971.

Polit, et al., (2006). *Essentials of Nursing Research: Methods, Appraisal and Utilization (6th edition)*. Lippincott Williams & Wilkins, Inc.

Serrano, A. C. (2016). *Practical Research `1: Quantitative Research*. Unlimited Books Library Services &

Publishing Inc.

Smith, P. E. (2003). *Taylor's Clinical Nursing Skills*. Lippincott Williams & Wilkins, Inc.

Toledo-Pereyra, L. H. (2012). *Ten Qualities of a Good Researcher*. Journal of Investigative Surgery, 25(4), 201 202. http://doi.10.3109/08941939.2012.701543.

Wa-Mbaleka, S. & Gladstone, R. K. (2018). *Qualitative Research for Senior High School*. Oikos Biblio Publishing House.

MODULE 2:

QUALITATIVE RESEARCH AND ITS IMPORTANCE IN DAILY LIFE

LEARNING OUTCOMES

At the end of this module, students should be able to:

1. Describes characteristics, strengths, weaknesses, and kinds of qualitative research

2. illustrates the importance of qualitative research across fields

Nature of Qualitative Research

Recall the discussion about the qualitative-quantitative dichotomy in the previous module. In that discussion, we emphasized the key differences between these two research approaches in terms of their focus, research design, data collection techniques, sampling, and data analysis.

Qualitative research is defined as an inquiry process of understanding a social or human problem based on building a complex, holistic picture formed with words, reporting details of informants, and conducted in a natural setting (Creswell, 1994). A quantitative research, on the other hand, is an inquiry into a social or human problem, based on testing a theory composed of variables, measured with numbers, and analyzed with statistical procedures, in order to determine whether the predictive generalization of the theory holds true (Creswell, 1994).

Several authors and researchers commonly define research as containing these features: detailed and systematic descriptions or interpretation of experiences, phenomena, situations, events, people and their beliefs and attitudes, cultural traditions among others. The idea of qualitative research is to gain deeper understanding of specific contexts and find meaningful knowledge for human consumptions (Amarado & Talili, 2017).

The choice of using qualitative research depends on the research objectives and nature of research problems. The same principle applies in deciding to use either qualitative or quantitative method. The problem or the topic determines what method to employ, and not the other way around.

Arce (2001) further described that in qualitative research, "the bulk of data consist of texts, pictures, maps, charts, and physical artifacts. A number may also be included; however, the resolution of the research problem is not dependent on procedures in statistical analysis.

Generally, a qualitative research design is used to describe life experiences or social phenomena and make sense by giving them significant meanings or meaningful significance through discernible patterns or novel discoveries. In qualitative research, the researcher makes sense of the world, scouring the trees to see the forest, as what Hollis (1994) would declaim, like the bee that gathers materials from the flowers of the garden and of the field, but transforms and digests them by a power of its own. Martens (2004) also defined qualitative research as consisting of detailed descriptions of situations, events, people, interactions, and observed behaviors; direct quotations from people about their experiences, attitudes, beliefs, and thoughts; and informed interpretation of the meaning of individual cultural artifacts in context.

Qualitative research is essentially concerned with systematic textual description and analysis, while quantitative research on testing relationships and establishes causality (association and cause and effect) using statistical analysis.

Schram (2003) laid down four guidelines to help clarify the purpose of qualitative research: descriptive (to describe), interpretive (to interpret), explanatory (to explain), and emancipatory (to emancipate).

Descriptive purposes are specifically aimed to document and describe the unique experiences in a given context. Interpretative purposes are oriented to unravel, illuminate and investigate categories of meanings and symbols. Explanatory purposes are geared to analyze and to clarify relationships of recurring themes and discernible patterns without causative, correlational or probabilistic association (except when complemented with quantitative analysis). Emancipatory purposes are used to generate suggestions and recommendations.

Furthermore, qualitative research is aimed at particularization while quantitative research is at generalization. Thus, qualitative study hardly does conclusion.

Particularization means the generated knowledge is applied to specific contexts or certain particularities (sample and locale of research). What is true to a few particular may not be true to others in general. It requires depth, i.e. digging deeper into a social phenomenon. On the other hand, generalization means the generated knowledge is applied to many others or to all. What is true to few particular must be true to general. It requires breath, i.e. applicability to as many as possible.

Again, qualitative research does not come up with a conclusion since the generated knowledge and findings are not intended to generalize.

How do we conduct qualitative research?

The following are common features of how qualitative research is done.

1. Qualitative researchers are interested in accessing experiences, interactions, and documents in their natural context and in a way that gives room to their particularities and the materials in which they are studied.

2. Qualitative research refrains from setting up a well-defined concept of what is studied and from formulating hypotheses in the beginning in order to test them. Rather, concepts (or hypotheses, if they are used) are developed and refined in the process of research.

3. Qualitative research starts from the idea that methods and theories should be appropriate to what is studied. If the existing methods do not fit to a concrete issue or field, they are adapted or new methods or approaches are developed.

4. Researchers themselves are an important part

of the research process, either in terms of their own personal presence as researchers or in terms of their experiences in the field and with the reflexivity they bring to the role – as are members of the field under study.

5. Qualitative research takes context and cases seriously for understanding an issue under study. A lot of qualitative research is based on case studies or a series of case studies, and often the case (its history and complexity) is an important context for understanding what is studied.

6. A major part of qualitative research is based on text and writing – from field notes and transcripts to descriptions and interpretations and finally to the presentation of the findings and of the research as a whole. Therefore, issues of transforming complex social situations (or other materials such as images) into texts – issues of transcribing and writing in general – are major concerns of qualitative research.

7. If methods are supposed to be adequate to

what is under study, approaches to defining and assessing the quality of qualitative research (still) have to be discussed in specific ways that are appropriate for qualitative research and even for specific approaches in qualitative research.

When to Use Qualitative Research?

When is it appropriate to use qualitative research? We conduct qualitative research because a problem or issue needs to be explored. This exploration is needed, in turn, because of a need to study a group or population, identify variables that cannot be easily measured or hear silenced voices.

These are all good reasons to explore a problem rather than to use predetermined information from the literature or rely on results from other research studies (Creswell & Poth, 2018).

1. We also conduct qualitative research because we need a complex, detailed understanding of the issue. This detail can only be established by talking directly with people, going to their homes or places of work, and allowing them to tell the stories unencumbered by what we

expect to find or what we have read in the literature.

2. We conduct qualitative research when we want to empower individuals to share their stories, hear their voices, and minimize the power relationships that often exist between a researcher and the participants in a study. To further deemphasize a power relationship, we may collaborate directly with participants by having them review our research questions, or by having them collaborate with us during the data analysis and interpretation phases of research.

3. We conduct qualitative research when we want to write in a literary, flexible style that conveys stories, or theater, or poems, without the restrictions of formal academic structures of writing.

4. We conduct qualitative research because we want to understand the contexts or settings in which participants in a study address a problem or issue. We cannot always separate what people say from the place where they say

it—whether this context is their home, family, or work.

5. We use qualitative research to follow up quantitative research and help explain the mechanisms or linkages in causal theories or models. These theories provide a general picture of trends, associations, and relationships, but they do not tell us about the processes that people experience, why they responded as they did, the context in which they responded, and their deeper thoughts and behaviors that governed their responses.

6. We use qualitative research to develop theories when partial or inadequate theories exist for certain populations and samples or existing theories do not adequately capture the complexity of the problem we are examining.

7. We also use qualitative research because quantitative measures and statistical analyses simply do not fit the problem. Interactions among people, for example, are difficult to capture with existing measures, and these measures may not be sensitive to issues such

as gender differences, race, economic status, and individual differences. To level all individuals to a statistical mean overlook the uniqueness of individuals in our studies.

Figure 2: **Summary description of when qualitative approaches are simply a better fit for our research problem.**

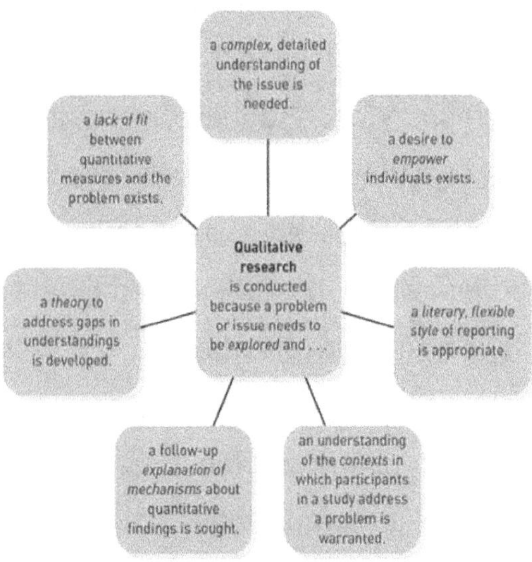

Strength and Weakness of Qualitative Research

Anderson (2010) enumerated the following strength and weaknesses of qualitative research.

Strengths

1. The study requires a few cases or participants. Data collected are based on the participants' own categories of meaning.
2. It is useful for describing complex phenomena.
3. Issues can be examined in detail and in-depth.
4. Interviews are not restricted to specific questions and can be guided or redirected by the researchers in real-time.
5. Subtleties and complexities about the research subjects or topic are often missed by more positivistic inquiries.
6. It provides individual case information.
7. Cross-case comparison and analysis can be conducted.
8. It provides understanding descriptions of people's personal experiences of phenomena (i.e the emic or insider's viewpoint).
9. It can describe in detail the phenomena as they are situated and embedded in local contexts.
10. The researcher is usually identifying contextual and setting factors as they relate to the phenomenon of interest.

11. The researcher can study dynamics (i.e documenting, sequential patterns, and change).
12. The researcher can use the primarily qualitative method of grounded theory to inductively generate a tentative but explanatory theory about the phenomenon.
13. It can determine how participants interpret construct (i.e., self-esteem and IQ).
14. Data are usually collected in naturalistic settings in qualitative research.
15. Qualitative approaches are especially responsive to local situations, conditions, and stakeholders' needs.
16. Qualitative data in the words and categories of participants lend themselves to exploring how and why particular phenomenon occur.
17. You can use an important case to vividly demonstrate a phenomenon to the readers.
18. It can determine idiographic causation (i.e., determination of causes of particular events).

Weaknesses

1. The knowledge produced might not apply to

other people or other settings (i.e., the finding might be unique to the relatively few people included in the research study).

2. Inflexibility is more difficult to maintain, assess, and demonstrate.

3. It is sometimes not as well understood and accepted as quantitative research within the scientific community.

4. The researcher's presence during data gathering which is often unavoidable in qualitative research can affect the subjects' responses.

5. Issues of anonymity and confidentiality can present problems when presenting findings.

6. It is difficult to make quantitative predictions.

7. It is more difficult to test hypothesis and theories with large participant pools.

8. It might have lower credibility with some administrators and commissioners of programs.

9. It generally takes more time to collect the data compared to quantitative research.

10. Data analysis is often time–consuming.

11. The results are more easily influenced by the researchers' personal biases and idiosyncrasies.

Kinds of Qualitative Research

Researchers collect data of the targeted population, place, or event by using different kinds of qualitative research design.

These are the four common kinds of qualitative research design.

1. **Narrative** collects stories from individuals (and documents, and group conversations) about individuals' lived and told experiences. These stories may emerge from a story told to the researcher, a story that is co-constructed between the researcher and the participant, and a story intended as a performance to convey some message or point. Thus, there may be a strong collaborative feature of narrative research as the story emerges through the interaction or dialogue of the researcher and the participant(s).

2. **Phenomenology.** It describes the common meaning for several individuals of their lived experiences of a concept or a phenomenon. it focuses on describing what all participants have in common as they experience a phenomenon (e.g., grief is universally experienced). The basic purpose of phenomenology is to reduce individual experiences with a phenomenon to a description of the universal essence (a "grasp of the very nature of the thing.

3. **Grounded Theory.** intended is to move beyond description and to generate or discover a theory, a "unified theoretical explanation" for a process or an action. Participants in the study would all have experienced the process, and the development of the theory might help explain practice or provide a framework for further research. A key idea is that this theory development does not come "off the shelf" but rather is generated or "grounded" in data from participants who have experienced the process. Thus, grounded theory is a qualitative research design in which the inquirer generates a general

explanation (a theory) of a process, an action, or an interaction shaped by the views of a large number of participants.

4. **Ethnography**. it focuses on an entire culture-sharing group. It describes and interprets the shared and learned patterns of values, behaviors, beliefs, and language of a culture-sharing group. As a process, ethnography involves extended observations of the group, most often through participant observation, in which the researcher is immersed in the day-to-day lives of the people and observes and interviews the group participants. Ethnographers study the meaning of the behavior, the language, and the interaction among members of the culture-sharing group.

5. **Case Study**. It is an in-depth examination of an individual, group of people, or an institution. Some of its purposes are to gain insight into a little–known problem, provide background data for broader studies, and explain socio-psychological and socio-cultural processes (Cristobal & Cristobal, 2017). A case study also

involves a comprehensive and extensive examination of a particular individual, group, or situation over a period of time. It provides information on where to conclude the impact of a significant event in a person's life (Sanchez, 2002).

Importance of Qualitative Research Across the Fields

Qualitative studies are important since research is not limited to collecting numerical data, but it also involves investigating the experiences of people and through obtaining insight from them. Through the analysis of human experiences, qualitative research becomes useful in determining the factors necessary for making sound decisions and improving the quality of life. It is also important in developing a deeper understanding of a phenomenon, which can help improve social interaction. Indeed, the impact of qualitative research is not only confined within the four corners of a classroom, it is also evident across various fields.

- **Humanities and Social Inquiry**. Qualitative research can help you understand the behavior and experiences of other people, like your classmate, neighbors, and even your fellow Filipinos. In turn, understanding their actions and experiences can help you become an effective and functional member of your school and community.

- **Culture and Arts**. Conducting qualitative research also helps you better understand people's culture. You also learn more about how the arts reflect the individuality of a culture or the person practicing it. Consequently, studies dealing with culture and the arts help in their propagation and preservation.

- **Sports**. Qualitative research can help you understand the problems of athletes and the challenges in implementing sports in order to contribute to their effective creation and implementation. In addition, undertaking a qualitative study can help you find out how crucial physical activities are in making citizens active and healthy.

- **Agriculture and Fisheries.** Qualitative research will give you information on the belief of farmers, their practices, and the challenges they experience. You can then use this information in identifying ways to increase food production.

- **Science and Technology.** Conducting qualitative research can help in improving technology and medical services. It can also help in generating science – and – technology-related issues.

- **Business.** You can utilize qualitative research in exploring the attitudes and experiences of people in companies and customers of a business. It can help you analyze human relations in the workplace, processes in the company, customer satisfaction, and sales and marketing activities.

- **Information and Communication Technology**. Finally, qualitative research can make us better understand how technology can supplement human communication and interactions. This can be done, for example, by examining the quality of human interactions in computer-mediated communication.

ASSESSMENT TASKS

I.   Direction: Write **S** if a qualitative approach is suitable for each given situation and **N** if not.

1. Determining the strength and weakness of literacy program.

2. Exploring the lived experience of teenagers with bipolar disorder.

3. Developing a new product or service.

4. Analyzing patients' perception of government hospitals.

5. Understanding the causes of miscommunication in the workplace.

6. Examining whether an increased amount of exercise helps senior citizens lose weight.

7. Determining whether exposure to CNN program increases the English proficiency of learners.

8. Studying the responses of Filipino to political advertisements.

9. Exploring the attitudes of Filipino youth towards Senate hearing on extrajudicial killings.

10. Investigating whether emotional quotient increases with intelligence quotient.

II. **Direction:** Identify the form of qualitative research depicted in the following scenario.

1. The meaning of death and pain of dying - why a mother grieves for the loss of a loved one.

2. The tribe in Mindanao has unique food production thru hunting with the tradition in their eating behavior and food practices.

3. The street children and their perspectives on the meaning of life habitat with a proverbial "roof under their head"

4. What is the world of orphans? Is being alone without parents to look up to a big constraint to pursue living?

5. The Ifugao of the Mountain Province and their indigenous marriage customs and traditions.

6. The making of Filipino heroes thru their mighty pens-from pre-Hispanic to

modern times.

7. A researcher immerses with the Badjao street dwellers to learn how they were able to migrate from Mindanao.

8. A researcher seeks to discover the events that transpired behind the assassination of Antonio Luna in Cavite in 1899 and discuss the implication of these events to history.

9. Examination of the common experiences encountered by a person with a spouse who is undergoing rehabilitation.

10. Life transformation in a remote village in Mindanao - Traditions and Values for Education.

III. **Direction:** Name the type of qualitative research best suited for the following topics.

1. The Mangyans' Burial Practices.

2. Relatives of Typhoon Victims.

3. Filipino Caregivers in Japan.

4. Travails of Senior Citizens at the LRT/MRT Stations.

5. Tanglawan Festival of San Joseño

IV. **Direction:** Discuss whether you agree or disagree with the following statement.

Qualitative approach can never be accurate and reliable. Hence, it is less important than quantitative research and should only be used as a supplement to the latter. It is also impossible for quantitative approach to supplement qualitative approach.

V. **Direction:** Explain how qualitative research can be used in each of the following fields of study. Make your explanation specific by providing a practical example. You may use a separate sheet for your answers.

Areas	Practical Implication
Arts and Humanities	
Sports	
Education	
STEM	
Business & Accounting	
Agriculture & Fisheries	
ICT	

PERFORMANCE TASK

Direction: Choose one of the listed qualitative studies and read it carefully. Your teacher may provide you with a printed copy of the article or may find it on Google Scholar. In the table below, identify the kind of qualitative research used by the authors of the article. Then, based on the kind of qualitative research used, identify the strength and weakness of the study. You may use a separate sheet for your answers.

Suggested Studies:

1. Unveiling the Mystical Lucban Pahiyas Festival (Rosaroso & Rosaroso, 2015).

2. Culture and Heritage of Tiwi, Albay, Philippines through the Lenses of Cultural Mapping (Ayo, 2020).

3. A Phenomenological Study on the Experiences of Carers of the Mentally ill on a Mental Health Facility in the Philippines (Redubla & Cuaton, 2019)

4. Lived Experiences of Tertiary Students in the Teaching of Philippine History Courses (Deligero-Badilles, 2017).

Title of Research:________________________________

Kind of Qualitative Research Used:

____

Strength	Weakness

Cited References and Suggested Readings

Anderson, A. (2010). *Presenting and evaluating qualitative research*. American Journal of Pharmaceutical Education, 74 (8). http://doi.10.5688/aj7408141.

Amarado, R. D. & Talili, I. N. (2017). *Qualitative Research: A Practical Approach*. Mutya Publication House. Inc.

Arce, W. (2001). *Systematic qualitative data research: An introduction for Filipino practitioners (2nd Edition)*. Ateneo de Manila – ORP.

Creswell, J. W. (1994). *Research Design: Qualitative and Quantitative Approaches.* SAGE Publication.

Creswell, J. W. & Poth, C. N. (2018). *Qualitative Inquiry & Research Design Choosing Among Five Approaches (4th edition)*. SAGE Publications, Inc.

Cristobal, A. P., & Cristobal, M. C. (2017). *Practical Research 1*. C & E Publishing, Inc.

Hollis, M. (1994). *Ants, Spiders, and Bees. Philosophy of Social Science*. Cambridge University Press.

Marten, B V. D V. (2004). *The Professional stranger. Ethnographic researcher. Research techniques and information management.* Syracuse University School of Information Studies.

Sanchez, C. A. (2002). *Methods and Techniques of Research, (Revised Edition)*. Rex Book Store, Inc.

Schram, T. (2003). *Conceptualizing Qualitative Inquiry.* Merril Prentice Hall.

MODULE 3:

IDENTIFYING THE INQUIRY AND STATING THE PROBLEM

LEARNING OUTCOMES
At the end of this module, students should be able to:

1. designs a research project related to daily life

2. writes a research title

3. describes the justifications/reasons for conducting the research
4. states research questions.

5. indicates scope and delimitation of research.

6. cites benefits and beneficiaries of research

7. presents written statement of the problem

Nature of Qualitative Research Problem

A research problem is a statement of an area of interest, a situation to be changed, a challenge to be removed, or a disturbing question in academic literature, in theory, or in practice that points to the need for meaningful understanding and intentional research (Samosa, et al., 2021). This description of a research problem reflects that its nature focuses on an issue or an opportunity that needs to be studied.

Research literature suggested that a good research problem usually possesses several traits that demonstrate clarity, logic, linguistic simplicity, and conceptual depth.

Specifically, Jimenez and Silin (2016) enumerated that a research problem should be:

1. **Significant.** One aim of the research is knowledge production. You should choose a topic that would be beneficial and would be of importance to building more knowledge in every individual in particular and at a larger scale for the society. The research problem should be worth – investigating must contribute to the knowledge and value to the field chosen, should improve educational practice,

and most importantly the human condition.

2. **Original.** The rise of the internet offers us a lot of information. Due to this, there have also been misuse and abuse of too much data and references. As a researcher, it is your responsibility to create new topics and solve new problems. Desire to be original and creative in selecting the subject of your study. There is nothing more rewarding than an authentic study.

3. **Feasible.** A good research problem is not too much lengthy. A research can be as equally excellent though done within a limited time. Being economical and practical as a researcher is vital. Choose a research problem that can be done within an adequate period of time.

4. **Researchable.** A good research problem is not too obscure. There shall be sufficient resource materials to add content to your study. Avoid research problems that might take too much of your time because of the lack of references.

5. **Current.** The issue to be tackled in your research must be first of all applicable and relevant to the current and proceeding generation. Moreover, If

your research is of current and trending issue, there would be a lot of references and materials you can use to gather data.

Abila and Fernandez, (2020), discusses three important features of research problems:

1. **Clarity of terms, concepts, signification, and limitations**. The research problem is typically expressed in a clear statement. The research problem is typically expressed in a question or interrogative sentence. It does not make vague claims, broad and sweeping generalizations, and careless assertions that are not backed by studies and by reality. If a student wants to do a quick test of the clarity of a research problem., he or she should ask: *Is the research problem clearly stated? Are there vague or ambiguous concepts or terms used in the statement of the research problem, research questions, or research objectives?*

2. **Feasibility to conduct**. The second trait of a research problem is that it presents a feasible and practicable issue on topic and method. A research problem must be realistic, logistical, and practical.

The practicability or feasibility of a research should be rooted in realistic access to the data or information as well as human participants. This means that if there is a set of information as well as human participants. This means that if there is a set of information that could not be collected ethically then the study is problematic. For instance, a researcher could not ask questions that involve potentially illegal information, which could be considered also as unethical information.

However, the statement of a research problem does not necessarily express the procedure or method of the study of the study, pose a value-laden question, or propose a broad proposition. If a student wants to do a quick test of the feasibility of a research problem, the student should ask: *Does the research problem promise too much in terms of what it aims to answer or achieve? Are there unethical or illegal information that will be collected? Can the researcher actually and practically conduct the planned research method/ is there financial cost of the research reasonable and realistic?*

3. **Depth in its intended Analysis**. The third fundamental feature of a research problem is that it has the potential to show a theoretical depth or understanding in what it tries to study or examine. This means that the research problem is informed or based on academic theory (or theories) that guide the discussion of the main concepts, issues of the research, and its findings or results.

There are two (2) general approaches in starting a qualitative research problem (Henson & Soriano, 2016).

1. **Instrumentalist** questions that focus on what to observe like *"how do school bullies behave in attacking a victim?* And

2. **Realist question** which incorporates belief, feelings, and intentions as fallible evidence to be used critically to test ideas about what is going on like *"How do school bullies express their interpersonal relations with their teachers and parents"* In formulating the qualitative questions, the researcher deals with the meaning of events and activities to the people involved in them, and how these can influence the physical and social

context of these events.

In summary, a research problem is a definite and clear statement of a study that requires a need for meaningful understanding, and deliberate and systematic study. The research problem avoids complexity and jargon, and it must be reasonable to conduct.

Purposes of a Research Problem

Samosa et al. (2021) enumerated the purposes of a research problem statement is to:

1. Introduce the reader to the significance of the subject being discussed.
2. Anchor the questions, theories, or conclusions for analysis to pursue.
3. It provides a brief statement about your paper's intent.
4. Place the subject in a clear sense that determines the boundaries of what is to be discussed.
5. Provide the results reporting process, indicate what is likely to be required to perform the analysis, and clarify how the findings would provide this knowledge.

Possible Aspects that can be studied using Qualitative Research.

According to Creswell (2014), qualitative study originated from several disciplines, which include anthropology, sociology, humanities, and evaluation. These disciplines highly recognize the value of doing field research, or "going directly to the social phenomenon under study and observing it completely as possible" to get a "full understanding of it" (Silverman, 2013).

Babbie (2008) identified the following aspects that can be utilized best when studying in field research.

1. **Practices.** Habits, customs, traditions, and behaviors such as washing of hands, storytelling, and tattooing.

2. **Episodes.** Life events or scenarios such as marriage and sickness societal events such as ouster, revolutions, or prosperity.

3. **Encounters.** Meeting between or among people and their interaction.

4. **Roles.** A look into people, the "positions" they take on, and "the behavior associated with those

positions" such as in the family, workplace, or indigenous groups.

5. **Relationship.** Action and experiences between "pairs or sets of roles" such as mother-child, politician – constituent, and supervisor-employee.

6. **Groups.** Sets of people sharing common characteristics or interests such as clubs and working groups.

7. **Organizations.** "formal organization such as hospitals and schools".

8. **Settlements.** Smaller units of society like communities, villages, and neighborhoods.

9. **Social worlds.** "ambiguous social entities with vague boundaries and populations such as "the sports world and 'wall street".

10. **Lifestyles or subcultures.** The way of living of a certain group of people such as "the elites, marginalized groups, or those with unique practices such as bikers, games, or nerds.

The Three C's of Qualitative Research Problem

1. **Circumstances.** First-hand observable account and vicarious experiences of the researcher in

encountering the problem.

2. **Contents.** Second source from scientific literature and documents highlighting certain findings and identifying certain fields that have not been covered yet.

3. **Construct.** Drawn from theories showing that a problem could be explained by a principle that has come shortcomings and could be researched.

Criteria in Evaluating Qualitative Research Problems.

Some criteria that can be used for evaluating qualitative research problems as follows:

1. The problem should not be too general or too specific.

2. The problem should be amenable to change as data are collected and analyzed.

3. The problem should not be biased with restrictive assumptions or desired findings.

4. The problem should be written in "how" and "what" forms to focus on describing the phenomena and,

5. The problem should include a central question as well as the participants and site.

How to Write the Qualitative Research Title

The research title usually serves as the show window of the entire research paper as it is frequently read the first (Amorado & Talili, 2017). It is generally crafted in a way that the intended readers gain an idea of the scientific inquiry. Being the final task after the research is completed, crafting the research title takes time as it is based on the guidelines or protocol prescribed by the publisher in the case of journal publication and organizer in the case of a research conference.

At the beginning of the research activity, researchers generally create a working title and get back to it after finishing the data analysis and interpretation of findings to reorient themselves on the research objectives and perhaps on the possibility of re-crafting the preconceived title.

The following guidelines are commonly used in writing a qualitative research title:

1. The title is reflective of the main objective or the salient findings of the study.

2. It lends international character especially when the paper is intended for international journal

publication.

3. It indicates the subject of the study as well as its scope.

4. It stimulates the interest of the readers.

5. It utilizes the current taxonomy (or word choice) from the field of study.

6. It ignores redundant phrases or wasteful words such as "An investigation of," "An analysis of," "A study of on," or similar constructions.

7. It may be crafted in declarative or interrogative statements.

8. It is written out with the letter of the first word capitalized, including that of the first word of a subtitle. All content words (nouns, verbs, adjectives, and adverbs) that come in between the first word and last word of the title are also capitalized.

9. The title can be crafted creatively.

10. It is written creatively satisfying the typical function – to explore and/or explain a world phenomenon, of a qualitative research.

In some instances, a subtitle is used along with the main title. It functions in the following ways:

1. It provides explication or explanation.

   Illustrative Example:

   The Joy of Social Work Administration: An Exploratory Qualitative Study of Human Service Administrators' Positive Perceptions of Their Work. (Watson & Hoefer, 2016).

2. It enhances the main title (oftentimes in a direct quote) which is literacy, if not, imaginative.

   Illustrative Example:

   Design and Development of Electric Motor Controller Trainer: An Instructional Device (Bajet, Guzman & Bajet, 2015).

3. It contextualizes the research.

   Illustrative Example:

   Student Retention in Higher Education in Turkey. (Aypay, Çekiç, & Boyaci, 2012).

4. It describes the temporal or progressive scope of the study.

   Illustrative Example:

   The Year – two Decline: Exploring the Incremental Experiences of a 1:1 Technology Initiative. (Swallow, 2015).

5. It reflects or identifies the research method or

approach used.

Illustrative Example:

Finding the Groove: A Grounded Theory Study on Leading Others to a Productive Path. (William, 2011).

Justifications for the Conduct of Research

The need to justify virtually everything that a researcher does makes research differ from other forms of inquiry. Research critics can challenge the validity or relevance of the findings if they believe there was something non-typical about the people selected for study, something biased in the way people are selected for study, something unfair about the groups compared, something wrong with the way the researcher phrased questions, and so forth. Every aspect of research design has an influence on what will be learned from the study.

Serrano enumerated some of the reasons in justifying the conduct of the research study.

1. Places the portion of the discussion in the academic in the academic context by showing that there are gaps in knowledge in the field

that merit a closer investigation.

2. Demonstrate that the work will fill this gap by adding knowledge in and understanding of the field.

3. Demonstrate the work hasn't been previously done, ensuring the intellectual contribution is indeed original.

4. Demonstration of a critical approach to scholarship. Show that the researcher has analyzed and critiqued the theories or methodologies in the field and that he knows the main arguments related to his topic.

5. Consider how the available research and existing scholarship support the research. How does it contradict the research? How will the research resolve the difference?

Therefore, the researcher needs to have a rationale for every aspect of his study. To see how this rationale makes difference, image that there are two different studies being read with similar design and research methods, but with different rationale? Which would be more persuasive to find out?

Illustrative Example of Justification of the Study

Worker Perceptions in Assumed Low-Risk Environments

The purpose of this research is to examine the personal perceptions and safety concerns of workers in assumed low-risk organizations. While high-risk organizations and professions, such as policing (Chappell & Di Martino, 2006), have been identified and studied in previous research, there is a lack of knowledge about the personal points-of-view of workers in assumed low-risk organizations regarding safety issues.

The broad topic of workplace violence has received attention, including from the government, but assumed low-risk environments are not the focus of that attention. Instead, the Occupational Safety and Health Administration (OSHA), while acknowledging that workplace violence occurs in all industries, is currently focusing on workplace violence issues regarding those in healthcare and social assistance jobs (Association of Safety Engineers, 2017).

As society faces increased threats regarding workplace violence, the types of organizations that are now at risk are changing. Years ago, people would not believe that children could be attacked while in the safety of their school (Chappell & Di Martino, 2006). "Just a few decades ago, the very notion that children would be murdered in their schools by other children was unthinkable" (Ruffini, 2006). The results of this project may provide insight into workers' perceptions of safety in currently assumed low-risk environments such as libraries and coffee shops, which are other environments that are typically considered safe by the general public. With the changes regarding what organizations are at-risk, understanding workers' perceptions of safety is beneficial to leaders in organizations because safety concerns have the potential to impact both the professional and personal needs of employees.

Explain the research focus and its relationship to the discipline or field of study that supports the need to conduct the proposed study.

According to Jain, Saeed, Arnaout, and Kortum (2012) major areas of concern in the workplace include stress, violence, and bullying. "At the organizational level, work stress can lead to a deteriorated work climate, and can have an impact on product and service quality as well as the image of the organization" (Jain et al., 2012). The exposure to stress in the workplace could lead to negative effects in an individuals' mental and physical health, as well as organizations' overall productivity and effectiveness.

The data collected through this research have the potential to be used to raise awareness of worker concerns in assumed low-risk environments, and to provide information for organizations to use in an effort to create or improve prevention plans and trainings regarding workplace violence. In so doing, assumed low-risk environments could potentially avoid becoming higher risk, as happened previously with schools (Chappell & Di Martino, 2006). Furthermore, the research results may provide organizations with information that potentially can be used to address the mental health needs of employees in assumed low-risk environments.

Describe the issue, situation, problem, or opportunity that supports the need to implement the study.

Explain how the outcome of your study will benefit practitioners and scholars

Research gap

Research gap is a research question that has not been addressed properly. Researchers and academicians often find it difficult to identify the research gap in the literature in their respective fields. Exploring the research gap is one of the most difficult tasks for researchers who are a novice or who are at the preliminary stage of their research.

According to Carey et al. (2011) "Audiences likewise researchers could use information about prioritized research gaps to understand areas of uncertainty and more quickly initiate studies". Robinson et al. (2011) opined that "the clear and explicit identification of research gaps is a necessary step in developing a research agenda, including decisions about funding and the design of informative studies". Identifying research gap from the literature is common practice but the criteria used seems to be ambiguous and vague. He added that research note suggested the reasons for research gap including insufficient or imprecise information, biased information, inconsistency or unknown consistency, and not the right information.

Research gap analysis is ambiguous and equivocal for novice, young researchers as they find it challenging to explore the research gap because of a lack of criteria or predetermined procedures. For example, identifying the broad area and then selecting the specific area can lead to the problem identification

Research gap essentially makes research publishable -it shows the researchers;

1. Is not just repeating existing research;
2. Has a deep understanding of the status of the body of knowledge in a chosen field;
3. Has conducted a research which fulfills that gap in the literature

Types of Research Gaps

1. Evidence Gap (Contradictory Evidence Gap).

An evidence gap occurs with a provocative exception arises if a new research finding contradicts widely accepted conclusions. This gap involves contradictions in the findings of the prior research. It occurs if results from studies allow for conclusions in their own right, but are contradictory when examined from a more abstract point of view. The identification

120

of contradictory evidence starts with analyzing each research stream. Subsequently, the results from these analyses need to be synthesized in order to reveal contradictory evidence (Müller-Bloch & Kranz, 2014).

Results from studies allow for conclusions in their own right but are contradictory when examined from a more abstract point of view (Jacobs, 2011; Müller-Bloch & Kranz, 2014; Miles, 2017).

Strategy Example and writing up the research gaps and selling the research proposal

> The researcher identified an apparent evidence gap in the prior research concerning_______________. Previous research has addressed several aspects of _______________: (1)_______________(cite two to three relevant articles), (2) _______________ (cite two to three relevant articles), and (3) _______________ (cite two to three relevant articles). However, the previous research has not addressed several contradictions in the findings concerning the prior research. The researcher has identified there is an evidence gap in the prior studies that are contradictory in the findings.

2. Knowledge Gap (Knowledge Void Gap).

The knowledge gap is a common gap in the prior research. There are two settings where a knowledge gap (knowledge void) might occur. First, knowledge may not exist in the actual field to theories and literature from related research domains. Second, it might be the case that the results of a study differ from what was expected (Müller-Bloch & Kranz, 2014).

Desired research findings do not exist (Jacobs, 2011; Müller-Bloch & Kranz, 2014; Miles, 2017)

Strategy Example and writing up the research gaps and selling the research proposal

> The researcher identified an apparent knowledge gap in the prior research concerning_____________. In addition, the prior research did not address the subject of _____________. This encompasses several unexplored dimensions that lately have attracted research attention in other disciplines (cite two to three relevant articles). The _____________ should be explored further to provide an understanding as to why such is not the case with _____________ .

3. Practical Knowledge Gap (Action-Knowledge Conflict Gap).

This kind of gap tends to be a discrepancy that can motivate new research in this direction. A practical–knowledge (action-knowledge) conflict arises when the actual behavior of professionals is different from their advocated behavior. In this case, research could seek to determine the scope of the conflict and to uncover the reasons for its existence (Müller-Bloch & Kranz, 2014).

Professional behavior or practices deviate from research findings or are not covered by research (Jacobs, 2011; Müller-Bloch & Kranz, 2014; Miles, 2017).

Strategy Example and writing up the research gaps and selling the research proposal

There is appears to be a practical- knowledge gap in the prior research. There is a lack of rigorous research in the prior literature. Some of these unexplored________ appear to be lacking in the practice of _______________field. The field of _______________ is ripe for an investigation of practical focus research on ___________Many of the prior studies focus on the theoretical aspects of the field of _______________. However, there are very few practical studies or action research in the field of _______________. This is an important and worthy of investigation in the context of _______________. An investigation of these issues is important because _______________. Furthermore, previous theoretical research has focused primarily on _______________ and very little practical- research has been done on ___________field

4. Methodological Gap (Methodology Void Gap).

A methodological gap is the type of gap that deals with the conflict that occurs due to the influence of methodology on research results. This gap addresses the conflicts with the research methods in the prior studies and offers a new line of research that is divergent from those research methods. It is noted that it might be useful to vary research methods, especially if certain research topics have been mainly explored using a singular or common method (Müller-Bloch & Kranz, 2014)

A variation of research methods is necessary to generate new insights or to avoid distorted findings (Jacobs, 2011; Müller-Bloch & Kranz, 2014; Miles, 2017).

Strategy Example and writing up the research gaps and selling the research proposal

The researcher identified a methodological gap in the prior research. There is a lack of _________________research designs in ____________. Based on the research we are trying implement as a research design, we found there is dearth in the prior research on_________ research designs. In this study we seek to establish a new inquiry on research designs with ___________. We seek to extend _________________ the research by addressing the gaps with _________________in the research methodologies with ____________.

5. Empirical Gap (Evaluation Void Gap).

An empirical gap is the type of gap that deals with gaps in the prior research. This conflict deals with the research findings or propositions need to be evaluated or empirically verified. For example, the empirical gap often addresses conflicts that no study to date has directly attempted to evaluate a subject or topic from an empirical approach (Müller-Bloch & Kranz, 2014).

Research findings or propositions need to be evaluated or empirically verified (Jacobs, 2011; Müller-Bloch & Kranz, 2014; Miles, 2017).

Strategy Example and writing up the research gaps and selling the research proposal.

There is appears to be an empirical gap in the prior research. There is a lack of rigorous research in the prior literature. Some of these unexplored________ appear to be important and worthy of investigation in the context of _________________________. An empirical investigation of these issues is important because _________________. Furthermore, previous research has focused primarily on qualitative research concerning _________________ . No study to date has directly attempted to empirically evaluate ____________. Very little empirical research has been done on ____________.

6. Theoretical Gap (Theory Application Void Gap).

The theoretical gap is the type of gap that deals with the gaps in theory with the prior research. For example, if one phenomenon is being explained through various theoretical models, similar to a methodological gap conflict, there might be a theoretical conflict. Researchers and scholars could examine whether one of those theories is superior in terms of the gap in the prior research. Theoretical gaps are a common occurrence in examining prior research on a phenomenon [Müller-Bloch & Kranz, 2014]

Theory should be applied to certain research issues to generate new insights. There is lack of theory thus a gap exists (Müller-Bloch & Kranz, 2014; Jacobs, 2011; Müller-Bloch & Kranz, 2014; Miles, 2017).

Strategy Example and writing up the research gaps and selling the research proposal

> The researcher identified an apparent theoretical gap in the prior research concerning________________. The theory on ________________is rather dated and the current studies bear the fruit of this theoretical gap. Some of the prior theory appear to be important and a foundation worthy of recognition. However, an investigation in terms of ________________ and theoretical development is warranted. An investigation of these issues is important because ________________ Furthermore, previous theoretical models need to embrace contemporary research in ________________ and related fields to provide a stronger theoretical basis for projects. The previous theory tends to focus primarily on ________________. It does not encompass new paradigms in ________________.

7. Population Gap

A population gap is a common gap recognized among researchers. There are always under-served populations that have been under-researched. This gap is the type of research regarding the population that is not adequately represented or under-researched in the evidence base or prior research (e.g., gender, race/ethnicity, age, and etic) (Robinson, et al, 2011).

Research regarding the population that is not adequately represented or under-researched in the evidence base or prior research (Robinson, et al, 2011).

Strategy Example and writing up the research gaps and selling the research proposal.

> Based on the review of the prior research, there is a population gap. Some of these sub-populations have been unexplored and under researched. The__________ appear to be important and worthy of investigation in the context of __________________________________. An investigation of this group is important because ___________________________. Furthermore, previous research has focused primarily on this population of __________________. Very little research has been done on ___________________.

The Problem and Its Background

This portion of your research should provide an overview of and rationale for the study. This includes background information that would focus attention on the importance and validity of the problem under investigation. It is a general orientation to the problem area. Describe your topic at the very start. A rationale to justify the problem must be provided. The opening statement should capture the interest of the reader.

The preparation of the introductory remarks entails reading a lot of literature in your field of concentration and being critical of what you read, attending professional lectures, colloquia, or seminars, subscribing to journal in your field, and building up some library materials.

Biron, De Jose & Abaigar (2018) asserted that one way of making an introduction is to define the major concepts to be used in the study. Another is to cite some conclusions or findings of previous research which prompted you to conduct a study or extension study on the problem. Describe the prevailing condition of the phenomenon today, if there are available statistics to be cited showing the importance of the problem then this could be a good support to your introduction. Some writers state concisely the objectives of their research incorporating explicitly the key statement concerning the problem to be investigated.

For good background, you can state the antecedents of your study, the reasons why this topic is being proposed relative to previous studies.

The Problem and its Background have the following essential elements.

1. Introduction

2. Statement of the Problem

3. Scope and delimitation of the Study

4. Significance of the Study

Illustrative Example

> This chapter present the different elements: the introduction which contains the rationale (an explanation of the reasons for the conduct of the research), the literature review and statistical foundation; the statement of the general and specific problem, the scope and delimitation which identifies the major variables, sub-variables and the indicators; the significance of the study which enumerates the beneficiaries of the study and the corresponding benefits each will receive.

The Introduction

The introduction is important in establishing the cognitive setting of the research (Cristobal & Cristobal, 2013). The introduction explains why this research is important or necessary or important. Begin by describing the problem or situation that motivates the research. Move to discuss the current state of research in the field; then reveal a "gap" or problem in the field. Finally, explain how the present research is a solution to that problem or gap. More so, tt has the following elements:

1. Rationalization of the need to research on the problem

2. Clarification of the important terminologies for the reader to easily understand what the research is about

3. Establishment of the degree of seriousness of the problem which prompted the researcher to look for solutions

The following questions will aid the researcher in formulating the introduction (Cristobal & Cristobal, 2017).

1. **What is the rationale of the problem?** This question is answered by sharing the reasons why the researcher decided to look for solutions to the problem. A rationale may include the narration of personal experiences, a description of an article read, a scene witnessed, news heard, or a theory that needs to be clarified. The researcher should describe the existing and prevailing problem

based on his or her experience. The scope may be local, national, or international. Ideally, the rationale can start from a global perspective to a more personal one.

2. **What is the setting of the problem?** The setting forms part of the delimitation of the study. It defines the geographic boundaries and certain demographic characteristics of the research. This describes the place where the research was conducted since the setting has a significant bearing on the variables being studied. In the description of the setting, its distinctive characteristics must be highlighted.

3. **What is the basic literature foundation of the study?** This is different from the review of the related theories, conceptual literature, and research literature. This part seeks to provide the researcher clarity on the terms or variables used in the study. The terms and variables must be clear to the researcher for an easy understanding of the readers. As such, sufficient background can assist the investigator in determining the boundaries of the study. This part is derived from different

literature sources. The use of various references is crucial in this part of the first chapter.

4. **How serious is the chosen research problem?** The researcher is tasked to identify the intensity and magnitude of the problem. When the gravity of the problem has already been described, he or she may then gauge the kind of action to be used to identify the problem. In most cases, the researcher at this point looks for statistical or quantitative evidence to assess the significance of the problem at hand.

5. **What is the general objective of the problem?** This is the general statement of the problem or the major tasks of the researcher to discharge and should also be the basis of the enumerated statements of specific problems.

6. **What is the overall purpose of the problem?** It is important to note that the researcher must be totally aware of the purpose of the research problem. He or she must fully understand the implications of the resulting findings of the study.

Illustrative Example of Introduction

**The Unheard Voices of Students:
Affective Filter
in Focus** (Lim,2020).

Emotion and cognition are often tagged as factors in learning a language. Many times, I have observed scenarios where students find difficulty in sharing ideas in the class not due to lack of knowledge but due to certain level of shyness which inhibits them to perform better in oral communication.

→ **Rationale**

This knowledge has been shared, not only in the context of this study, but as well as abroad. Lin's (2008) research on affective filter hypothesis among Taiwanese university students found that affective competence affected the students in knowledge acquisition. The study used natural approach of teaching such as the incorporation of games, English songs and movies. This methodology further informs teachers that facilitating emotional health can be done in a most typical manner (Berho & Defferding, 2005).

→ **Setting of the Problem**

A research was also undertaken by Marcial (2016) in the University of the Philippines Los Baños. The study showed that even students at the university had already reported anxiety at a lower rate and that the students' level of anxiety had a strong connection to their self-perceived use of English in both formal and informal conversation

→ **Literature Foundation**

Findlay & Coplan (2009) concluded that the family environment and situation is assumed to play a significant role in in the development of shyness among the children. If children experience high levels of family stress during a young age, they are more likely to experience shyness during the middle childhood years and beyond. Parents who experience high long-standing arguments with their children may increase the chance of developing shyness in their children. Children may also develop a more dependent relationship with parents as well as a strong passive stance with other peers and new people (Feng, Shaw, & Moilanen, 2011). This captures the use of English language outside the classroom and at home.

Since shy children are at an elevated risk of higher levels of anxiety, they also have an increased risk of depression; they report feeling sad more frequently than non-shy children (Eggum et al., 2012). Increase levels of anxiety contribute to lower results of performances at school. In addition, nervous students as well as other extremely insecure students have poorer scores than other students.

Social functioning is also decreased which leads to poorer relationships and more stressful school experience (Wood, 2006). Shy children may have academic struggles as well. They experience an increase levels of stress from being with peers and teachers. Their cognitive abilities are taxed (Hughes & Coplan, 2010).

Setting of the Problem

Seriousness of the Problem

This results to a reduction in their cognitive resources which should have been used for learning and paying attention. Hence, lower grades, lower standardized test scores and higher levels of unfinished work of students can be attributed to the increase level of stress.

Seriousness of the Problem

An important method for helping shy students from a teacher's standpoint is to develop positive teacher–child relationship (Arbeau, Coplan & Weeks, 2010; Pianta & Stuhlman, 2004). Other than the traditional role of teaching academic skills, the teachers are responsible for controlling children's activity level. Intimate teacher and child relationships are negatively associated with school avoidance and positively related to prosocial behavior. The teachers reported that timid children are more inclined to develop intimate, close relationships with one or two friends. Positive relationships between teachers and students promote children's long-term social and academic improvement and are especially helpful for the adjustment of shy students in school (Coplan & Rudasill, 2016).

Setting of the Problem

Hence, the current researcher was inspired to delve into looking the struggles of students with high affective filter; how students with high affective filter cope their inability to perform well in the class, and what expectations students have from teachers to lessen their high affective filter.

General Objective

> This study was viewed using Krashen's (1982) affective filter hypothesis Several main factors in the success of learners in Second Language Acquisition should be related to the emotional state of the student as stressed by Krashen (1982).
>
> The achievement of learners in learning the English language in English as a second language classroom relies heavily on the learner 's enthusiasm and involvement in the lesson plus the faith and trust they have in their teacher

General Purpose

Statement of the Problem

A problem statement is a brief description of the issues that need to be addressed by a problem-solving team and should be presented to them (or created by them) before they try to solve the problem. On the other hand, a statement of the problem is a claim in one or two sentences in length that outlines the problem addressed by the study. More so, Trinidad (2018), elucidated that statement of the problem starts with a declarative account of the main research problem that will be investigated. This is usually a paragraph that encapsulates the realities to be investigated, the variables to be studied, and a summary of the methods to be applied. Connectedly, Chan, et al (2008), asserted that statement of the problem should be in consonance with the title of the study.

Taking aside, Creswell and Clark (2014) provide the following criteria in writing the purpose statement:

1. It should use single and not compound sentences.
2. It should clearly express the purposes of the study.
3. It should include the central phenomenon.
4. It should use qualitative words such as
    a. Report (or reflect) the stories (e.g., narrative research)
    b. Describe the essence of the experience (e.g., phenomenology)
    c. Discover (e.g., grounded theory)
    d. Seek to understand (e.g., ethnography)
    e. Explore a process (e.g., case study)
5. It should identify the participants in the study.
6. It should state the research site.

A sample pattern for the purpose statement is provided below.

> The purpose of this **(narrative, phenomenological, grounded theory, ethnographic, and case study research)** is to **(understand, describe, develop, discover)** the **(central phenomenon of the study)** for (the participant) at (the site). At this stage in the research, the (central phenomenon) will be generally defined as **(a general definition of the central concept).**

Illustrative Example of Statement of the Problem

> **Campus Bullying in The Senior High School:**
> **A Qualitative Case Study (Galabo, 2019)**
>
> The purpose of this qualitative case study was to describe the campus bullying experiences of senior high school students, their problems encountered, their emotional struggles, their coping strategies and even their insights and realizations that would be useful in making interventions in the future.

The general problem is followed by an enumerated of the specific problems. These problems are usually stated as questions that the researcher seeks to answer. Therefore, the specific problems must meet the following criteria (Cristobal & Cristobal, 2017).

1. They must be in question form.

2. They define the population and the samples of the study (respondents).
3. They must identify the variables being studied.

Research Questions

Research questions serve as guide posts in research. The research topic, general issue, challenge, knowledge gap, or concern you which to address in your investigation, as well as the purposes of your study, are concretized in your research questions (Clamor-Torneo & Torneo, 2018). A qualitative research question is a question about some process, issue, or phenomenon that is to be explored. It is a general, open-ended, and overarching question that you would like to answer. From this overarching research question, you can frequently narrow the purpose of a qualitative study to more specific questions. It can be helpful to state the general purpose of the study and then state a number of subquestions that break the overall research question into components that will be investigated.

More so, qualitative inquiry allows one to answer questions about the nature of social phenomena under study rather than the prevalence of the phenomena. This means that all aspects of the phenomenon will be dissected and described and possibly an attempt will be made to understand how the phenomenon is built-up, what the relationships are between the different parts, and what influences the absence or presence of certain parts.

The research questions will be the focus of your inquiry. They will be the basis for your data gathering instruments and the queries that you would need to address all throughout your research.

Roles of Research Questions (Punch, 1998., & Silverman, 2013).

The following are the roles of research questions.

1. **They organize the research and give it direction and coherence**. Your questions will serve as your guide from the start of your research until the end. In the beginning, you plan how to get answers to these questions by coming up with a research design, data gathering procedure, and tools. In qualitative research, it is normal to encounter a lot of data.

You might feel intimidated by it, but let the research questions be the basis of your data analysis. Keep them in mind as your study.

2. **They delimit the research, showing its boundaries.**

3. **They keep the researcher focused**. Since the research questions clearly limit the scope of the topic you wish to address, you can focus your attention on answering these. You can keep coming back to your research questions and have them always at the back of your mind when planning your study, gathering data, analyzing data, and coming up with a conclusion.

4. **They provide a framework when you write your research.** your paper can be organized according to your research questions. Depending on what emerged from your data gathering phase, you may address one question per chapter. The sections of your paper will reflect your answer to your research questions.

5. **They point to the methods and data that will be needed.** As mentioned in previous modules, there is a certain inquiry that requires either a qualitative or a quantitative research methodology.

According to Creswell and Clark (2014), there are two types of research questions in qualitative research. These are as follows:

1. **Central questions.** These are the most general questions that can be asked.
2. **Sub-question.** These questions. These questions subdivide the central question into more specific topical questions and are only limited in number.

Creswell and Clark (2014) also provide some guidelines in formulating the research question in qualitative research:

1. The question should begin with words such as "how" or "what".
2. The readers should be informed of the information that will be discovered, generated, explored, identified, or described in the study.

3. The question "What happened?" should be asked to help craft the description.

4. The question "What was the meaning to people of what happened?" should be asked to understand the results.

5. The question "What happened over time?" should be asked to explore the process.

In addition, Creswell and Clark (2004) also provide the following scripts as a guide in designing qualitative central and sub-questions:

1. **Central question script**

   a. "What is the meaning of/what does it mean to (central phenomenon)?"

   b. "How would (participants) describe (central phenomenon)?"

2. **Sub-question script**

   a. "What (aspect) does (participant) engage in as a (central phenomenon)?"

Illustrative Example of Research Questions

> **Campus Bullying in The Senior High School:**
> **A Qualitative Case Study (Galabo, 2019)**
>
> 1. What are the campus bullying experiences of senior high school students?
> 2. What are the coping mechanisms of bullied senior high school students?
> 3. What are the realizations and insights the students learned?

Types of Qualitative Research Questions

1. **Exploratory Questions.** This is form of question looks to understand something – without influencing the results with preconceived notions. The objective of asking an exploratory question is to learn more about a topic without attributing bias or preconceived notions to it.

   Illustrative Examples:

   a. What is the effect of personal technology on today's youth?

   b. What is the experience of identifying as LGBTQ in the foster care system?

2. **Predictive Questions.** As the name entails, these questions seek to understand the intent or future outcome surrounding a topic or action. These types of questions use past information to predict reactions to hypothetical events.

   Illustrative Example:

   Are millennials more likely to buy a product after a celebrity promotes it?

3. **Interpretive Questions.** Look to gather

feedback on a certain topic or concept without influencing the outcome. They ask questions on how a group makes sense of shared experiences and attributes meaning to various phenomena.

Illustrative Examples:

a. How do preschoolers in a play-based program handle transitions between activities?

b. How do people who witness domestic violence understand how it affects their current relationships?

Criteria for Evaluating Research Questions

The following are the criteria for evaluating the research questions in qualitative research (Bryman, 2008).

1. They should be clear, in the sense of being intelligible.

2. They should be researchable. That is, they should allow you to do research in relation to them. This means that they should not be formulated in terms that are so abstract that

they cannot be converted into researchable terms.

3. They should have some connection(s) with established theory and research. This means that there should be literature on which you can draw to help illuminate how your research questions should be approached. Even if you find a topic that has been scarcely addressed by social scientists, it is unlikely that there will be no relevant literature (e.g., on relevant or parallel topics).

4. Your research questions should be linked to each other. Unrelated research questions are unlikely to be acceptable since you should be developing an argument in relation to unrelated research questions.

5. They should at the very least hold out the prospect of being able to make an original contribution – however small – to the topic.

6. The research questions should be neither too broad (so that you would need a massive grant to study them) nor too narrow (so that you cannot make a reasonably significant

contribution to your area of study).

Research Objectives

Objectives are goals or academic expectations that researchers set in the study. Objectives are also referred to as aims. Generally, there are one general or main objectives, which may refer to a statement about the overall direction of the study. Consequently, student researchers may identify specific objectives, called sub-objectives that may refer to a particular topic that they want to investigate. These sub-objectives must be within the scope of the main objective of the research but may refer to one aspect of the study. It is advised that one sub-objective may reflect one aspect of the research.

According to Marquez-Fong and Tigno (2016), the easy way to formulate research objectives is to derive a general objective from the research question and transform it into an infinitive clause. An infinitive clause begins with the infinitive form of a verb (to + verb).

From the main objectives, you can derive at least two or three specific objectives that will guide your data gathering and analysis. These specific objectives should be stated clearly such that they are clearly and definitely related to the data you will obtain. They represent subsequent actions that will help you achieve the general objective and should follow a logical sequence based on how you will analyze your data.

Action Verbs used to Write Basic Research Objectives

1. **Cognitive Domain**
    a. **Knowledge.** List, define, tell/state, describe, identify, show, label, collect, tabulate, quote, name, recognize, recall, memorize, select, recognize, enumerate, record, match, read/view.
    b. **Comprehension.** summarize, describe interpret, associate, distinguish, estimate, differentiate, discuss (rehash), extend, translate, convert, indicate, classify, paraphrase.
    c. **Application**. apply, demonstrate, calculate, complete, illustrate, show, solve, examine,

modify, relate, change, classify, experiment, discover, prepare, operate, conduct.

d. **Analysis**. Analyze, separate, explain, connect, divide, arrange, compare, explain, infer, 'weed out', estimate, dissect, 'break down', discuss.

e. **Synthesis.** combine, integrate, modify, rearrange, substitute, plan, create, design, invent, compose, formulate, prepare, generalize, rewrite, argue, write, produce, theorize, incorporate.

f. **Evaluation**. assess, decide, rank, grade, test, measure, recommend, convince, judge, explain, discriminate, support, conclude, summarize, appraise, evaluate, contrast, compare, criticize, support, prioritize.

2. **Affective Domain**

a. **Receive Phenomena**. become aware, choose.

b. **Respond Phenomena**. Asks, complies, greets, participates, practices.

c. **Value initiates**. Invites, joins, shares, proposes.

d. **Organize Values**. Adheres, alters, integrates, completes.

   e. **Internalize Value**. Acts upon listens (willingly), influences others.

3. **Psychomotor Domain**

   a. **Perception.** choose, select, pick out.

   b. **Ready to act**. begin, prepare, volunteer.

   c. **Respond.** copy, trace, follow, reproduce.

   d. **Mechanism**. assemble, calibrate, lift/load, type

   e. **Adaptation.** adapt, alter, modify, change.

   f. **Originate**. compose, construct, design/develop, create (new).

Illustrative Example of Research Objectives

**Kpopped!: Understanding the Filipino Teens'
Consumption of Korean Popular Music
and Videos (Alanzalon, 2018)**

In general, the study attempted to understand why the Filipino teens are active consumers of Korean popular music and videos.

Specifically, the study aimed:

1. To measure the consumption of the Filipino teens through their frequency of consuming Korean popular music and videos;
2. To determine the different ways Filipino teens' consumed Korean popular music and videos;
3. To identify the different cultural offerings, present in Korean popular music texts that appealed to the Filipino teens;
4. To determine how the presence of cultural offerings influenced the consumption of the Filipino teens;
5. To know how the consumption of Kpop content gratified the different needs of the Filipino teens;
6. To find out how the gratification of needs served as a motivation for the Filipino teens' continued consumption of Korean music and videos

> **Semantic Feature of Philippine English: A Qualitative Analysis (Dayon, 2018)**
>
> In this study, I intended to primarily describe the semantic feature of Philippines English in the Davao region.
> *Specifically, I aimed to achieve the following objectives:*
> 1. To analyze the semantics of words or phrases as seen in student composition, print media, billboard ads, virtual communication, and office communication;
> 2. To describe the semantic feature of Philippine English as evidently discovered in multiple sources of data; and,
> 3. To draw out implications of the findings to education practice.

Scope and delimitation of the study

Scope and limitation of the study is an important section of a thesis, dissertation, and research paper. This includes the coverage of the study are, the subjects, the research instruments, the research issues or concerns, the duration of the study, and the constraints that have a direct bearing on the results of the study (Flores, 2016).

The study should indicate the coverage of the study (scope) and the variables excluded (delimitation). Ariola (2006) stressed that the limitation of the study indicates the variables that are to be contained/studied in the research study, while delimitation of the study is those which are not part (excluded) of the study. Since we cannot study or include everything in the environment, the weaknesses and shortcomings of the study should be indicated in this section. There has to be a limit in the study variables by considering time, money, materials, personnel, among others. In writing this section, the first paragraph should contain the scope and the second paragraph contain the delimitation.

Illustrative Example of Scope and delimitation

Kpopped!: Understanding the Filipino Teens' Consumption of Korean Popular Music and Videos (Alanzalon, 2018)

This study focused primarily on the Kpop fandom among the Filipino teens, regardless of gender and socio-economic status. Using the methods of survey and focus interviews, the study described the processes of the fans' consumption of Kpop media. It also determined the cultural aspects present in Kpop that Filipino teens could relate with, and how the content gratified the needs of the fans.

In this study, it shall be understood that Kpop not only refers to the music per se, but also the videos with Kpop idols and group in it including official music videos and other television shows featuring Kpop artists. In South Korea, Kpop artists frequently appear in talk, variety, and reality shows. These television shows were included in the media text that served as the basis of the Kpop audience's response. Only the television shows featuring Korean artists Girls' Generation, Super Junior, Shinee, SS501 and U-Kiss were included in the study.

In addition, the researcher focused on understanding the consumption of the fans by describing the cultural offerings of Kpop in the survey questionnaires, as well as the different ways of how Kpop gratified the needs of the fans. It did not attempt to look into other reasons such as other economical, psychological and sociological reasons, but only focused on the four different cultural offerings (language, visuals, cultural capitals, story) and the gratification of the four types of needs (information, personal identity, social interaction, entertainment). The term "fandom" in this study shall be understood as the emotionally involved consumption of media texts, as opposed to the gathering of people with the same interest for an artist or media content.

Also, the study did not attempt to generalize the Filipino teenage Kpop fans, but rather isolated cases and attempted to understand the individual fandom of the Filipino fans by means of focus interviews.

Illustrative Example of Scope and delimitation

Campus Bullying in The Senior High School:
A Qualitative Case Study (Galabo, 2019)

This qualitative inquiry is delimited only to the identified three students who are frequently reported, noted, and observed as victims of bullying at Optaciano Hilay National High, Manambulan, Tugbok District, Davao City. These participants were officially enrolled in the senior high school for the School Year 2017 – 2018. Bullies were not included in this study. One of the weaknesses of this study was the limited number of participants in which their shared experiences may not truly represent the reality that of the majority of the population in the entire City of Davao. Besides, since it utilized qualitative method, this cannot make generalization or general conclusion about campus bullying. However, the researcher made sure that trustworthiness and credibility of the participants were dealt with utmost safeguard.

Significance of the Study

Researches will be of no value if they do not contribute something specific to a body of knowledge or to some intended beneficiaries. The significance of the study is that part of the thesis, dissertation, and research paper that allows the researcher to state the value, importance, and or contributions that the study is expected to add to a particular disciple and to society in general (Salmorin, 2006).

The significance or importance of the study contains an explanation or discussion of any or all of the following (Bermudo, et al., 2010).

1. The intended or target beneficiaries of the study. Simply, the researcher should be able to identify WHO will benefit from the results of the investigation. The beneficiaries of the study vary according to the topic investigated. For researches that focused on the academic performance of students, the beneficiaries or end-users could be the students, teachers, administrators, parents, and others.

2. The specific benefits each of the intended clients/end-users may get out of the results of

the investigation. The concrete benefit that each client or end-user will get from the investigation is written after the data have been gathered, analyzed, and interpreted. However, for purposes of research proposal preparation, the researcher merely projects HOW the client or end-user will get benefit from the results of the investigation. The discussion is usually written from the general perspective. Once the result of the study is identified, the benefit that each client will get from the research will change. In other words, a justification for why there is a need to conduct the study is explained and discussed in this portion.

3. The contribution of the study to a body of knowledge.

Calderon (1993) stresses that any or all of the following may be included under the importance of the study, to wit:

1. The rationale, timeless, and/or relevance of the study. The rationale, timeless, and/or relevance of the study to existing conditions must be explained or discussed.

2. Possible solutions to existing problems or improvements to unsatisfactory conditions.

3. Who are to benefits and how they are to be benefited? It must be shown who are the individuals, groups, or communicates that may be placed in a more advantageous position on account of the study.

4. Possible contribution to the fund of knowledge.

5. Possible implications. It should be discussed here that the implications include the possible causes of the problem discovered, the possible effects of the problems, and the remedial measures to solve the problems. The implication also includes the good points of the system which ought to be continued or to be improved if possible.

Phrases in Expressing Significance of the Study

1. Researchers may find the findings useful as…

2. This study will encourage them to…

3. It will also serve as a basis in the study of…

4. This study will contribute to….

5. This study provides….

6. This study can help boost the…

7. Through this study, students will become aware of…

8. The result of this study will provide some insights and information on how they…

Illustrative Example of Significance of the Study

Kpopped!: Understanding the Filipino Teens' Consumption of Korean Popular Music and Videos (Alanzalon, 2018)

The primary reason for the researcher's interest in undertaking a study about Kpop was her own fascination for it. Although guided by her own reasons for consuming Kpop, she wanted to objectively look at the phenomenon. The researcher was also surprised that no other studies have tackled the Kpop fandom in the country considering the multitude of Filipino Kpop fans and its overwhelming popularity since 2009.

The researcher firmly believes that through this study, the Filipino teenage kpop fans may gain understanding of their fandom, and how their consumption of Kpop media content affects their decisions and participation in many activities in their lives. The study could encourage fans to be critical of the media's direct effects on their daily decisions. Also, the researcher was convinced that Kpop fans spend a considerable amount of their allowances on buying Kpop media products. This study could make Filipino parents understand their children's fascination for such foreign media products.

The findings of this study could strengthen and contribute to the studies on the appreciation of Filipinos of foreign media content. Also, it is an update on the studies of phenomenon and mania produced by the media, and the formation of fandom in the Philippines based on novelty and fads. Consequently, this research probed on the effects of the media on its audience, and posited that the audience is active.

The study may become the basis for Korean entertainment companies to recognize the Philippines' strong potential as a market for their products. This would also be beneficial to Kpop fans who demand easier access. Although some companies, both local and Korean, already recognize the Filipino market, it can't be denied that Kpop's reach in the Philippines is still not as widespread as compared to other Asian countries.

Also, this study maybe a basis for broadcast networks and producers to create strategies targeting Kpop fans as potential audience. The local media may also use the findings to recognize the factors that attract Filipino fans to Kpop content and use these strategies to improve local media content.

This study also encourages the audience to become critical and responsive to the media content presented to them. This way, they can contribute to the betterment of the local media through their active participation in the feedback process, thus creating a healthy relationship between the media and the society.

Lastly, the spread of Kpop may cultivate a better relationship between Filipino and Korean nationals residing in the Philippines, fostering an open society as it promotes intercultural relativism which opens the critical minds of the Filipinos to foreign cultures.

Illustrative Example Significance of the Study

Campus Bullying in The Senior High School: A Qualitative Case Study (Galabo, 2019)

This study explored the different experiences of bullying in the campus including its effects and consequences to victims, their coping mechanisms and insights learned. The experiences of the participants may serve as lessons to all students, teachers, parents and the entire community in order to be aware of the negative effects of bullying to both the victims and bullies. Through this study, preventive measures could be possibly discovered which may minimize, if not eliminate, bullying inside the school premises. Findings of this research could lead to a better understanding of campus bullying that would encourage school administrators, guidance counselors, teacher, advisers and subject teachers formulate policies in addressing the said problem. Once bullying is carefully dealt with, students may be motivated to learn and eventually academic standings would be improved.

ASSESSMENT TASKS

I. **Direction:** Identify the following research title according to their functions.

1. Exploring School Counselors' Perception of Vicarious Trauma.

2. Permission -Seeking as an Agentive Tool for Transgressive Teaching: An Ethnographic Study of Teachers Organizing for Curricular Change.

3. "This Ain't the Project: A Researcher's Reflections on the Local Appropriates of Our Research Tools.

4. "I know Down to My Ribs": A Narrative Research Study on the Embodied Adults Learning of Creative Writers.

5. Latino Parents and Teachers: Key Players Building Neighborhood Social Capital.

6. Investigating a New World: Thoughts on Kindergarten Literacy and Arts Integration.

7. A Classroom at Home: Children and the Lived of MOOCs.

8. Exploring the Phenomenology of Suicide

9. Interpretive and Critical Phenomenology

Crime Studies: A model Design.

10. Tribal College Transfer Students Success at Four–Year Predominantly White Institutions.

II. **Directions:** Make a good and creative title to the following problem – situation for a qualitative inquiry. From the questions you made, create a good and interesting title. Here is an example of a title for the question: "What is the school bully phenomenon (central phenomenon) in public secondary school?

Title: School Coercers Strike Again – How to Pull Away from a Bully

1. The meaning of death and pain of dying: why a mother grieves for the loss of a loved one.

2. A tribe in Victoria, Mindoro uses unique food production thru hunting with their tradition in their food–eating habits, behavior, and practices.

3. How the alternative learning system originated from its early beginning to its

contributions to the prevent educational system.

4. The group of students' fraternity brotherhood and its implications to the spirits of oneness.

5. The streets children and their perspectives on the meaning of life habitat with the proverbial "roof under their heads".

6. The aim of developing computer skills for "baby boomers" (old teachers) must first establish a need before a self–help manual is developed.

7. What is the world of orphans? Is being alone without parents to look up to a big constraint to pursue living?

8. Teachers in schools who "sell" goods for a lucrative income.

9. The Ifugao of the Mountain Province and their indigenous marriage customs and traditions.

10. The making of Filipino heroes thru their mighty pens: from pre-Hispanic to modern times.

III. **Directions:** Read the following situation and write a research question to start a qualitative inquiry.

1. **The Self – supporters.**

   High school students are too young to take responsibility – some of them engage in part-time jobs to augment income with various reasons to describe their self-supporting struggles in life. Describe their social world at an early stage of taking work as a disciple on top of their dream to acquire a diploma.

2. **Is there Life after Showbiz?**

   Showbiz personalities despite their popularity want to finish school. But how? Behind the glitters of the movie, the world is a great desire to pursue education through an alternative learning system (ALS) or home study program. There are cases of success and failure in this plan.

3. **People with Special Abilities**

   People show their best and great pride in what they do, despite certain handicaps. But this is not a reason to give up hope instead, they rise and shine. What drives these people to achieve and believe in themselves even physically and mentally, their social world is not complete.

IV. **Directions.** From the main research question, break it down to small questions like "what is the school bully phenomenon (central question) in public secondary school?" as the main question. The sub-question is:

a. What social relationship (aspect) do students, teachers, and parents (participant) engage in with a school bully (central phenomenon)?

b. What is the form of bullying experienced by high school students?

c. What are the strategies of the school to prevent school bully?

1. The Self – supporters' sub-questions

2. Life after Showbiz sub-questions

3. People with Special Abilities sub-questions.

V. **Directions:** Based on the sample introduction

below, identify the different parts of the sample introduction. Use a crayon or coloring pen to highlight the paragraph/s and then label which part they correspond to.

Kpopped!: Understanding the Filipino Teens' Consumption of Korean Popular Music and Videos (Alanzalon, 2018)

Since the advent of media, there has been an influx of ways and opportunities for fans to express their admiration for a popular narrative or text. Fans send fan letters through snail mail, or visit their idols on shoots and productions. And now especially with the dawn of new media such as the Internet and cellphone, the audience and the fans have a faster avenue to express their thoughts. After an episode of a drama series aired, fans would rally online to talk about their thoughts on the recent episode minutes after the broadcast. Andrejevic's study on the productivity of online fans found that viewer thoughts on an episode can change the way writers and producers create future episodes. Through different media, celebrities and broadcast programs are now more reachable for the fans. It is the same way that even fans from one country can access media content from another country. The world has become borderless, and media and fan activities are just two aspects of globalization that brought about the openness of the world.

Therefore, it is no surprise that even a Mexicana named Thalia and four chinky-eyed men from Taiwanese group F4 captured the hearts of the Filipinos. Marimar and Meteor Garden were game-changers in the programming landscape of the Philippines and created a cult-following among Filipinos. Their penetration in the mainstream media and the openness of the Filipinos to foreign media products brought upon the Korean Wave in the country. Since 2003, Korean dramas have become a staple in Philippine television. Studies show that the Philippines was only one of the many shores that the Korean wave, also known as Hallyu, affected. Hallyu is the rapid spread of the Korean entertainment industry in Asia.5 In addition, Korean pop music (Kpop) is also popular in Japan, China and Taiwan.

In the Philippines, Filipinos were only drawn to Korean dramas. However, June 2009 saw the debut of Korean music videos (MVs) in MYX Music Channel. Since then, Kpop as a media content, has become a staple in the programming of said channel, and created a fandom especially among the Filipino teenage fans. Korean songs entered MYX music charts and stayed for weeks. Music companies distributed Korean albums in the country, and most of these albums were best sellers in music stores. As an answer to the fans' clamor for Kpop content, MYX channel launched Asia Myx in December 2009, and Pop Myx Kpop Edition in May 2010. The year 2010 marked another milestone for the Kpop fandom among Filipino teens. Numerous Kpop groups like Shinee, 4minute, FT Island, Super Junior, U-kiss,Beast, Kim Hyunjoong and Rain visited the Philippines to perform.

In addition, more than two thousand Kpop fans gathered for the first ever Philippine Kpop Convention held in the Philippines International Convention Center on December 10, 2009. Various fan clubs and organizations joined hands to establish the Philippine Kpop Committee, and since its inception in late 2009, numerous projects and events have been held like parties and charitable events.

From observation, it is clear that Filipino fans join social groups to mingle with people with the same interest, as proven by the subculture of Kpop fans in the country flamed by activities of fan clubs and organizations.

However, it is very interesting to note that there have been no studies attempting to understand the Kpop fandom among the Filipino teens. What is the reason for their active consumption of Kpop media texts? What aspects of Kpop media content contribute to the Filipino teens' liking and appreciation? Do Kpop media texts gratify the various needs of the Filipino fans which contribute to their regular consumption? These questions fueled the researcher's interest in understanding the Filipino teens' consumption of Korean popular music, videos and artists.

PERFORMANCE TASKS

Design and Make the Problem and its Background

TASK 1: Creating a Title for the Research Study

The impression you create at the start of your research paper is very important. Your title should catch the readers' attention while properly informing them about the main focus of your research study. Make a list of three (3) possible titles for your qualitative research paper using the problem you wrote in Module 1 and Module 2. Try to make the main title intriguing and the subtitle descriptive.

TASK 2: Justification of the Study

Providing justification for your research topic stemmed solely from the outcome of your literature review. From the review, it may be that the methodologies previous studies employed did not adequately explain the phenomenon; it may be that new methodology in another field of studies may contradict the existing knowledge about the phenomenon and offer fresh insight which you may want to apply; it may be that the way the problem and its associated concepts were approached and defined was problematic and it may be that contemporary problem has falsified at the previous claims about the issue you are investigating. By the time you do through review, any of the aforementioned points will come out and that will help provide a good justification for your research. Write a draft of the justification of your study on a separate sheet of paper.

TASK 3: Research Questions

Coming from the three (3) titles you wrote, choose one which is you are interested to explore. Write the central research question for this title.

TASK 4: Research Objectives

From the chosen research title of your study. Construct the objectives of your study based on the research questions.

TASK 5: Introduction

From the chosen research problems or title. Formulate the introduction of your study by answering the following questions.

1. What is the rationale for your chosen problem?
2. Describe the setting where your study is to be conducted.
3. What are terms, variables, or concepts that need to be defined, clarified, or described to you and your reader?
4. Look for related literature that defines the main concepts of your study provide at least three (3) references per concept. Provide a brief description of each.
5. Determine the significance of your chosen problem. Research contextual evidence of its "gravity". Provide the details (and references) of this.

6. What are the general objectives or overall purpose of the study?

TASK 6: Scope and Delimitation of the Study

In the field of research, scope and delimitation refer to parameters that prevent researchers from pursuing further studies due to time and budgetary constraints. Some researchers must explore a subject area and find results within a specific period of time. Having a time limit is delimitation because it excludes the opportunity for individuals to make further discoveries in their subject areas, which influences the amount of information that can be relayed to an audience. Now, you are ready to write down the scope and delimitations of your research for the study.

TASK 7: Significance of the Study

Impactful research enables changes that make a positive difference to individuals, groups, organizations, and society as a whole (beneficiaries). Benefits may include, for example, incremental, minute improvement to the lives of large segments of the population, as well as deep, transformative influences upon the personal or professional lives of small numbers of individuals. In this task enumerate possible people who would benefit from your research study. Correspondingly indicate the benefits they will obtain from your research study.

Rubric for Writing the Problem and its Background

Criteria	Excellent 16-20	Very Good 11-15	Good 6-10	Need Improvement 1-5
Introduction	The introduction of the study is well developed.	The introduction of the study is fairly well developed.	The introduction of the study is not well constructed	The introduction of the study is badly written.
Statement of the Problem	The research problem is clearly stated and supported by high-quality (strong) evidence.	The research problem is fairly well stated, but it provides evidence that is not as strong it could be.	The research problem is not clearly stated, and it lacks quality evidence for support.	The research problem is not properly stated, and no evidence supports the problem.
Significance of the Study	The importance and relevance of the research are clearly explained.	The importance and relevance of the research are fairly explained.	The importance and relevance of the research are not clearly explained.	The introduction does not state the significance of the study.
Scope and limitation of the study	The scope of the study including the areas that will	The scope of the study including the areas that will	The scope of the study including the areas that will	The introduction does not include the

	not be covered is clearly defined.	not be covered is fairly defined.	not be covered is not clearly defined.	scope and limitation of the study.
Justification of the Study	The research justification is well stated based on the purpose of the study. The statement follows all the guidelines for formulating research justification	The research justification is fairly well stated based on the purpose of the study. The statement follows greater than 80% of the guidelines for formulating research justification	The research justification is unclear. The statement follows less than 80% of the guidelines for formulating a hypothesis.	The research justification does not support the purpose of the study. The statement fails to follow the guidelines for formulating research justification
Definition of Terms	The key terms used in the research are clearly defined. The operational and conceptual definitions are clearly stated.	The key terms used in the research are fairly defined. The operational and conceptual definitions are fairly stated.	The key terms used in the research are not clearly defined. The operational and conceptual definitions are not clearly stated.	There are no definitions of terms.
Overall Quality of the Research Introduction	The introduction articulates clear, reasonable research questions given the purpose, design, and methods of the proposed study. All constructs and variables have been appropriately defined. Propositions are clearly supported by	Although a research issue is identified, the statement of the problem is too broad, or its description fails to establish its importance. The research purpose, questions, hypotheses, or constructs and variables are poorly formed, ambiguous, or not logically	A relevant research issue is identified. Research questions are succinctly stated, connected with the research issue, and supported by the literature. Constructs and variables have been identified and described. Connections are	The statement of the problem, significance, purpose, questions/ hypotheses, or definitions of constructs and variables were omitted or inappropriate.

	the literature. All elements are mutually supportive.	connected to the description.	established with the literature.	

Cited References and Suggested Readings

Abila, S. & Fernandez, C. J. (2020). *Practical Research 1: Introduction to Qualitative Research for Senior High School.* Anvil Publishing House.

Alanzalon, S.M. (2011). *Kpopped! Understanding the Filipino Teens' Consumption of Korean Popular Music and Videos*. Unpublished Undergraduate Thesis, University of the Philippines College of Mass Communication.

Amarado, R. D. & Talili, I. N. (2017). *Qualitative Research: A Practical Approach*. Mutya Publication House. Inc.

Ariola, M.M. (2006). *Principles and Methods of Research.* Rex Book Store, Inc.

Barbie, E. (2008). *The Basics of Social Research (3rd Edition).* Thomson Wadsworth.

Birion, J.C., De Jose, E. G., & Abaigar, R.R. (2018). *Guide to Thesis and Dissertation Writing.* Unlimited Books Library Services & Publishing Inc.

Bryman, A. (2008). *Social Research Methods (3rd Edition).* Oxford University Press.

Carey, T., Yon, A., Beadles, C., & Wines, R. (2011). *Use of Research Gaps from Systematic Reviews to Inform Research Priorities*. http://www.shepscenter.

Clamor – Torneo, H. S., & Torneo, A.R. (2018). *Practical Research 1: An Introduction to Qualitative Research.* Sibs Publishing House, Inc.

Chan, E.I., Canapi, M. R., Bernales, R.A., Orozco, M.N., Pasigui, R.E.,& Vidal, CJ. E. *Research in Various Discipline: Seeing Through the Process of Writing*. Mutya Publishing House Inc.

Creswell, J. W. (2014). *Research Design: Qualitative, Quantitative, and Mixed Methods Approaches*. Sage Publication, Inc.

Cristobal, A. P., & Cristobal, M. C. (2013). *Research Made Easier: A Step-by-Step Process*. C & E Publishing, Inc.

Cristobal, A. P., & Cristobal, M. C. (2017). *Practical Research 1*. C & E Publishing, Inc.

Dayon, C. A. (2018). Semantic *Feature of Philippine English: A Qualitative Analysis*. Asian Society of Teachers for Research, Inc.

Flores, M.F. (2016). *Methods of Research in Business Education*. Unlimited Books Library Services & Publishing Inc.

Galabo, N. R. (2019). *Campus Bullying In The Senior High School: A Qualitative Case Study*. International Journal of Scientific & Technology Research, 8 (4).

Henson, R. M., & Soriano, R. F. (2016). *Qualitative Research: Word of Reality Dissections.* Mutya Publishing House Inc.

Jacobs, R. L. (2011). *Developing a Research Problem and Purpose Statement, in The Handbook of Scholarly Writing and Publishing*. Jossey-Bass.

Jimenez, M. M., & Silin, M. S. (2016). *Research in Daily Life: Practical Research 1.* Jenher Publishing House Inc.

Lim, R. A. (2020). *The Unheard Voices of Students: Affective Filter in Focus*. International Journal of Research and Innovation in Social Science (IJRISS), 4, (9).

Marquez- Fong, SE. R. & Tigno, C. R. (2016). *Practical Research 1*. Vibal Group, Inc.

Miles, D.A. (2017). *A Taxonomy of Research Gaps: Identifying and Defining the Seven Research Gaps*. Doctoral Student Workshop: Finding Research Gaps – Research Methods and Strategies, Dallas, Texas.

Müller-Bloch, C. & Kranz, J., (2014). *A Framework for Rigorously Identifying Research Gaps in Qualitative Literature Reviews.* The Thirty Sixth International Conference on Information Systems, Fort Worth.

Robinson, K., Saldanha, I. & McKoy, N.A. (2011). *Development of A Framework for to Identify Research Gaps Systematic Reviews*. Journal of Epidemiology, 64(1), pp. 1325-1330.

Salmorin, M. E. (2006). *Methods of Research*. Mindshapers Co., Inc.

Samosa, R.C., Magulod, G.C., Capulso, L.B., Delos Reyes, R.J., Gigawin, R.R., Luna, AR. F.,Maglente, S.S., Orte, CJ.S., Olitres, BJ.D., Pentang, J.P. Vidal, CJ. E., & Obrero, M. P. (2021). *How to Write and Publish Your Dissertation*. Beyond Books Publication.

Samosa, R.C., Magulod, G.C., Capulso, L.B., Delos Reyes, R.J., Luna, AR. F., Maglente, S.S., Orte, CJ.S., Olitres, BJ.D., Pentang, J.P. Vidal, CJ. E. (2021). *How to Write and Publish Your Thesis*. Beyond Books Publication.

Silverman, D. (2013). *Doing Qualitative Research (4th Edition).* Sage Publications Ltd.

Serrano, A. C. (2016). *Practical Research 1 on Qualitative Research.* Unlimited Books Library Services & Publishing Inc.

Summers, J. (2011). *Guidelines for Conducting Research and Publishing in Marketing: From Conceptualization Through the Review Process.* Journal of the Academy of Marketing Science, 29(4), pp. 405-415.

Trinidad, J. O. (2018). ***Researching Philippine Realities: A Guide to Qualitative, Quantitative, and Humanities Research.*** Ateneo De Manila University Press.

MODULE 4:

LEARNING FROM OTHERS AND REVIEWING THE LITERATURE

LEARNING OUTCOMES
At the end of this module, students should be able to:

1. selects relevant literature.

2. cites related literature using standard style (APA, MLA or Chicago Manual of Style)

3. synthesizes information from relevant literature.

4. writes coherent review of literature.

5. follows ethical standards in writing related literature.

6. presents written review of literature.

Literature Review

Research proposals and reports typically have a section – often an entire chapter in a thesis, dissertation, or research paper – that describes theoretical perspectives and previous research findings related to the problem at hand. Its function is to review – to "look again" at (re + view) – what others have done in areas that are similar, although not necessarily identical to, one's own topic of investigation.

A research literature review is a systematic, explicit, and reproducible method for identifying, evaluating, and synthesizing the existing body of completed and recorded work produced by researchers, scholars, and practioners (Fink, 2014).

The literature review in qualitative research can be used in several ways. It can be used to explain the theoretical underpinnings of the research study, to assist in formulation of the research question and selection of the study population, or to stimulate new insights and concepts throughout the study. Qualitative researchers often integrate the literature review throughout their study, working back and forth between the literature and the research (LeCompte & Preissle, 1993). Still, there are two schools of thought about the use of literature reviews in qualitative research. According to one school of thought, it is important to conduct a thorough literature review on your research topic before collecting data.

Strauss and Corbin (1990) specified several different ways in which a literature review conducted before data collection can be of value:

1. The literature review can be used to stimulate theoretical sensitivity toward concepts and relationships that prior literature has repeatedly identified and that therefore appear to be meaningful and significant. Because of their apparent significance, you might want to bring these concepts into the situation you are studying to identify the role they might play. For example, if the concept of isolation is repeatedly identified in the literature as being significantly related to creative achievement and you are studying creative achievement in underprivileged children, you might want to look for evidence of how isolation relates to

creative achievement in your study.

2. The literature can stimulate questions. The literature can assist you in deriving an initial list of pertinent questions to ask or behaviors to observe.

3. Finally, the literature can provide some information about the situations and populations that you need to study so that you can uncover phenomena that are important to the development of your theory. For example, in a study of creativity, the literature might indicate that you should look at individuals who are experiencing various emotional states because mood might be an important variable in the development of your theory of creativity.

According to the second school of thought, the researcher should set aside any preconceived notions (including published literature) and use a fully exploratory approach in which interpretations and additional research questions, hypotheses, and theory emerge from the data collected. From this perspective, you should initially familiarize yourself with the literature only enough to make sure that the study you are planning to conduct has not already been done. Only after you have collected your data do you conduct a thorough literature review to try to integrate what you have found with the literature.

Role of Literature Review (Leedy & Ormrod, 2021)

An extensive literature has many benefits.

1. It can help you ascertain whether other researchers have already addressed and solved your research problem or at least some of its subproblems.
2. It can offer new ideas, perspectives, and approaches that may not have occurred to you.
3. It can inform you about other individuals who conduct work in this area – individuals whom you may wish to contact for advice or feedback.
4. It can alert you to controversial issues and gaps in understanding that have not yet been resolved – issues and gaps you might address in your own work.
5. It can show you how others handled

methodological and design issues in studies similar to your own.

6. It can reveal sources of data you may not have known existed.

7. It can introduce you to assessment tools that other researchers have developed and effectively.

8. It can help you interpret and make sense of your findings and ultimately, help you tie your results to the work of those who have preceded you.

9. It can bolster your confidence that your topic is one worth studying, especially if you find that others have invested considerable time, effort, and resources in studying it.

Types of Sources for a Literature review

Researchers need to familiarize themselves with the types of sources before they begin to search for information related to the research question. The following are the types of sources includes general, primary, secondary, and tertiary sources (Clemente, Julaton., & Orleans, 2016).

1. **General references** are sources that are first accessed by a researcher to give them information about other sources such as research articles, professional journals, books, monographs, conferences, proceeding, and similar documents.

2. **Primary sources** are those that provide first-hand information about experts' and other researchers' publications. These publications contain findings that are directly communicated to the readers and interested parties. Authors' information for future correspondences may also be found in these publications.

3. **Secondary sources** are those written by authors that describe another researcher's works. These materials or documents may contain only summaries or interpretations of the research reports rather than a complete description of them. Good secondary sources are articles on a meta-analysis of studies conducted in a period of time because they can provide research gaps and over-studied areas of a research field. Secondary sources include

textbooks, single-authored books, books edited by different authors with each contributing to a collection of chapters on a single topic.

4. **Tertiary sources** are books and articles based on secondary sources. It synthesizes and explains the work of others.

However, Henson and Soriano (2016) enumerated the suggested sources for literature review.

1. **Textbooks.** Collection of writing in a subject is such as annuals (compact books of facts dealing with any topic) and scholarly handbook, sometimes referred to a s *vade mecum* (Latin phrase which means "go with me") or pocket reference that is intended to be carried at all times, generally compendiums of information in a particular field or about a particular technique.

2. **Encyclopedia.** All-embracing compilations of information with a multi-faceted approach to a subject and a compendium of all knowledge with bibliographies that provide specific sources, classified either as subject encyclopedias containing overview articles

summarizing what is known about topics in a specific discipline, and legal encyclopedia on laws as a useful source.

3. **Dictionaries.** Alphabetical arrangements of words and their meanings, an abbreviated type of subject encyclopedia that lists and defines a basic and specialized term in a particular field providing meanings for abbreviation, jargon, and slang.

4. **Annual Reviews**. Yearly summaries of current research activities useful for selecting and refining research topic or question, finding information or sources, and updating bibliographies.

5. **Bibliographies**. List of citations to sources. Is an alphabetical listing by author, list of citations to sources ranging from "works cited" list at the end of books and articles to complete independent publications and annotation by giving a brief summary of the content of the article or book, possibly a comment on its quality either as appended or attached with at the end of an article, chapter

or book.

6. **Indexes**. Provide a way of finding additional materials, arranged by subject headings sometimes by authors, occasionally by journals with a list of articles in research publications by subject area and sometimes by the author, different types of indexes like periodical indexes with a specific date or issue copy, and even the pages for a specific article usually arranged by subject heading sometimes by author.

7. **Abstracts.** Paragraph–length summaries or considerations of study articles published in books/journals; paragraph or sentence–length summaries of original of a research articles, thesis, review, conferences proceedings, or any in-depth analysis of a particular subject or discipline, and is often used to help the reader quickly ascertain the paper's purpose.

8. **Scholarly Journals.** Vehicles for reporting current studies conducted by academic/professional organizations.

9. **Professional/Trade Periodicals.** Provide

important sources of information and insight in a given field.

As you select work to read and sources to use in your research, your research, you should be able to evaluate the materials with regard to the primary or secondary nature of the source, the objectivity of the source, the qualifications of the author, and the level of the source.

Some Criteria in Evaluating Literature Sources

1. **Type of source.** A particular work may be primary or secondary source according to your purpose; primary sources are basic materials with little or no annotation or editorial alterations, such as manuscripts, diaries, letters, interviews, and laboratory reports, while secondary sources are derived from materials with analysis interpretation and commentary on primary materials.

2. **Objectivity.** When the source has no bias or prejudice caused by the author's affiliations or allegiances, whether economic, political,

religious, or philosophical; try to discern the writer's point of view and evaluate the work accordingly.

3. **Qualification of the Author.** Credentials of an author for writing the work, such as academic degrees, professional experience, and status in the field that may influence the choice of a source.

4. **Level.** Determine the level of work in areas such as diction, sentence structure, complexity and assumed background knowledge, some find sources are too technical and advanced or some works written for a wide audience that is too general or simplistic for your research.

Types of Literature Reviews

Literature reviews are pervasive throughout various academic disciplines, and thus you can adopt various approaches to effectively organize and write your literature review. The following are the various types of literature reviews:

1. **Argumentative Review** this form examines literature selectively in order to support or

refute an argument, deeply embedded assumption, or philosophical problem already established in the literature. The purpose is to develop a body of literature that establishes a contrarian viewpoint. Given the value-laden nature of some social science research [e.g., educational reform; immigration control], argumentative approaches to analyzing the literature can be a legitimate and important form of discourse. However, note that they can also introduce problems of bias when they are used to make summary claims of the sort found in systematic reviews.

2. **Integrative Review** is considered a form of research that reviews, critiques, and synthesizes representative literature on a topic in an integrated way such that new frameworks and perspectives on the topic are generated. The body of literature includes all studies that address related or identical hypotheses. A well-done integrative review meets the same standards as primary research in regard to clarity, rigor, and replication.

3. **Historical Review** few things rest in isolation from historical precedent. Historical reviews are focused on examining research throughout a period of time, often starting with the first time an issue, concept, theory, phenomena emerged in the literature, then tracing its evolution within the scholarship of a discipline. The purpose is to place research in a historical context to show familiarity with state-of-the-art developments and to identify the likely directions for future research.

4. **Methodological Review** a review does not always focus on what someone said [content], but how they said it (method of analysis). This approach provides a framework of understanding at different levels (i.e. those of theory, substantive fields, research approaches, and data collection and analysis techniques), enables researchers to draw on a wide variety of knowledge ranging from the conceptual level to practical documents for use in fieldwork in the areas of ontological and epistemological consideration, quantitative and

qualitative integration, sampling, interviewing, data collection and data analysis, and helps highlight many ethical issues which we should be aware of and consider as we go through our study.

5. **Systematic Review** this form consists of an overview of existing evidence pertinent to a clearly formulated research question, which uses pre-specified and standardized methods to identify and critically appraise relevant research, and to collect, report, and analyze data from the studies that are included in the review. Typically, it focuses on a very specific empirical question, often posed in a cause-and-effect form, such as "To what extent does A contribute to B?"

6. **Theoretical Review** The purpose of this form is to concretely examine the corpus of theory that has accumulated in regard to an issue, concept, theory, phenomena. The theoretical literature review help establish what theories already exist, the relationships between them, to what degree the existing theories have been

investigated, and to develop new hypotheses to be tested. Often this form is used to help establish a lack of appropriate theories or reveal that current theories are inadequate for explaining new or emerging research problems. The unit of analysis can focus on a theoretical concept or a whole theory or framework.

As you can see, the literature is dispersed all throughout the thesis, dissertation, and research paper.

Literature review is usually organized in this way:

1. Discussion of literature on the phenomenon being studied.
2. Discussion of previous studies done on the topic, their methods, and main findings.
3. Discussion on relevant theories about the topic.
4. Synthesis of the literature review and critical issues in the current existing body of knowledge.

Steps in Conducting the Literature Review

There are several ways to do a literature review, but the advisable way is for you to approach it in a systematic manner.

Adapted from Creswell (2014), the steps below present a method for accomplishing the literature review.

1. Identifying keywords or main ideas from your research topic or from your initial reading of related materials on the topic.

2. Search for possible references materials from a library at your school, city, or nearby college or university using the keywords you have identified. You may also use references available at home, such as encyclopedia and other publications. You may also look for materials from the internet. Make use of online journal database such as ERIC (Educational Resources Information Center), google scholar, and EBSCO. The college or university library may also provide you access to such online database.

3. Come up with a list of related books or articles

about your research topic. Creswell (2014), recommends prioritizing books and journal articles as they are accessible.

4. Skim through these reference materials. Evaluate how relevant they are in addressing your research problem. Select those that you would like to review more deeply.

5. Critically review the articles and books that you think will help you understand the phenomenon you are studying. You may write summaries of the most relevant articles. Use an appropriate style guide in citing literature.

6. Organize your literature review. Connect key ideas and structure relevant concepts thematically. Define how your study fills in gaps in existing literature or contributes to the knowledge base about the topic.

7. Write the review of related literature section of your research. Utilize various strategies to avoid plagiarism.

Parts of the Literature Review

After gathering notes from the different sources reviewed, the researchers prepare the final review. Most literature reviews consist of the following parts.

1. **Introduction.** It describes the nature of the researcher's problem and explains what led the researcher to investigate the question. The summary presents the main topics covered in the literature review section.

2. **Body.** It briefly reports what experts think or what other researchers have found the research problem. Studies done on one key element or factor of the research problem are reviewed under the topic followed by studies done on other aspects of the problem. The common findings of several studies are summarized in one or two sentences and only when necessary, some specific findings of each study may be presented.

3. **Summary/synthesis.** It "ties together" the major findings of the studies reviewed. It presents a general picture of what has been known or thought of about the problem to date.

It points out similar results, as well as conflicting findings.

4. **Conclusion.** This part presents the course of action suggested by the literature. Based on the state of knowledge revealed by the literature, the researcher could further justify the need for his/her study.

Literature Review Strategies (Samosa et. al, 2021)

The following are brief descriptions of techniques that you might use in your literature review. Choose the approaches that are the most pertinent to your rhetorical situation.

1. **Summary.** Briefly state the argument and main points of relevant research.
2. **Synthesis.** Combine ideas in order to form an integrated theory or system through critical evaluation, compare/contrast, etc.
3. **Analysis**. Closely examine the elements or structure of the research and interpret through the lens of the field.
4. **Evaluation.** Assess the research based on criteria you choose, state, and explain. Support

your evaluation with research.

Illustrative Example of Literature Review

Thesis Statement:

Service-learning programs implemented in American undergraduate universities since 2000 have not only proven beneficial for the individuals or organizations being served but also for the participating students by offering opportunities for academic, emotional, and social growth.

Prior studies have identified many benefits for educational institutions from service-learning programs. These benefits include positive perceptions of the university by the community (Miron & Moely, 2006), enhanced student retention rates (Eyler et al., 2001), positive teaching and learning outcomes such as greater student involvement and participation in class (Caruso et al., 2007), and increased opportunities for meaningful research and scholarly activities (Strand et al., 2003).

In this study and related research, the individuals serving are university students who are collaborating with the community partner. The studied benefits to individuals serving include cultural awareness sharing (Crabtree, 2008), as well as networking opportunities and application of classroom learning to real-world issues (Bowen et al., 2009).

Ultimately, service-learning stimulates student learning and engages students in their surrounding communities. Service learning creates new goals for students such as personal development, career development, moral development, academic achievement, and "reflective civic participation" (Lamb et al., 1998). These types of projects allow students to utilize material learned in the classroom to improve societal conditions.

Integrating concepts and theories learned in the classroom with everyday life makes students more capable of highlighting the importance of each course. Additionally, material learned in business courses can be applied to benefit the community through a variety of tangible services, such as business planning or marketing new programs. Service learning is an excellent way for students to apply their course lessons to real-world situations and concurrently benefit the community.

Tips in Organizing Literature Review

1. Your new professional persona requires that you use only certain types of sources for your literature review: peer-reviewed sources. You cannot generally cite items from the popular

press or from the internet. The internet sometimes does contain appropriate sources but doing google search is going to waste your time.

2. For a research report, the rule by the Publication Manual says "Discuss the literature but they do not include an exhaustive historical review". Each study cited in your literature review is cited for a specific purpose. For example, you may stress the method in one and findings in another. You should not summarize exhaustively every study in your review. However, you will need to provide a paragraph or two on those studies even though the published articles only offer a sentence or two about relevant research studies.

3. When you attempt to summarize the method of a published study that contains several conditions or several similar experiments with small variations, concentrate on one experiment or condition and describe it clearly. Then you will be able to mention the variations very briefly and they will be clear.

4. For a study of instructional methods, describe one method, the tasks, and the dependent measure. Then, you can briefly note that other groups were identical except for the instructional methods – which you then describe.

5. After gathering all your notes, it is time to organize them for the review, keep in mind the point you are making about each study. This will help you introduce the paragraph containing the details. There should be some evidence of linear logic in the introduction, but the students sometimes find themselves without good reasons for sequencing a particular set of studies. When this happens, they introduce paragraphs with phrases like, Pagulayan (2021) found out that..." or Pagulayan (2021) also did a study of ..." but this type of writing introduces a common problem: failing to show the connections among the studies in the review.

6. The word also is not always a good term to link studies together. But you might want to make

the point that the two researchers did some things very similar. Perhaps you have decided to build a case for someone's theory by adding more evidence. If this is true, then say so. Alternatively, you might prefer to emphasize that this study appears similar to another, but an important difference remains and you want to explain it.

7. Knowing why you are including a particular study will give you a much better idea of where to include it. In this way, your paragraphs will begin with more natural transitions and have appropriately clear topic sentences. Once again, keep in mind that your own literature review will contain more details than are included in the articles you read. It is now time to take a look at these types of transitions.

8. Your literature review is not the place for your opinions. If you find the sample in an experiment to be very small, you can only call attention to that fact if someone else has found different results with a similar but larger sample. Perhaps the author has noted a

problem in his or her own discussion section; if so you then have tacit permission to cite the author's own misgivings. You may speculate about contradictory findings, but once again be careful not to be critical of the work of either author. Try not to write about what authors did not do unless you are contrasting it with what you are about to do or with what you are about to do or with what someone else did.

9. Do not forget the rules on verb tenses in your literature review. You are reporting on work that has been completed. Therefore, use past tense (found) or present perfect (have found). Even your own has already been completed by the time you report the results.

10. Most reviews start with an introduction of their own of two to three paragraphs. This introduction, like that of the empirical research report, sets the context for the work: why this is an important issue, what sorts of people and how many have these problems or concerns, what are the public policy and/or practice issues that are affected by this problem. The

things to be careful of here, is not to underestimate the expertise of your audience.

11. One good method is to organize around competing theoretical models. Some studies support one theory or model and some studies support another. Sometimes there are three or four models. If you think of your reading in these terms, then you will be likely to end by making a point about which model seems to be the most reasonable, given the evidence.

The Synthesis

The last part of Chapter II is the synthesis of the review of related literature and studies. The synthesis is usually one of the shortest subparts in a thesis, dissertation, and research paper but is often one of the most difficult to write.

The synthesis of the related literature and study must logically summarize and combine into a coherent whole the survey findings and ideas of other researchers and authors through the researcher's own words and logical views.

In other words, the synthesis is not a summary

of chapter II. It is a part that puts the survey materials in a logical perspective, vis a vis the researchers' study. The researcher will do well if, in his own words, he will synthesize or bring together the survey's major findings and conclusion by pointing out the similarities as well as the differences between his study and those of others.

Guidelines in Writing the Synthesis (Salmorin, 2006).

1. The synthesis is written after the surveyed and chosen materials have been thoroughly read and examined by the researcher in terms of major findings, conclusions, and recommendations of the other authors and researchers.

2. The synthesis should be concisely written and should not be more than two pages. A one–page synthesis is usually enough for most research papers.

3. Very lengthy or complex sentences should be avoided in writing the synthesis.

4. Brief citations of ideas or findings of other researchers/authors can be done to enhance

the researcher's own logical views of the entire materials in Chapter II.

5. The synthesis puts the present study in the context or the light of other studies by other researchers. Both similar and contradictory findings can be placed in the synthesis in very concise citations.

In-text Citations (University of Monash, 2021).

An in-text citation is the brief form of the reference that you include in the body of your work. It gives enough information to uniquely identify the source in your reference list. Insert an in-text citation when your work has been influenced by someone else's work, for example, when you directly quote someone else's work or when you paraphrase someone else's work.

The in-text citation consists of author surname(s)/family name (s), in the order that they appear on the actual publication, followed by the year of publication of the source that you are citing. For direct quotes, make sure to include page or paragraph numbers.

Illustrative Example:

> (Samosa, 2021, p. 31).

Page numbers are not normally included when paraphrasing but may be included if desired.

The in-text citation is placed immediately after the information being cited. If your citation is at the end of a sentence, ensure the full stop is placed after the reference. If quoting or citing a source that has been cited within another document, mention the original source together with the secondary reference details;

Illustrative Example:

> (Samosa, 2020, as cited in Pagulayan,

In this case, only the secondary reference (i.e. Pagulayan, 2021) should be included in the reference list.

Please note, however you should use secondary sources only where you are unable to obtain a copy of the original, or the original is not available in English.

In-text citations are usually included in the

word count of your document. For citations in parentheses with two authors, the '&' symbol is used. If the author citation forms part of your sentence the word 'and' must be used.

Illustrative Examples:

> (Samosa & Pagulayan, 2021)
> Samosa and Pagulayan (2021) indicate that...

The placement of citations can be important depending on the emphasis you wish to apply If you wish to quote or paraphrase an author and want to emphasize the author, then your citation becomes 'author prominent.'

Illustrative Example:

> Samosa (2012) has concluded that...

If you wish to emphasize the information you have paraphrased or quoted from an author, then your citation becomes 'information prominent'.

Illustrative Example:

> .. as evidenced from a recent study
> (Samosa, 2012).

Illustrative Examples of in-text citations

1. One author

Rule: Surname of the author, no initials or suffixes such as Jr. The year of publication is also included

Illustrative Examples:

> ...This was seen in an Australian study (Conger, 1979).
> Conger (1979) has argued that...
> In 1979, Conger conducted a study which showed that...

2. Two authors

Rule: Cite both surnames every time the reference occurs in the text

Illustrative Examples:

> (Davidson & Harrington, 2002)
> Davidson and Harrington (2002) ...

3. Three to five authors

Rule: Cite all surnames and publication year the first time, thereafter only the first surname followed by et al. Note: There is a full-stop (.) after al (see below).

Illustrative Examples:

> The first time cited: ...(Brown, Soo, & Jones, 1990).
> Brown,Soo, and Jones (1990)...
> thereafter:
> ...(Brown et al., 1990).
> Brown et al. (1990)...

4. Six or more authors

Rule: Cite only the surname of the first author followed by et al. and the year from the first citation. Note: There is a full-stop (.) after al (see below). Include all authors, up to seven, in the reference list. Please see the instruction for eight or more authors on the introductory page of this guide.

Illustrative Examples:

> .... (Girad-Perregaux et al., 2003).
> Girad-Perregaux et al. (2003)...

5. Different authors: same surname

Rule: Add the initials of the author's first or given name/s to their surname to distinguish them.

Illustrative Examples:

> P. R. Smith (1923) to distinguish from S. Smith (1945) ...
> (S. A. Brown & Jones, 1961) to distinguish from (W. O. Brown & Smith, 1985).

6. Multiple authors: ambiguous citations

Rule: If a multiple (3+) author citation abbreviated with et al. looks the same as another in-text citation similarly shortened, add enough surnames to make a distinction, followed by a comma and et al.

Illustrative Examples:

> ...(Brown, Shimamura, et al., 1998) to distinguish from (Brown, Taylor, et al., 1998).

7. Multiple works: by the same author

Rule: When cited together give the author's surname once followed by the years of each publication, which are separated by a comma.

Illustrative Examples:

> ...(Brown, Shimamura, et al., 1998) to distinguish from (Brown, Taylor, et al., 1998).

8. Multiple works: by same author AND same year

Rule: If there is more than one reference by an author in the same year, suffixes (a, b, c, etc.) are added to the year. Allocation of the suffixes is determined by the order of the references in the reference list, not by the order in which they are cited. Suffixes are also included in the reference list, and these references are listed alphabetically by title. If cited together, list by suffix as shown below.

Illustrative Examples:

> Stairs (1992b)... later in the text ... (Stairs, 1992a).
> ...(Stairs, 1992a, 1992b).

9. **If the author is identified as 'anonymous'**

   Rule: Use Anonymous in place of the author's surname.

   Illustrative Example:

   > ... (Anonymous, 1997)

10. **Unknown author**

    Rule: Give the first few words of the title. If the title is from an article or a chapter use double quotation marks. If the title is from a periodical, book brochure or report then use italics.

    Illustrative Example:

    > ...the worst election loss in the party's history ("This is the end," 1968).

11. Corporate or group of authors

Rule: If an organization is recognized by abbreviation, cite the first time as follows:

Illustrative Examples:

> .. (Australian Institute of Health and Welfare [AIHW], 2005)
> **Note:** [AIHW] is in square brackets for the initial in-text citation and thereafter as
> ... (AIHW, 2005).
> However, if abbreviation not widely known, give the name in full every time:
> ... (Australian Research Council, 1996)

12. Multiple references

Rule: List the citations in alphabetical order and separate with semicolons.

Illustrative Example:

> ... (Burst, 1995; Nguyen, 1976; Turner & Hooch, 1982).

13. Citing specific parts of a source

Rule: For a direct quote the page number(s) must be given. Indicate page, chapter, figure, table, etc. as specifically as possible. Use accepted abbreviations, i.e. p. for page, para. for paragraph.

Illustrative Examples:

As one writer put it "the darkest days were still ahead" (Weston, 1988, p. 45).
Weston (1988) argued that "the darkest days were still ahead" (p. 45).
This theory was put forward by Smith (2005, chap.7)

14. Quote from an electronic source

Rule: Where page numbers are not provided use paragraph numbers.

Illustrative Example:

...(Chang, 2001, para. 2)

15. Personal communications

Rule: These include private letters, e-mail, and conversations. As personal communications are not accessible to others, they are not included in the reference list. However, an in-text citation is required.

Illustrative Example:

... (R. Smith, personal communication, January 28, 2002).
R. Smith (personal communication, January 28, 2002)...

16. Citation of a secondary source: (i.e a source referred to in another publication)

Rule: APA 6th specifies that secondary citations should ONLY be used where the original is unavailable (for example, out-of-print). Wherever possible, read and cite the original source. The original source is not available, only include the details of the source you actually read. In the example below, the original source would be Farrow (1968), which you saw cited in a paper by Ward and Decan (1988).

Illustrative Examples:

... (Farrow, 1968, as cited in Ward & Decan, 1988).
Farrow (1968, as cited in Ward & Decan, 1988) ...
Ward and Decan (1988) cited Farrow (1968) as
finding...

17. **Citing legislation or legal cases.** The way you cite legislation or legal cases depends on whether you read the actual legislation or read about it in another source. If it is the latter, the legislation/case should be treated as a secondary source.

18. **Rule (Legislations):** The *title of the legislation and the year* (jurisdiction). Note: include the jurisdiction the first time the act is cited. The

jurisdiction can be dropped with subsequent citations.

Illustrative Examples:

> The *Medical Treatment Act 1988* (Vic) states......
>
> by virtue of s. 25.1 of the *Aged Care Act 1997* (Cth).....
>
> ..."A restrictive intervention may only be used on a person....." (*Mental Health Act 2014* (Vic), s. 105)
>
> as a **secondary source**
>
> ....*Occupational Health and Safety Act 2004* (Vic)

Rule (Cases): The *title of the case* (year). Note: Include the year with the first citation. The year can be dropped in subsequent citations.

Illustrative Examples:

> According to the case of *Rogers v Whitaker* (1992).....
> as a **secondary source**
> .....*Chappel v Hart* (1988) (as cited in Forrester & Griffiths, 2010)

19. Websites (but not a specific document on that site)

Rule: When citing an entire website, it is sufficient to give the address of the site in the text. No reference list entry required.

Illustrative Example:

> Apple is one of the most visited consumer technology websites in the world (http://www.apple.com).

Rule: Family name and year of publication.

Illustrative Examples:

> In a recent article on the role of quantitative analysts Loeper (2019) states…
>
> The role of quantitative analysts has been recently reviewed (Loeper, 2019)

21. Web page with corporate author

Rule: Organization name and year of publication.

Illustrative Examples:

> A webpage regarding educational programs and discounts offered by Samsung (2019) states…
>
> Extensive information on education programs and discounts are offered by one of the world's largest telecommunications companies (Samsung, 2019)

22. Web page, unknown author

Rule: Give the first few words of the title. If the title is from an article use double quotation marks. Also include the year of publication.

Illustrative Example:

> An Australian government agency recommend checking rainwater tanks in Queensland ("Unsealed rainwater tanks", 2019)

23. Web page, no date

Rule: Use the letters n.d. - an abbreviation of the words 'no date'.

Illustrative Examples:

> In a self-published autobiographical article audiovisual organisation Bose (n.d) mention...
>
> The company's history is outlined in a self-published autobiography (Bose, n.d.)

24. Market Reports/Industry databases, no individual author

Rule: Cite the database or Market Report publisher as the author.

Illustrative Examples:

> An industry report on infrastructure construction in China by IBISWorld (2019) asserts...
>
> Infrastructure construction in China was summarized in a recent industry report (IBISWorld, 2019).

25. Market Reports/Industry databases, author

Rule: Family name and year of publication.

Illustrative Example:

> In an industry report on Australian accommodation Smith (2019) states…
>
> Australian accommodation options were recently reviewed (Smith, 2019).

presentation.

For on-text citation

Samosa (2021) _stressed_ that …

> (emphasized, mentioned, cited, stated, clarified, elucidated, verified, made, clear, adduced, trajected, deduced, enthralled, permeated, denoted, connoted, impinged, bashed, struck, hit, swiped, thudded, slammed, rammed, propensed, propelled, inclined, trailblazed, indicated, catalyzed, noted, demonstrated, explained, leveraged, focused, averred, underscored, valued, highlighted, undermined, exposed, featured, advised, demanded, engrossed).

Samosa (2021) _enlisted_ the….

> (Determined, identified, enumerated, shared, contributed, disseminated, laid down, presented, arranged, concretized)

Samosa (2021) _asserted_ that ….

> (ascertain, viewed, discerned, adduced, resonated, coined, banked on, construed, accentuated, opined, hypothesized, theorized, articulated, conceptualized, reconceptualized, made appropriate, and relevant, approached, referred to, recognized)

Samosa (2021) _anticipated_ that…

(assumed, projected, premised, presupposed, expected)

Samosa (2021) _defined_….

(elaborated, analyzed, redefined, presented, expounded)

The finding of Samosa (2021) _aimed_ to….

(portrayed, defined, endeavored, explored, navigated, rediscovered, revealed, showed, apprised, thrived at, carried its purpose, settled, discovered, investigated, uncovered, unraveled, attempted, intended, expedited, unveiled, revealed, unleashed, aspired, desired, targeted, insisted, traveled, journeyed, walked with, went through, walked through).

The results of Samosa's study (2021) _began_…

(started, impetused, commenced, incubated, initiated, resumed, prompted, established, built, grounded, embedded, founded, laid upon, impounded by, anchored on, maneuvered, propelled, geared towards, entered, came in, knocked, fueled, instigated, triggered, provoked).

The study of Samosa (2021) _implied_ that….

(indicated, implicated, impacted, affected, alluded, hinted, inferred, insinuated, suggested, recommended, intimated, pressed, posited, postulated, prodded, spurred, pushed, forwarded, moved, proposed, recommended, insisted, accorded, assigned, designated).

The intervention of Samosa (2021) _resolved_…

(solved, mitigated, redeemed, regenerated, resumed, transformed, resolved, reformed, changed, metamorphosized, innovated, renovated, repaired, remade, distressed, restored, extricated, fulfilled, expiated, retrieved, rewinded, recovered, replenish, rejuvenated, satisfied, kept, met, filled, completed, answered, responded, addressed, compiled, conduced, progressed, developed, improved, changed, innovated, facelifted, improved, mitigated, cured, treated, recuperated, relieved, shifted, tansfered, moved, changed, forced, compelled, obliged, volunteered).

The idea of Samosa (2021) on research _complemented_…

(complimented, paralleled, aligned with, threaded, pipelined, connected, interconnected, interwined, included, integrated, correlated, incorporated, inserted, related, combined, lifted, moved, immersed, emerged, amalgamated, united, merged, mixed, differentiated, discerned, related, took, similarities, included)

The study of Samosa (2021) _revealed_…

(redeemed, showed)

The discovery of Samosa (2021) _stopped_…

(ceased, quit, perpetuated, proliferated, diminished, reduced, dwindled, lessened, receded, declined, eliminated, deleted, removed)

The study of Samosa (2021) *agreed*…

(conformed, affirmed, liked, ensured, assured, guaranteed, accepted, kept, took, supported, took side with, considered, joined, included, enioined)

Samosa (2021) *opposed* that…

(argued, reciprocated, negated, transgressed, violated, juxtaposed, commented, compared, resisted, contradicted, objected, negated, resisted, opted, chose, neglected, ignored, denied, condemned, warned, lied, denied, corrected, set aside, set apart, worsened, apprehended, punished, offended, appealed, excluded, separated, left).

Samosa (2021) *assessed*….

(evaluated, accounted, examined, appraised, reviewed)

Samosa (2021) *investigated*….

(analyzed, studied, probed, reviewed, reflected on, proved, validated, applied, evidenced, revisted).

The study of Samosa *concluded* that

(synthesized, surmised, generalized, summarized)

The study of Samosa (2021) *led* to ….

(created, reached out, brought about, made a way to became)

Samosa (2021) *remembered…*

> (recalled, applied, observed, understood, comprehended, reminisced, remembered, encountered, faced, experienced, applied, hoped for, look forward to, granted, accorded).

Samosa (2021) *requested…*

> (pleaded, summoned, pleased, honored)

Samosa (2021) *praised…*

> (commended, appreciated, instilled, developed, honed, harnessed, obtained, achieved, reached, gained, gotten, excelled, bested, succeeded, triumphed, conquered, conquested).

Conjunctions & Transitional Markers for in-text citation

In connecting concepts

> (Likewise, and, more so, moreover, also, in addition, more than, similarly, like, relatively, concomitant to, cognizant to, affirmatively, in juxtaposition, engagingly, connectedly, interconnectedly, in correlation, proportionally, relatively, similarly, congruently).

In citing examples, elaboration, and discussion.

(Just like, on the same way (hand, end), to enumerate, listed down, just like, somewhat like, for example, to explain, to expound, elaborate, given the chance, to elaborate, to substantiate, accordingly, in details, comprehensively, tantamount to, in detail, in capsule, in a nutshell, accordingly, in retrospect, clearly, as per, deemed, subsequently, explicably)

In contrast

(However, on the hand, on the other end, but on the other side, compared with, unlike, in contradictory (contrast), paradoxically, opposite wise, on the other hand, on the contrary, reciprocally, oppositely).

In synthesizing

(therefore, thus, hence, henceforth, so that, so because, that is why, due to, caused by, thereby, as such, thereby, in summary, in conclusion, in effect, that is why, in turn, definitely, in general, as a whole, holistically, entirely, truly, constantly, logically, operationally, absolutely, apparently)

In transitioning concepts and ideas

(meanwhile, as such, in a way, consequently, taking aside, cognizantly, paramount to, concomitantly, in request for, in favor of, in quest for, looking forward to, behaviorally, emergently)

In stressing a point or position on an issue.

(Definitely, precisely, absolutely, entirely, irrevocably, soundly, strongly, perfectly, impeccably, intensively, concisely, ultimately, needlessly, seemingly, optimally, preferably, proportionally, as ground, as a result, as a matter of fact, in fact, subsequently, painstakingly, apparently, significantly, incessantly, presumably, legally, competitively, seriously, perfectly, intentionally, essentially, really, immeasurably, enticingly, unquestionably, emphatically, consistently, consistently, effectively, efficiently, enticingly, unconsciously, propositionally, probably, approximately, anticipatedly)

Conceptual Framework

(Interestingly, vehemently, amazingly, unbelievably, inevitably, intentionally, presumably, notably, remarkably, commendably, impartially, noticeably, sequentially, immeasurably, continuously, uninterruptedly, sustainably, seemingly, requisitely, instantly, impressively, accurately, tangibly, in accordance to, deemed, essential, necessarily, critically).

At the outset of planning your research, you set the study into a framework that justifies the study and explains its structure or design. This framework is like a foundation for a house. It provides the essential support for the study components and also clarifies the context of the study for the reader, much like a house blueprint. By constructing this framework, you not only justify and explain the study to others but also check your understanding of the need for the study, how the study is aligned with the problem identified for the study.

Before exploring the various understanding of conceptual frameworks in-depth, it is helpful to compare multiple definitions of the terms. Some authors view conceptual and theoretical frameworks as synonymous. Interestingly, some research design authors do not provide a description or definition of either conceptual or theoretical framework, even if they discuss theory; for example in Leedy and Ormrod (2021). Please note this omission from the text does not justify excluding a conceptual framework from a study. A conceptual framework provides the orientation to the study and assists both the researcher and the reader in seeing how the study contributes to the body of knowledge on the topic, how elements of the study align, and how the study design and methodology meet rigorous research standards (Crawford, 2020). In summary, a conceptual framework is incredibly important.

Ravitch and Riggan (2017) presented the most

comprehensive understanding of the conceptual framework. Indeed, they devoted an entire book to the topic. Their main point was that a conceptual framework is an argument for the study and that argument has two parts: first, the argument establishes the importance of and intended audience for the study. Second, the argument demonstrates alignment among research questions, data collections, and data analysis, as well as the use of rigorous procedures to conduct the study. They posited that the conceptual framework both informs and describes the development of research questions, design selections, data collection, data analysis, and presentation of findings.

A major contribution to the idea of conceptual framework presented by Miles, et al. (2014) is the graphical representation of the conceptual framework. They promoted spending significant time in developing and presenting the conceptual framework. That process encourages a closer assessment of how study variables are related, how study participants are characterized, and how data collection instruments are selected.

Maxwell (2013) discussed conceptual frameworks in relation to qualitative research design. For Maxwell, the conceptual and theoretical frameworks are synonymous. Maxwell presented the terms as synonymous because he viewed the conceptual framework as presenting a theory of the phenomenon under investigation. A major point of Maxwell's contribution is that researcher must build, or construct, the conceptual framework from personal experience, prior research, and published theory into a coherent representation of the study.

Marshall and Rossman (2016) described conceptual framework as providing a rationale for the study. The idea of rationale is close to Ravitch and Riggan (2017) view of conceptual framework as an argument for the study. Marshall and Rossman also emphasized the importance of grounding a conceptual framework in the literature published on the topic under study.

All definition demonstrates the importance of the relationship of the conceptual framework to the roots of the study purpose and the alignment of study parts. They also indicate ways that a conceptual framework makes the construction of a study clearer, cleaner, and more straightforward.

Purpose of Conceptual Frameworks

To construct an informative conceptual framework, the researcher must understand the purpose of a conceptual framework. Different authors present the purpose of conceptual framework as argumentation for the study (Marshall & Rossman, 2016; Ravitch & Riggan, 2017). Other authors see the conceptual framework as explanatory (Anfara & Mertz, 2015; Miles et al., 2014). Merriam & Tisdell (2016) viewed the conceptual framework, which they termed theoretical framework, as generating elements of the research design and methods, whereas Robson & McCartan (2016) emphasized variable relationships and relationships and research design. Marxwell (2013) combined the purposes of the conceptual framework into clarification, explanation, and justification.

Purposes of conceptual frameworks according to different authors:

1. Argue for why the topic matters and why the

proposed design and methodology are appropriate and rigorous (Ravitch & Riggan 2017).

2. Explain the relationship among key factors/variables/constructs of the study (who and what will be studied) (Miles et al. 2014).

3. Clarify, explain, and justify methods (Maxwell, 2013).

4. Specify variable relationship and research design (Robson & McCartan, 2016).

5. Argue for study in terms of meaning and contribution to improving the human condition (Marchall & Rossman, 2016).

6. Generate study problem, research questions, data collection, data analysis, and interpretation of findings (Merriam & Tisdell, 2016).

7. Explain variable relationships (Anfara & Mertz, 2015).

From this, the purposes of conceptual frameworks include the following:

1. **Argumentation** focuses on the importance of studying the topic, the appropriateness of the

design, and the rigor of the methods.

2. **Explanation** stresses the relationship among who and what will be studied.

3. **Generation** gives rise to the problem, research questions, and methods of a study.

Sources of Conceptual Frameworks

A source for a conceptual framework is the principal element forming the basis for the development of the framework (Ravitch & Riggan, 2017). You may think of it as the impetus for the conceptual framework. These are three sources for a conceptual framework.

1. **Experience.** Ravitch and Riggan (2017), Maxwell (2013), Robson and McCartan (2016), Marshall and Rossman (2016), and Booth, Colomb, Williams, Bizup, and Fitzgerald (2016) all allowed for personal interests, experiences, intuitions, and hunches as stimuli for a conceptual framework, although none of them believed that personal experience alone is sufficient. For example, your personal

experience observing leadership styles in an organization may stimulate in you a desire to conduct a study on a certain aspect of leadership, but a literature review might reveal that that aspect has already been deeply studied or that there is scant support in the profession for investigating that aspect. Personal issues may point you in the direction of a study topic, but the topic must have meaning for others in the field. In other words, there must be evidence that others in the field share your concern and that addressing the concern will advance knowledge. Such evidence rests in literature and a theoretical base to support a conceptual framework for a study.

2. **Literature.** An essential source for your conceptual framework is the published research literature related to your topic. Ravitch and Riggan (2017), Maxwell (2013), Robson and McCartan (2016), Merriam and Tisdell (2016), and Marshall and Rossman (2016) advocated for rooting the conceptual

framework in the literature associated with the topic of study. Of singular importance is that your study is based on a need documented from the literature. For example, following the idea in the prior paragraph, your personal experience may point to a desire to study a certain aspect of leadership. Of importance, though, is that you find out from the literature the extent to which that aspect has already been studied, what is still not understood about it, and whether or not the discipline needs to remedy the lack of knowledge (Booth et al., 2016). The literature review provides the evidence for the argumentation contained in a conceptual framework.

3. **Theoretical Framework**. An additional source for your conceptual framework is a theory (Anfara & Mertz, 2015; Marshall & Rossman, 2016; Maxwell, 2013; Ravitch & Riggan, 2017; Robson & McCartan, 2016), and this source is expressed in the theoretical framework. The study may be focused on generating a new theory or on the testing theory that has already

been constructed (Creswell & Poth, 2018). For example, your study may focus on describing how leaders distribute power in an organization. In other words, the focus is on developing an explanation, or theory, of how power distribution functions in a certain kind of organization. Or your study may focus on testing some theory of power distribution that has already been developed to determine if it accurately explains how power is distributed within a certain group. Whether generating or testing theory, the conceptual framework contains the theoretical framework, or theoretical context, for the study.

Table 2: Sources of Conceptual Frameworks

As shown in Figure 2, there are three sources,

or stimuli, for creating a conceptual framework: (1) experience, (2) literature, and (3) theory. Although personal experience may instigate a research idea, personal experience is not sufficient to support a conceptual framework for a research study. The conceptual framework must be rooted in the professional literature. The literature provides the rationale for the study by exposing what is not yet known or understood about a phenomenon. The third source for a conceptual framework is theory, integrated as the theoretical framework. Is there already a theory that needs to be tested? Is there no existing viable theory of the phenomenon and does one need to be developed? Thus, experience may prompt a conceptual framework, the literature must provide the argumentation for pursuing the research idea, and the study must be situated in relation to generating or testing theory.

Constructing a conceptual framework: Suggested 'how to' steps

As there is no single, best format for making an argument, there is also no single 'right' way to construct a conceptual framework. As stated previously, a sound conceptual framework provides a clearly articulated point of reference from which the researcher can make sense of the dynamic nature of the research process. As new insight emerges and adjustments are made, the conceptual framework will remain the focal or the reference point.

The effective construction of a conceptual framework requires certain skills from the researcher, for example:

1. contextual awareness by understanding the world as dynamic interaction of multiple events and trends.
2. general knowledge and meaning-making abilities
3. logical reasoning and common sense
4. basic understanding of the potential causal relationships between multiple variables
5. a measure of linguistic acumen (e.g. suitably apply dictionary meanings of words and its usage in different social settings)
6. model-building skills
7. the ability to answer the 'what-if', 'what', 'how', 'where', and 'when' questions related to

research topics and titles.

In the absence of some of the above-mentioned skills, researchers or 'emerging researchers' may simply brainstorm ideas with a more senior, experienced colleague or their thesis/dissertation adviser.

The following are the steps in constructing a conceptual framework of the study.

1. **Choose the topic.** The topic describes the field of study, for example, public finance, project management, or human resource management. Therefore, the topic should be within the researcher's field of interest and/or specialization.

2. **Choose the title.** Typically, a title should focus on the study and illustrate the relationship between variables, for example, 'the significance of leadership for organizational excellence', where 'leadership' and 'organizational excellence' are key constructs.

3. **Isolate the key concepts and/or constructs in the title**. Identify the specific variables described in the literature and determine how

these are potentially related.

4. **Do a literature review and identify related concepts and variables.** Review relevant and updated research on the title of the study in general and the concepts and constructs in particular. Consult preferably peer-reviewed textbooks and established scientific journals because these are more reliable sources of information.

5. **Generate the conceptual framework.** In this phase, the researcher should be in a position to construct at least a basic conceptual framework by using the information gathered from the literature review. The study's problem statement provides a reference for constructing the conceptual framework. The purpose of such a framework is to illustrate the research approach in graphical form to aid understanding of the research approach and design.

Presentation of Conceptual Frameworks

There are two ways to present a conceptual framework—graphically and narratively. If you are crafting a research study for a thesis or dissertation, your institution will probably expect that, at a minimum, you describe the conceptual framework narratively, with optional figures to support clarity of presentation

1. **Graphic Presentation.** Some authors favor a diagrammatic portrayal of a conceptual framework using a concept map, with or without an accompanying narrative (Marshall & Rossman, 2016; Maxwell, 2013; Merriam & Tisdell, 2016; Miles et al., 2014; Robson & McCartan, 2016). A concept map is a pictorial portrayal of relationships. It shows how one idea or concept connects to other ideas or concepts. Miles et al. (2014) provided several fine examples of graphic presentations and concept maps describing conceptual frameworks.

   Miles et al. (2014) noted that forcing the graphic onto one page rather than multiple text pages allows you to see and adjust all the parts of the study as a unit as well as to see inconsistencies and contradictions. Going through this process lends cohesiveness to the study design. You should expect development of the graphic to be an iterative process with several versions until it finally accurately represents the study. During this iterative process, how you are writing about the study in text and how you are graphically representing the study become mutually informative and mutually formative. Miles et al. further suggested that you should challenge yourself to avoid overly global graphics with ubiquitous two-way arrows that do not clearly demonstrate the flow of the study.

Like Miles et al. (2014), Robson and McCartan (2016) advocated presenting the conceptual framework in graphic format. Robson and McCartan provided six specifications for developing that graphic

a. Contain the graphic on one page.

b. Include multiple inputs, such as prior research, including pilot studies; relevant theories; hunches with regard to the phenomenon or variable relationships; and thoughts of other professionals in the field.

c. Attain internal consistency within the graphical map.

d. Expect to produce multiple iterations of the framework graphic.

e. Include an item, rather than exclude it, if unsure.

f. Simplify the graphic as you learn from experience.

If you attend to each of the six specifications listed, you will develop a solid graphical presentation of your conceptual framework

2. **Narrative Presentation.** Ravitch and Riggan (2017) were less supportive of a graphical presentation. Although they saw that graphical and narrative presentations of the conceptual framework can work well, they preferred a text-based presentation of conceptual framework when there is a question about presentation. Ravitch and Riggan provided strong examples

of narratively presented conceptual frameworks in relation to design, data collection, data analysis, and presentation of findings.

Illustrative Example of Conceptual Framework:

Kpopped!: Understanding the Filipino Teens' Consumption of Korean Popular Music and Videos (Alanzalon, 2018)

In translating the theoretical framework into specific concepts used in this study, the researcher specified the audience to be Filipino teenage Kpop fans. The media content was understood as Korean popular music, videos and television shows.

The facets of Cultural Proximity theory was translated into more specific concepts such as language, visuals, cultural capitals, and stories. Language referred to the languages present in Korean music and videos. On the other hand, visuals represented aesthetic elements in the media content. Cultural Capital included history, jokes, idioms and traditions.

exclusive to the Korean culture, whereas stories referred to sets of values and themes present in the text. The information processing of the Kpop fans referred to their different patterns and ways of consuming Kpop media content. On the other hand, the theoretical model of the different media purposes provided by McQuail was retained in the conceptual framework. Information was the knowledge that fans gained from the exposure to Kpop media content. Personal Identity referred to the fans' personal growth, personality changes, dreams, goals and aspirations that were gained or lost during the process of consuming Korean music and videos. Social Interaction pertained to the social relationships with family, friends and fellow fans that have been affected by the fans' Kpop fandom. And lastly, entertainment denoted how Kpop provided happiness, amusement, diversion and other entertaining purposes to the consumers.

Theoretical Frameworks

The definitions of the conceptual framework are confounded by the fact that some authors do not differentiate between conceptual and theoretical frameworks. Maxwell (2013), Robson and McCartan (2016), and Merriam and Tisdell (2016) consider the terms synonymous. Anfara and Mertz (2015) do not explicitly relate conceptual and theoretical frameworks, but they imply a synonymous relationship between them. Some authors (Marshall & Rossman, 2016; Miles et al., 2014) offer no discussion of the relationship between conceptual and theoretical frameworks.

Merriam and Tisdell (2016) defined theoretical framework as "the underlying structure, the scaffolding or frame of your study", which seems close to some of the definitions of conceptual framework provided earlier. Anfara and Mertz (2015) defined theoretical frameworks as "any empirical or quasi-empirical theory of social and/or psychological processes, at a variety of levels . . . that can be applied to the understandings of phenomena".

A clear definition of theoretical frameworks and the relationship between theoretical and conceptual frameworks comes from Ravitch and Riggan (2017). They defined theoretical frameworks as follows:

> In the case of theoretical frameworks, the "parts" referred to in this definition are theories, and the thing that is being supported is the relationships embedded in the conceptual framework. More specifically, we argue that the parts are formal theories; [sic] those that emerge from and have been explored using empirical work.

Ravitch and Riggan (2017) required that the theoretical framework be based on published, identifiable theories. Private conceptualizations or theoretical constructions do not qualify. In addition, they held that the theoretical framework resides within the conceptual framework and is not synonymous with it. In other words, the conceptual framework presents the overall structure of the study, and the theoretical framework within it explains the relationships that are explored within the study.

Ravitch and Riggan (2017), the theoretical framework should do the following

1. **Identify the theory cluster.** A theory cluster combines theories into categories, such as theories of learning style, organizational communication, and language acquisition.

2. **Identify specific theories relevant** to that cluster, including the originator or source and the major propositions and hypotheses of each theory.

3. Identify the theory selected for the study. This includes specifying the specific theory within the cluster that will be used, the propositions of the theory that relate to the specific study, and the review of prior studies using that theory as a focus.

4. State how the study will contribute to the body of knowledge related to the theory.

Illustrative Example of Theoretical Framework

**Campus Bullying in The Senior High School:
A Qualitative Case Study (Galabo, 2019)**

This study considered some relevant theories of bullying in the school as presented by Rigby (2003). Firstly, the developmental theory on bullying which emphasized that bullying begins in early childhood when individuals begin to assert themselves at the expense of others in order to establish their social dominance. They tend at first to do so crudely, for instance by hitting out at others, especially those less powerful than themselves, in an attempt to intimidate them. Besides, as children develop they begin to employ less socially reprehensible ways of dominating others.

Verbal and indirect forms of bullying become more common than physical forms. In time, the kind of behavior that is generally labeled as "bullying" becomes relatively rare. Secondly, the theory of attributions to individual differences which explained that the broad explanations in terms of developmental processes and environmental influences fail to take into account individual differences between people that may lead to interactions that result in one person bullying another.Thirdly, bullying as a sociocultural phenomenon wherein this perspective seeks to explain bullying as an outcome of the existence of specified social groups with different levels of power. The focus is typically on differences which have a historical and cultural basis, such as gender, race or ethnicity and social class. Major emphasis has been placed upon differences associated with gender. Society is seen as essentially patriarchal. Males are seen as generally having more power than females as a consequence of societal beliefs that males should be the dominant sex. In order to maintain their dominance, boys feel justified in oppressing girls. It is sometimes claimed that bullying tends to be associated with racial or ethnic divides. It is argued that some ethnic groups are more powerful than others whom they seek to dominate. Typically, the less powerful are the victims of colonialism. The sociocultural perspective on bullying can have striking implications for how a school approaches the problem of bullying. Attention is directed towards how the school curriculum in its broadest sense can influence children to accept and respect sociocultural differences. It is suggested that not only should the school curriculum explicitly and directly address issues related to differences in gender, race or ethnicity and social class in order to counter prejudice and discrimination, but importantly the mode of delivery of the curricula should indirectly address bullying through the stimulus it provides to cooperative problem-solving, emotional sensitivity and independent critical thinking. Fourthly, bullying as a response to group and peer pressures within the school is an approach that has

However, the context is not defined according to sociocultural categories such as gender, race and class. There is first a broad social context consisting of the behaviors and attitudes of members of the entire school community. Individuals are seen as influenced to a degree by their perceptions of what may be called the school ethos, and student welfare policies may be systematically directed towards its improvement (Smith, et al., 2000). Secondly, students are powerfully influenced by a smaller group of peers with whom they have relatively close association. Such groups are typically formed within a school on the basis of common interests and purposes, and provide support for group members. The implications for schools are that they must be aware of the roles played by groups as distinct from individuals. They need to identify groups and work with them. Several methods have been devised for working with groups of children who have bullied or are suspected of bullying others. Lastly, bullying from the perspective of restorative justice which recognizes that some children are more likely than others to be involved in bully/victim problems as a consequence of the kind of character they have developed. Children who bully others typically feel little or no pride in their school and are not well integrated into the community (Morrison, 2002).

The interface between conceptual and theoretical frameworks

The literature does not always delineate clearly between theoretical and conceptual frameworks. There are generally three perspectives evident in a relationship between conceptual and theoretical frameworks.

1. Conceptual and theoretical frameworks are viewed as synonymous (Maxwell 2005; Saunders et al. 2015).
2. Conceptual framework is considered as much broader in scope than a theoretical framework (Eisenhart, 1991; Ravitch & Riggan 2017).
3. theoretical framework is understood as part of a conceptual whole (Imenda, 2014; Jacard & Jacoby, 2010; Kumar 2014).

Closer inspection of the above-mentioned perspectives indicates that authors ascribe a particular meaning to the notion of 'theory' (as applied in theoretical frameworks). Scholars who regard theoretical frameworks as broader than conceptual frameworks seemingly understand 'theory' in terms of meta-, grand- or macro-level theory or as a theoretical model in which the study is embedded (Maree, 2012).

This implies that a conceptual framework is rooted in the research traditions, paradigms, and approaches of a particular discipline such as (Van der Waldt, 2017) includes phenomenology, grounded theory, ethnomethodology, symbolic interactionism, feminism, and postmodernism.

Scholars who view theoretical frameworks as part of conceptual frameworks understand theory in terms of a micro-range where it informs specific concepts or constructs. In this regard, Kelly (2010) argued that micro-range theories guide research in at least four ways:

1. provides a contextual orientation for the study by focusing attention on the specific aspects under investigation
2. serves as an instrument to conceptualize and classify concepts and constructs
3. summarizes what is already known about the object of study, including empirical generalizations, and systems of relationships between propositions; also pinpoint gaps in existing knowledge
4. predicts results or findings of the research.

In this latter sense, theoretical frameworks may also refer to existing established theories or researchers' own theorizing, for example, assumptions, presuppositions, premises, or hypotheses (Sutton & Staw 1995; Torraco 1997)

Apart from the first perspective, namely, those conceptual and theoretical frameworks are synonymous, it has concurred fully with both the second and third perspectives mentioned previously, depending on the definition of the concept of 'theory'.

A conceptual framework is informed by theory to imbed the study philosophically, epistemologically, and methodologically (second perspective). However, such a framework is also broader than a theoretical one (third perspective). The reason is that concepts and constructs identified in the conceptual framework will guide the application of theory on a micro-level.

Ethical standards in Writing Related literature

You must observe the following ethical standard in writing literature review.

1. An ethical writer always acknowledges the contribution of others and the source of his/her ideas.

2. Any verbatim text taken from another author

must be enclosed in quotation marks.

3. We must always acknowledge every source that we use in our writing; whether we paraphrase it; summarize it, or enclose its quotations.

4. When we summarize, we condense, in our own words, a substantial amount of material into a short paragraph or perhaps even into a sentence.

5. Whether we are paraphrasing or summarizing we must always identify the source of our information.

6. When paraphrasing and/or summarizing others' work we must reproduce the exact meaning of the other author's ideas or facts using our words and sentence structure.

7. In order to make substantial modifications to the original text that result in a proper paraphrase, the author must have a thorough understanding of the ideas and terminology being used.

8. A responsible writer has an ethical responsibility to readers, and to the author/s

from whom, we borrow, and whenever possible, to use one's own words when paraphrasing.

9. When in doubt as to whether a concept or fact is common knowledge provide a citation.

10. Authors who submit a manuscript for publication containing data, reviews, conclusions, etc., that have already been disseminated in some significant manner (e.g., published as an article in another journal, presented at a conference, posted on the internet) must clearly indicate to the editors and readers the nature of the previous dissemination.

11. Authors of complex studies should heed the advice previously put forth by Angell & Relman (1989). If the results of a single complex study are best presented as a "cohesive" single whole, they should not be partitioned into individual papers. Furthermore, if there is any doubt as to whether a paper submitted for publication represents fragmented data, authors should enclose other papers

(published or unpublished) that might be part of the paper under consideration (Kassirer & Angell, 1995).

12. Because some instances of plagiarism, self-plagiarism, and even some writing practices might otherwise be acceptable (e.g., extensive paraphrasing or quoting of key elements of a book) can constitute copyright infringement, authors are strongly encouraged to become familiar with basic elements of copyright law.

13. While there are some situations where text recycling is an acceptable practice, it may not be so in other situations. Authors are urged to adhere to the spirit of ethical writing and avoid reusing their own previously published text unless it is done in a manner consistent with standard scholarly conventions (e.g., by using quotations and proper paraphrasing).

14. Authors are strongly urged to double-check their citations. Especially, authors should always ensure that each reference notation appearing in the body of the manuscript corresponds to the correct citations listed in the

reference section in the manuscript. In addition, authors should also ensure that all elements of a citation (e.g., spelling of authors' names, volume number of journals, pagination) are derived directly from the original paper, rather than from a citation that appears on a secondary source. Finally, authors should ensure that credit is given to those authors who first reported the phenomenon being studied.

15. The references used in a paper should only be those that are directly related to its contents. The intentional inclusion of references of questionable relevance for purposes of manipulating a journal's or a paper's impact factor or a paper's chances of acceptance is an unacceptance practice.

16. Authors should follow a simple rule: strive to attain the actual published paper. When the published paper cannot be obtained, cite the specific version of the material being used, whether it is conference presentation, abstract, or an unpublished manuscript.

17. Generally, when describing others' work, do

not rely on a secondary summary of that work. It is a deceptive practice, reflects poor scholarly standards, and can lead to a flawed description of the work described.

18. If an author must rely on a secondary source (e.g., textbook) to describe the contents of a primary source (e.g., an empirical journal article), s/he should consult writing manuals used in her discipline to follow the proper convention to do so. Above all, always indicate the actual source of the information being reported.

19. When borrowing heavily from a source, authors should always craft their writing in a way that makes clear to readers which ideas are their own and which are derived from the source being consulted.

20. When appropriate, authors have an ethical responsibility to report evidence that runs contrary to their point of view. In addition, evidence that we use in support of our position must be methodologically sound. When citing supporting studies that suffer from

methodological, statistical, or other types of shortcomings, such laws must be pointed out to the reader.

21. Authors have an ethical obligation to report all aspects of the study that may impact the independent replicability of their research.

22. Researchers have an ethical responsibility to report the results of their studies according to prior plans. Any post hoc manipulations that may alter the results initially obtained, such as the elimination of outliners or the use of alternative statistical techniques, must be clearly described along with an acceptable rationale for using such a technique.

23. Authorship determination should be discussed before commencing a research collaboration and should be based on established guidelines.

24. Only those individuals who have made substantive contributions to a project merit authorship in a paper.

25. Faculty-student collaboration should follow the same criteria to establish authorship. Mentors

must exercise great care to neither award authorship to students whose contributions do not merit it, nor to deny authorship and due credit to the work of students.

26. Academic or professional ghost authorship in the sciences is ethically unacceptable.

27. Authors must become aware of possible conflict of interest in their own research and to make every effort to disclose those situations (e.g., stock ownership, consulting agreements to the sponsoring organization) that may pose an actual or potential conflict of interest.

Definition of Terms

Definition of Terms is usually an annex to a work (book, research paper, pamphlet, etc.) either at the beginning or more likely near the end with a list of acronyms, jargon, credits, etc. This is an important part of a research paper or report in which the key or important terms in the study are clearly defined.

Type of Functions (Cariño, 2021)

1. **Conceptual** is the universal meaning that is attributed to a word or group of words and

which is understood by many people.

2. It is abstract and most general in nature. The usual source of the conceptual definition is the dictionary which is the reference book of everyday language.

3. **Operational definition** is the meaning of the concept or term used in a particular study. Unlike the conceptual definition, it is stated in a concrete term in that both types of the definition are to state first the conceptual followed by the operational.

4. **Function** establishes the rules and procedures the investigation will use to measure variables.

5. It provides unambiguous meaning to terms that otherwise can be interpreted in different ways.

Writing the Definition of Terms (Ragma, 2019)

1. Include only key terms from the title and research problems.

2. The terms should be arranged alphabetically and should be defined operationally using complete sentences.

3. Conceptual or "dictionary" definitions should be

documented as to reference.

4. A term may start with its conceptual and followed by its operational definitions.

5. Usually, a maximum of 10 items is defined in qualitative research.

Illustrative Example of Definition of Terms

Kpopped!: Understanding the Filipino Teens' Consumption of Korean Popular Music and Videos (Alanzalon, 2018)

The following terms shall be understood in context with the study. The researcher provided this section in order to inculcate the meaning of various terms in relation with the current research endeavor.

Active Consumption – consuming Kpop texts repeatedly and in a regular basis. Consumption – the act of using/utilizing Kpop media content.

Convention – a big scale gathering of fans with the same interest, most of the time filled with activities relating to the object of fandom.

Cultural offerings – facets of the Cultural Proximity Theory used in this study to describe the content of foreign media texts.

Entertainment company – the agency that manages the assets, schedules, and production of materials of the Kpop artists (e.g.: YG Entertainment, SM Entertainment, JYP Entertainment).

Fan – a person with an intense enthusiasm or attachment to Korean popular music, videos and artists.

Fan Club – an organized fandom established by a group of Kpop fans who share the same interest for a certain subject of their attention and enthusiasm.

Idol – a singer trained by an entertainment company marketed as an idol for the general public (e.g.: Girls' Generation, Super Junior, Shinee, SS501, U-Kiss).

Korean Popular Music (Kpop) – a genre of pop music that originated from South Korea and performed by Korean idol singers and groups.

Kpop Music Video (MV) – the official music video of a Kpop song originally performed by a Kpop artist and produced by their official Korean entertainment companies.

Kpop Video Clips – clips containing Kpop artists or their music; maybe videos from television shows.

Media Content – other music, video clips, and music videos which contain or are related in anyway to Kpop or Kpop artists.

Needs – the different psychological or sociological necessities/wants of the fans that are gratified by consuming Korean popular music and videos.

Online Forums – Internet communities where fans can post, download, and exchange comments, messages, pictures, videos with fellow fans.

Teenager – in this study, Filipinos of age 15-19.

ASSESSMENT TASKS

I. **Paraphrasing One Sentence**

Directions: Read the following published sentence and then paraphrase it—that is, rewrite it in your own words. You do not need to repeat every element. Instead, try changing the focus of the sentence while preserving the meaning of the original. Figure out the in-text citation that corresponds to the source information provided. Then add a parenthetical citation to your paraphrased sentence. Use the standard citation formats.

Published Sentences

Leaders who lack emotional and social competence undoubtedly can become a liability to organizations, directly leading to employee disengagement, absenteeism, stress-disability claims, hostile-workplace lawsuits, and increased health care expenses.

Source Information

Document type: Journal article (Section 10.1)

Authors: Kenneth Nowack and Paul Zak Publication year: 2020 • Article title: Empathy enhancing antidotes for interpersonally toxic leaders

Journal information: Consulting Psychology Journal:

Practice and Research, Volume 72, Issue 2, pages 119–133.

DOI: https://doi.org/10.1037/cpb0000164

II.   **Summarizing Multiple Sentences**

Directions: Read the following published sentences and summarize the authors' findings in your own words in one sentence. Figure out the in-text citation that corresponds source information provided. Then add a narrative citation to your paraphrased sentence. You do not need to re-cite the works that are already cited in the published sentences

Published Sentences

    Research suggests that people exercise less when demands in their job or studies increase (Englert & Rummel, 2016; Oaten & Cheng, 2005; Sonnentag & Jelden, 2009). Building upon these findings, the present study investigated the relationship between university students' implicit theories about willpower and the amount they exercise during their final examination period. We hypothesized and found that students with a limited theory about willpower— those who believed that their self-control resembles a limited resource—exercised significantly less than students with a nonlimited theory during this stressful period (about 220 min less over the course of 2 weeks).

Source Information

Document type: Journal article (Section 10.1)

Authors: Katharina Bernecker and Jule Kramer

Publication year: 2020

Article title: Implicit theories about willpower are associated with exercise levels during the academic examination period

Journal information: Sport, Exercise, and Performance Psychology, Volume 9, Issue 2, pages 216–231

DOI: https://doi.org/10.1037/spy0000182

III. **Writing a Long Paraphrase**

Directions: Read the following published paragraphs and summarize them in your own words in two to three sentences (a long paraphrase). Do not repeat every idea. Instead, highlight important findings and accurately represent the meaning of the original. Figure out the in-text citation that corresponds to source information provided. Then add either a parenthetical or narrative citation to your first sentence. You do not need to re-cite the works that are already cited in the published paragraphs.

Published Paragraphs

Food selectivity is the most frequently documented and well-researched feeding problem associated with autism spectrum disorder (ASD). It most often involves strong preferences for starches and snack foods, coinciding with a bias against fruits and vegetables. Associated mealtime difficulties include disruptive mealtime behavior (e.g., tantrums, crying), rigidity surrounding eating (e.g., only eating in a specific location, requiring certain utensils), and avoidance of certain food items based on the sensory characteristic (e.g., texture).

Severe food selectivity in ASD most often involves deficits in dietary variety, not volume, and children with ASD typically consume enough food to meet gross energy needs (Sharp, Berry, et al., 2013; Sharp et al., 2014). Because children with ASD typically consume an adequate volume of food, this may explain why, historically, feeding concerns in ASD have been overlooked in relation to other areas of clinical concern. The clinical picture, however, for food selectivity in ASD is more complicated from a nutritional and medical standpoint and requires looking beyond anthropometrics to determine the overall impact of atypical patterns of intake, including enhanced risk for underlying dietary insufficiencies and associated poor health outcomes (e.g., obesity).

Source Information

Document type: Edited book chapter (Section 10.3)

Chapter authors: T. Lindsey Burrell, William Sharp, Cristina Whitehouse, and Cynthia R. Johnson

Publication year: 2019

Chapter title: Parent training for food selectivity in autism spectrum disorder

Book editors: Cynthia R. Johnson, Eric M. Butter, and Lawrence Scahill

Book title: Parent training for autism spectrum disorder: Improving the quality of life for children and their families

Chapter page range: 173–202

Publisher: American Psychological Association

DOI: https://doi.org/10.1037/0000111-008

PERFORMANCE TASKS

Design and Make a Literature Review

1. From your approved research title and statement of the problem write a literature review. The structure of your literature review should have the following:

    a. A synopsis of the subject, problem, or theory under contemplation, along with the purposes of the literature review.

    b. Dissection of works under review into themes or categories (e.g., activities that support a particular position, those that propose an entirely new way).

    c. An explanation of how each work is alike to and differs from the others.

    d. Conclusion as to which parts are best considered in the argument of the pertinent area of research.

2. From your initial readings, construct the most feasible theoretical - conceptual framework of the study. What are your variables of interest? What theory or larger field of study are your variables anchored on? What will not be covered by your

theoretical-conceptual framework?

3. Give a very short explanation of your theoretical - conceptual framework. Deduce the overall goals of the study based on your theoretical-conceptual framework.

4. Submit a five-ten pages literature review. It must have an introduction, a body, a conclusion as well as citations.

Rubric for Writing the Literature Review

Criteria	Excellent 16-20	Very Good 11-15	Good 6-10	Need Improvement 1-5
Organization	The structure is intuitive and sufficiently inclusive of important constructs and variables of the proposed study.	A workable structure has been presented for presenting relevant literature related to the constructs and variables of the proposed study.	The structure of the literature is review is weak; it does not identify important ideas, constructs, or variables related to the research purpose, questions, or context.	The structure of the literature review is incomprehensi ble, irrelevant, or confusing.
Literature Review	The narrative integrates critical and logical details from the peer-viewed theoretical and research	Key constructs and variables are connected with relevant, reliable theoretical and research literature.	A key construct or variable is not connected with the research literature, selected literature is from	The review of literature is missing; it consists of nonresearched -based articles. Prepositions are irrelevant, inaccurate, or inappropriate.

	literature. Each key construct and variable is grounded in the literature.		unreliable sources. Literary supports are vague or ambiguous.	
Mechanics	There are no errors in punctuation and spelling	There are almost no errors in punctuation, capitalization, and spelling.	There are many errors in punctuation, capitalization, and spelling.	There are numerous and distracting errors in punctuation, capitalization, and spelling.
Citations	All works are cited done in the correct format with no errors	Some works are cited in the correct format. Inconsistent is evident	Few works are cited but done in the correct format.	No sources are cited in the review.

Cited References and Suggested Readings

Alanzalon, S.M. (2011). ***Kpopped! Understanding the Filipino Teens' Consumption of Korean Popular Music and Videos***. Unpublished Undergraduate Thesis, University of the Philippines College of Mass Communication.

Anfara, V. A., & Mertz, N.T. (2015). ***Theoretical framework in qualitative research (2nd edition)***. Sage Publication, Inc.

Angell M, Relman AS. (1989). ***Redundant publication.*** New England Journal of Medicine, 4;320 (18):1212-4. https://doi:10.1056/NEJM198905043201812.

Cariño, C. E. (2021). ***Tourism and Hospitality Research***. Mindshapers Co., Inc.

Clemente, R. F., Julaton, A B. E., & Orleans, A. V. (2016). *Research in Daily Life 1*. Sibs Publishing House, Inc.

Crawford, L. M. (2020). *Conceptual and Theoretical Framework in Research.* Sage Publications, Inc.

Creswell, J. W. (2014). *Research Design: Qualitative, Quantitative, and Mixed Methods Approaches*. Sage Publication, Inc.

Eisenhart, M. (1991). *Conceptual frameworks for research circa 1991: Ideas for a cultural anthropologist; implications for mathematics education research*. Psychology of Mathematics Education, Blacksburg, VA.

Fink, A. (2014). *Conducting research literature review*. Sage Publication, Inc.

Henson, R. M., & Soriano, R. F. (2016). *Qualitative Research: Word of Reality Dissections.* Mutya Publishing House.

Kassirer JP, Angell M. (1995). *Redundant publication: a reminder*. New England Journal of Medicine. 17;333 (7):449-50. https://doi:10.1056/NEJM199508173330709.

Kelly, M. (2010). *The role of theory in qualitative health research.* Family Practice 27(3), 285–290. https://doi.org/10.1093/fampra/cmp077.

Kumar, R. (2014). *Research methodology: A step-by-step guide for beginners (4th edition).* Sage Publication, Inc.

LeCompte, M. D., & Preissle, J. (1993). *Ethnography and Qualitative Design in Educational Research* (2nd Edition). Academic Press.

Leedy, P. D., & Ormrod, J. E. (2021). *Practical Research: Planning and Design (25th edition).* Pearson Education Limited.

Maree, J.G. (2012). *Complete your thesis or dissertation*

successfully: Practical guidelines. Juta, Cape Town.

Marshall, C. & Rossman, G. B. (2016). *Designing qualitative research (6th Edition).* Sage Publications, Inc.

Maxwell, J., (2005). *Qualitative research design: An interactive approach*. Sage Publications, Inc.

Merriam, S.B., & Tisdell, E. J. (2016). *Qualitative Research: A Guide to design and implementation (4th Edition).* Jossey-Bass.

Miles, M. B., Huberman, A. M., & Saldana, J. (2014). *Qualitative data analysis: A methods sourcebook.* Sage Publications, Inc.

Ragma, F. G. (2019). *Research 1: Qualitative Research*. Mindshapers Co., Inc.

Ravitch, S. M., & Riggan, M. (2017). *Reason & rigor: How conceptual framework guide research (2nd edition).* Sage Publications, Inc.

Robson, C., & McCartan, K. (2016). *Real-world research (4th edition)*. Wiley.

Salmorin, M. E. (2006). *Methods of Research*. Mindshapers Co., Inc.

Samosa, R. C., et.al. (2021). *Inquires, Investigation, and Immersion*. Beyond Books Publication.

Saunders, M.N.K., Gray, D.E., Tosey, P. & Sadler-Smith, E. (2015). *Concepts and theory building: A guide to professional doctorates in business and management*. Sage Publications, Inc.

Strauss, A., & Corbin, J. M. (1990). *Basics of qualitative research: Grounded theory procedures and techniques*. Sage Publications, Inc.

Sutton, R.I. & Staw, B.M. (1995). *What theory is not'*. Administrative Science Quarterly, 40(3), pp. 371–384.

https://doi.org/10.2307/2393788.

Torraco, R.J. (1997). ***Theory-building research methods***. Human resource development handbook: Linking research and practice.

University of Monash (2021). ***Citing and referencing: In-text citations.*** https://guides.lib.monash.edu/citing-referencing.

Van der Waldt, G. (2020). ***Constructing conceptual frameworks in social science research.*** The Journal for Transdisciplinary Research in Southern Africa 16(1), a758. https://doi.org/10.4102/td.v16i1.758.

MODULE 5:

UNDERSTANDING DATA AND WAYS TO SYSTEMATICALLY COLLECT DATA

LEARNING OUTCOMES

At the end of this module, students should be able to:

1. chooses appropriate qualitative research design.

2. describes sampling procedure and sample.

3. plans data collection and analysis procedures

4. presents written research methodology.

5. utilizes materials and techniques to produce creative work.

Qualitative Research Design

Design is a word that means a plan or something that is conceptualized by the mind. As a result of mental activity characterized by unfixed formation of something but an extensive. Cristobal & Cristobal (2017), defined research design as a plan which structures a study to ensure that the data collected and generated will contain the information needed to answer the initial inquiry as fully and clearly as possible. Interconnection of things, it serves blueprint or a skeletal framework of the study (Baraceros, 2019).

Think of the research design as a puzzle. It is composed of several pieces such as research questions, literature review, research approach, data collection methods, and data analysis methods. All of them to be aligned and linked; all of them need to address one another. Your research questions will dictate the type of data you will need and the evidence you will gather. They will also influence your data collection and analysis methods. Similarly, your literature review will make you aware of how researchers approached the phenomenon under study before. This would help you situate and start your inquiry about the research problem.

Now, in coming up with the research design, researchers often need to think about and weigh options on the following (Silverman, 2013):

1. Kinds of information and evidence needed to address the research questions.
2. Process of obtaining information.
3. Explanation for choosing a particular data collection method over others.
4. Method for analyzing acquired information.
5. Advantages and limitations of using the chosen data analysis procedure.

Bueno (2016), enlisted the consideration in describing your research design.

1. Analyze critically the utility of the design.
2. Describe how the design will help you in the conduct of the study.
3. Highlight problems in developing a suitable design.
4. Refers to an appropriate and accepted design.

Determining a research design requires careful plan on the most appropriate approach to carry out the objectives or purpose of the study. Qualitative research follows a bottom-up framework. The bottom-up framework starts where the quantitative methods end. For quantitative methods, the flow starts with a general rule or a theory. This will be narrowed down to a hypothesis, followed by an experiment, and lastly, confirmation of the result leading to verification of the theory or rejection of it (Gaddi, 2019).

Qualitative research starts with experience or a set of observable phenomena. Qualitative researchers dwell on possible patterns or similarities from which a hypothesis or cluster will be formed based on these patterns. From, it a theory will then be subjected for approval by testing it on different groups that may share related experiences.

In qualitative research the data gathered are presented from the perspectives of the respondents, so the biases of the researcher do not influence nor distort the data collection, interpretation, and analysis (Posecion, Go, & Albano, 2011). Researcher avoid describing a selected aspect of behaviors, for qualitative methods avoid established hypotheses or a priori knowledge, thereby any variable becomes the focus of the research. Researchers engaged in qualitative research are participant–observers themselves. They participate and record their observations and experiences in diaries while participating in the very act they are describing. In some cases, the study involves non – participant observation. The researcher records his/her observations of the events, but without the use of a questionnaire or other research tools. It aims to "reconstruct accurately what the respondents experience to understand the issues from the perspectives of the subjects themselves.

Qualitative design is useful, not only in providing rich descriptions of complex phenomena but in constructing or developing theories or conceptual frameworks and in generating hypothesis to explain those phenomena.

A wide range of tested qualitative research designs is available to address these challenges. The selection of method, or design will be tailored to the questions being studied and the setting for research.

Narrative Inquiry

Narrative collects stories from individuals (and documents, and group conversations) about individuals' lived and told experiences. These stories may emerge from a story told to the researcher, a story that is co-constructed between the researcher and the participant, and a story intended as a performance to convey some message or point. Thus, there may be a strong collaborative feature of narrative research as the story emerges through the interaction or dialogue of the researcher and the participant(s).

Narrative researchers can select from various types of narratives for guiding the collection of stories (Casey,1996). Here is a brief description of some popular approaches and an example for further reading.

1. A **biographical study** is a form of narrative study in which the researcher writes and records the experiences of another person's life.

2. **Autoethnography** is written and recorded by the individuals who are the subject of the study

(Ellis, 2004; Muncey, 2010). Muncey (2010) defines autoethnography as the idea of multiple layers of consciousness, the vulnerable self, the coherent self, critiquing the self in social contexts, the subversion of dominant discourses, and the evocative potential. They contain the personal story of the author as well as the larger cultural meaning for the individual's story.

3. A **life history portrays** an individual's entire life, while a personal experience story is a narrative study of an individual's personal experience found in single or multiple episodes, private situations, or communal folklore (Denzin, 1989).

4. An **oral history** consists of gathering personal reflections of events and their causes and effects from one individual or several individuals (Plummer, 1983). Narrative studies may have a specific contextual focus, such as stories told by teachers or children in classrooms (Ollerenshaw & Creswell, 2002) or the stories told about organizations (Czarniawska, 2004).

Oral history may draw upon diverse research methods and be guided by the interpretive framework (Janesick, 2013).

Procedures for Conducting Narrative Research (Creswell, 2014).

1. **Determine if the research problem or question best fits narrative research.** Narrative research is best for capturing the detailed stories or life experiences of a single individual or the lives of a small number of individuals.

2. **Select one or more individuals who have stories or life experiences to tell, and spend considerable time with them gathering their stories through multiple types of information.** Clandinin and Connelly (2000) refer to the stories as "field texts." Research participants may record their stories in a journal or diary, or the researcher might observe the individuals and record field notes. Researchers may also collect letters sent by the individuals; assemble stories about the

individuals from family members; gather documents such as memos or official correspondence about the individuals; or obtain photographs, memory boxes (collection of items that trigger memories), and other personal–family–social artifacts.

3. **Consider how the collection of the data and their recording can take different shapes**. Riessman (2008) illustrates different ways that researchers can transcribe interviews to develop different types of stories. The transcription can highlight the researcher as a listener or a questioner, emphasize the interaction between the researcher and the participant, convey a conversation that moves through time, or include shifting meanings that may emerge through translated material.

4. **Embed information about the context of these stories into data collection, analysis, and writing.** Narrative researchers situate individual stories within participants' personal experiences (their jobs, their homes), their culture (racial or ethnic), and their historical

contexts (time and place). Being context-sensitive is considered essential to narrative inquiry (Czarniawska, 2004).

5. **Analyze the participants' stories using the process of reorganizing the stories into some general type of framework called restorying**. The researcher may take an active role and "restory" the stories into a framework that makes sense. This framework may consist of gathering stories, analyzing them for key elements of the story (e.g., time, place, plot, and scene), and then rewriting the stories to place them within a chronological sequence (Ollerenshaw & Creswell, 2002). Cortazzi (1993) suggests that the chronology of narrative research, with an emphasis on sequence, sets narrative apart from other genres of research. One aspect of the chronology is that the stories have a beginning, a middle, and an end. Similar to basic elements found in good novels, these aspects involve a predicament, conflict, or struggle; a protagonist, or main character; and a sequence

with implied causality (i.e., a plot) during which the predicament is resolved in some fashion (Carter, 1993). Further, the story might include other elements typically found in novels, such as time, place, and scene (Connelly & Clandinin, 1990). The plot, or storyline, may also include Clandinin and Connelly's (2000) three-dimensional narrative inquiry space: the personal and social (the interaction); the past, present, and future (continuity); and the place (situation). This storyline may include information about the setting or context of the participants' experiences. Beyond the chronology, researchers might detail themes that arise from the story to provide a more detailed discussion of the meaning of the story (Huber & Whelan, 1999). Thus, the qualitative data analysis may be a description of both the story and themes that emerge from it. A postmodern narrative writer, such as Czarniawska (2004), adds another element to the analysis: a deconstruction of the stories, and unmaking of them by such analytic strategies as exposing dichotomies, examining silences, and attending to disruptions and contradictions. Finally, the analysis process consists of the researcher looking for themes or categories; the researcher using a micro linguistic approach and probing for the meaning of words, phrases, and larger units of discourse such as is often done in conversational analysis (Gee, 1991); or the researcher examining the stories for how they are produced interactively between the researcher and the participant or performed by the participant to convey a specific agenda or message (Riessman, 2008).

6. **Embed a collaborative approach in the collection and telling of stories.** Clandinin & Connelly (2000) describe active involvement of participants as central to their work that is, "Narrative inquiry is a way of understanding experience; it is a collaboration between research and participants, over time, in a place or series of places, and in social interactions with milieus" (p. 17). As researchers collect

stories, they negotiate relationships, smooth transitions, and provide ways to be useful to the participants. In narrative research, a key theme has been the turn toward the relationship between the researcher and the researched in which both parties will learn and change in the encounter (Pinnegar & Daynes, 2007). In this process, the parties negotiate the meaning of the stories, adding a validation check to the analysis (Creswell & Miller, 2000). Within the participant's story may also be an interwoven story of the researcher gaining insight into her or his own life (Huber & Whelan, 1999). Also, within the story may be epiphanies, turning points, or disruptions in which the storyline changes direction dramatically. In the end, the narrative study tells the story of individuals unfolding in a chronology of their experiences, set within their personal, social, and historical context, and including the important themes in those lived experiences. "Narrative inquiry is stories lived and told," said Clandinin and Connolly (2000,

p. 20).

7. **Present the narrative in written form.** Adapt the following general reporting structure as appropriate: an introduction to familiarize the reader with the participant(s) and the intended purpose for the story; research procedures to provide a rationale for use of a narrative and details about data collection and analysis; telling of the story to theorize about participant lives, with narrative segments; and patterns of meaning articulated around events, processes, epiphanies, or themes; and a final interpretation of the meaning of the story. It is not uncommon for researchers to find this process challenging "because it is at this point that we make our texts visible to public audiences, unknown audiences who may be far removed from the lived and told experiences of participants" (Clandinin, 2013, p. 50).

Figure 3: Procedures for Conducting Narrative Research

Methods of Data Collection:

1. In-depth unstructured and semi-structured interviews.

2. Autobiographical writings, poetry, and other narrative documents.

3. Photograph and other visual materials.

Methods of Data Analysis

1. Identification of Narrative themes, threads, and tensions.

2. Recording of narratives into a coherent chronological or thematic story.

Phenomenology

Phenomenology it describes the common meaning for several individuals of their lived experiences of a concept or a phenomenon. it focuses on describing what all participants have in common as they experience a phenomenon (e.g., grief is universally experienced). The basic purpose of phenomenology is to reduce individual experiences with a phenomenon to a description of the universal essence (a "grasp of the very nature of the thing.

Procedures for Conducting Phenomenological Research (Creswell, 2014).

1. **Determine if the research problem is best examined by using a phenomenological approach.** The type of problem best suited for this form of research is one in which it is important to understand several individuals' common or shared experiences of a phenomenon. It would be important to understand these common experiences in order to develop practices or policies or to

develop a deeper understanding of the features of the phenomenon.

2. **Identify a phenomenon of interest to study, and describe it.** Examples of a phenomenon include emotional states such as anger and social constructs such as professionalism. A phenomenon can also involve gaining understandings of a clinical descriptor—for example, what it means to be underweight or a professional descriptor like what it means to be a wrestler. Moustakas (1994) provides numerous examples of phenomena that have been studied.

3. **Distinguish and specify the broad philosophical assumptions of phenomenology**. For example, one could write about the combination of objective reality and individual experiences. These lived experiences are furthermore "conscious" and directed toward an object. To fully describe how participants, view the phenomenon, researchers must bracket out, as much as possible, their own experiences.

4. **Collect data from the individuals who have experienced the phenomenon by using in-depth and multiple interviews**. Polkinghorne (1989) recommends that researchers interview from 5 to 25 individuals who have all experienced the phenomenon. The participants are asked two broad, general questions (Moustakas, 1994): What have you experienced in terms of the phenomenon? What contexts or situations have typically influenced or affected your experiences of the phenomenon? Other open-ended questions may also be asked, but these two, especially, focus attention on gathering data that will lead to a textual and structural description of the experiences and ultimately provide an understanding of the common experiences of the participants. Other forms of data may also be collected, such as observations, journals, poetry, music, and other forms of art. van Manen (1990) mentions taped conversations; formally written responses; and accounts of

vicarious experiences of drama, films, poetry, and novels.

5. **Generate themes from the analysis of significant statements.** Phenomenological data analysis steps are generally similar for all psychological phenomenologists who discuss the methods (Moustakas, 1994; Polkinghorne, 1989). Building on the data from the first and second research questions, data analysts go through the data (e.g., interview transcriptions) and highlight "significant statements," sentences, or quotes that provide an understanding of how the participants experienced the phenomenon. Moustakas (1994) calls this step horizonalization. Next, the researcher develops clusters of meaning from these significant statements into themes.

6. **Develop textural and structural descriptions.** The significant statements and themes are then used to write a description of what the participants experienced (textural description). They are also used to write a description of the context or setting that

influenced how the participants experienced the phenomenon, called structural description or imaginative variation. Moustakas (1994) adds a further step: Researchers also write about their own experiences and the context and situations that have influenced their experiences. We like to shorten Moustakas's procedures and reflect these personal statements at the beginning of the phenomenology or include them in a methods discussion of the role of the researcher (Marshall & Rossman, 2015).

7. **Report the "essence" of the phenomenon by using a composite description.** From the structural and textural descriptions, the researcher then writes a composite description that presents the "essence" of the phenomenon, called the essential, invariant structure (or essence). Primarily this passage focuses on the common experiences of the participants. For example, it means that all experiences have an underlying structure (grief

is the same whether the loved one is a puppy, a parakeet, or a child).

8. **Present the understanding of the essence of the experience in written form.** The practice of phenomenological inquiry is considered by Max van Manen (2014) to be inseparable from the practice of writing. He goes on to explain that one of the challenges with writing is that "one must bring into presence a phenomenon that cannot be represented in plain words" (p. 370). There are numerous "ways" for communicating phenomenological research including by systematic exploration, meaning the phenomenon is placed in the context of existential (e.g., temporality or spatiality) or by organizing the account reflective of an ever-deepening understanding of the phenomenon experienced. A general reporting structure includes an introduction to familiarize the reader with the phenomenon and in some cases, a personal statement of experiences from the researcher (Moustakas, 1994);

research procedures to provide a rationale for the use of phenomenology, and philosophical assumptions and details about data collection and analysis; a report of how the phenomenon was experienced with significant statements; and a conclusion with a composite description of the essence of the phenomenon.

Figure 4: Procedures for Conducting Phenomenological Research

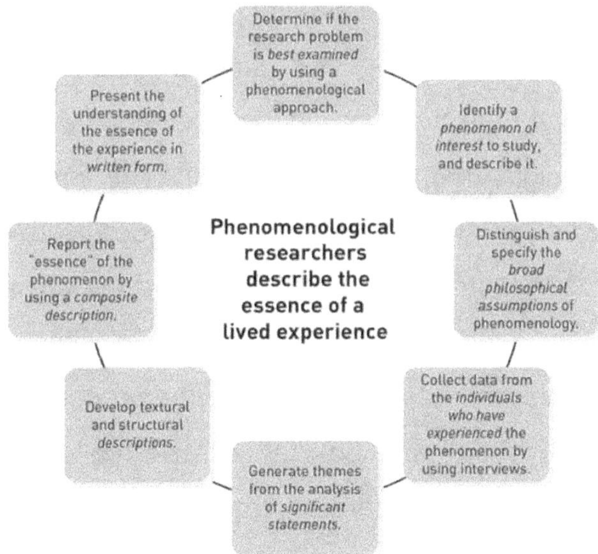

Methods of Data Collection

1. In-depth, semi-structured interviews.
2. Purposive sampling individuals.

Methods of Data Analysis

1. Search for meaningful concepts that reflect various aspects of the experience.
2. Integration of those concepts into a seemingly typical experience.

Grounded Theory

Grounded Theory is intended is to move beyond description and to generate or discover a theory, a "unified theoretical explanation" for a process or an action. Participants in the study would all have experienced the process, and the development of the theory might help explain practice or provide a framework for further research. A key idea is that this theory development does not come "off the shelf" but rather is generated or "grounded" in data from participants who have experienced the process. Thus, grounded theory is a qualitative research design in which the inquirer generates a general explanation (a theory) of a process, an action, or an interaction shaped by the views of a large number of participants.

Procedures for Conducting Grounded Theory Research (Creswell, 2014).

1. **Determine if grounded theory is best suited to study the research problem**. Grounded theory is a good design to use when a theory is not available to explain or understand a process. The literature may have models available, but they were developed and tested on samples and populations other than those of interest to the qualitative researcher. Also, theories may be present, but they are incomplete because they do not address potentially valuable variables or categories of interest to the researcher. On the practical side, a theory may be needed to explain how people are experiencing a phenomenon, and the grounded theory developed by the researcher will provide such a general framework.

2. **Focus the interview questions on understanding how individuals experience the process and identify the steps in the process (What was the process? How did it**

unfold?). After initially exploring these issues, the researcher then returns to the participants and asks more detailed questions that help to shape the axial coding phase, such as these: What was central to the process (the core phenomenon)? What influenced or caused this phenomenon to occur (causal conditions)? What strategies were employed during the process (strategies)? What effect occurred (consequences)? These questions are typically asked in interviews, although other forms of data may also be collected, such as observations, documents, and audiovisual materials. The point is to gather enough information to fully develop (or saturate) the model. This may involve 20 to 60 interviews.

3. **Theory-building emerges through the simultaneous and iterative data collection, analysis, and memoing processes.** In memoing, the researcher writes down ideas about the evolving theory throughout the data procedures in an effort to discover patterns (Lempert, 2007). The role of memoing as an

essential habit for theory development is highlighted by Corbin and Strauss (2015): "Writing memos should begin with the first analytical session and continue throughout the research process" (p. 117) and "memos begin as rudimentary representations of thought and grow in complexity, density, clarity, and accuracy as the research progresses" (p. 117).

4. **Structure the various analysis procedures as open, axial, and selective coding and follow traditions.** In open coding, the researcher forms categories of information about the phenomenon being studied by segmenting information. Within each category, the investigator finds several properties, or subcategories, and looks for data to dimensionalize, or show the extreme possibilities on a continuum of the property.

5. **In axial coding, the investigator assembles the data in new ways after open coding.** In this structured approach, the investigator presents a coding paradigm or logic diagram (i.e., a visual model) in which the researcher

identifies a central phenomenon (i.e., a central category about the phenomenon), explores causal conditions (i.e., categories of conditions that influence the phenomenon), specifies strategies (i.e., the actions or interactions that result from the central phenomenon), identifies the context and intervening conditions (i.e., the narrow and broad conditions that influence the strategies), and delineates the consequences (i.e., the outcomes of the strategies) for this phenomenon. Researchers are advised when focusing on a particular theory component (i.e., condition) the "explanation needs to remain at a conceptual level and use selected data fragments to provide supporting evidence" (Birks & Mills, 2015, p. 130).

6. **In selective coding, the researcher may write a "storyline" that connects the categories.** Alternatively, propositions or hypotheses may be specified that state predicted relationships. A model can serve as a helpful visual representation of the relationships among categories.

7. **Articulate a substantive-level theory for communication purposes**. A substantive-level theory is written by a researcher close to a specific problem or population of people. The substantive-level theory may be tested later for its empirical verification with quantitative data to determine if it can be generalized to a sample and population (Creswell & Plano Clark, 2011). Alternatively, the study may end at this point with the generation of a theory as the goal of the research.

8. **Present the theory as a discussion or model.** Writing is intertwined into every aspect of conducting grounded theory research and how a grounded theory is presented depends on the audience and the process being explained (e.g., see Birks & Mills, 2015; Charmaz, 2014; Corbin & Strauss, 2015). A general reporting structure includes an introduction to familiarize the reader with the process (or action) that the theory is intended to explain, research procedures to provide a rationale for grounded theory and details about

data collection and analysis, a theory description involving the major categories from open coding, conditions around core phenomenon from axial coding, and a proposition describing the interrelationships of categories in the model from selective coding. A model can be a useful to provide a summative, concise visual representation of the theory and conclude with a discussion of the theory and (if appropriate) connections and contradictions with extant literature, significance of findings, and implications and limitations.

Figure 5: Procedures for Conducting Grounded Theory Research

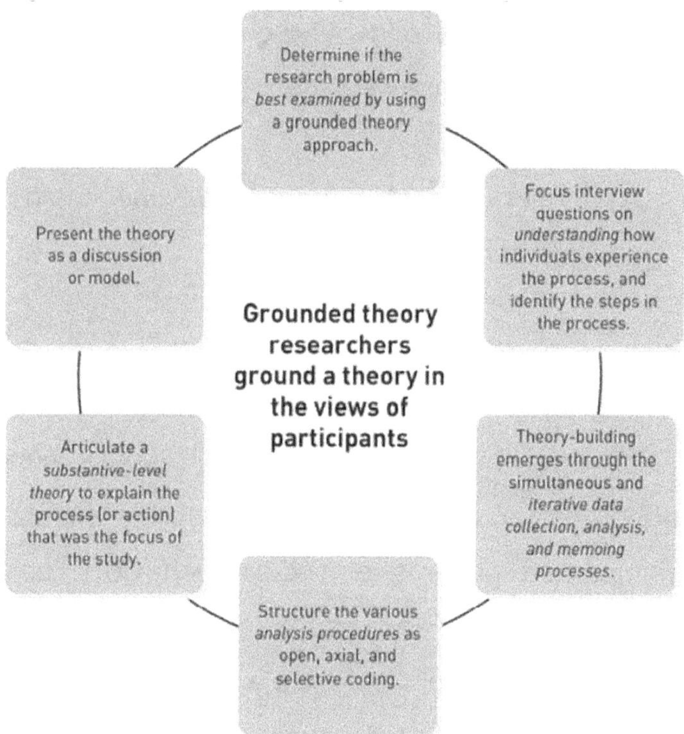

Methods of Data Collection

1. Interview
2. Theoretical sampling in order to saturate theoretical categories.
3. Any other relevant data sources.

Methods of Data Analysis

1. Systematic method of coding the data into categories and identifying interrelationships.
2. Continual interweaving of data collection and data analysis.
3. Construction of a theory from the categories and interrelationships.

Ethnography

Ethnography it focuses on an entire culture-sharing group. It describes and interprets the shared and learned patterns of values, behaviors, beliefs, and language of a culture-sharing group. As a process, ethnography involves extended observations of the group, most often through participant observation, in which the researcher is immersed in the day-to-day lives of the people and observes and interviews the group participants. Ethnographers study the meaning of the behavior, the language, and the interaction among members of the culture-sharing group.

Procedures for Conducting an Ethnography (Creswell, 2014).

1. **Determine if ethnography is the most appropriate design for studying the research problem.** Ethnography is appropriate if the needs are to describe how a cultural group works and to explore the beliefs, language, behaviors, and issues facing the group, such as power, resistance, and dominance. The literature may be deficient in actually knowing how the group works because the group is not in the mainstream, people may not be familiar with the group, or its ways are so different that readers may not identify with the group.

2. **Identify and locate a culture-sharing group to study.** Typically, this group is one whose members have been together for an extended period of time so that their shared language, patterns of behavior, and attitudes have merged into discernable patterns. This may also be a group that has been marginalized by society. Because ethnographers spend time

talking with and observing this group, access may require finding one or more individuals in the group who will allow the researcher in—a gatekeeper or key informants (or participants).

3. **Select cultural themes, issues, or theories to study about the group**. These themes, issues, and theories provide an orienting framework for the study of the culture-sharing group. It also informs the analysis of the culture-sharing group. The themes may include such topics as enculturation, socialization, learning, cognition, domination, inequality, or child and adult development (LeCompte et al., 1992). As discussed by Hammersley and Atkinson (1995), Wolcott (1987, 1994, 2008a), and Fetterman (2010), the ethnographer begins the study by examining people in interaction in ordinary settings and discerns pervasive patterns such as life cycles, events, and cultural themes.

4. **Determine which type of ethnography to use to study cultural concepts.** Perhaps how the group works needs to be described, or a

critical ethnography can expose issues such as power, hegemony, and advocacy for certain groups. A critical ethnographer, for example, might address inequity in society or some part of it; use the research to advocate and call for changes; and specify an issue to explore, such as inequality, dominance, oppression, or empowerment.

5. **Gather information in the context or setting where the group works or lives**. This is called fieldwork (Wolcott, 2008a). Gathering the types of information typically needed in an ethnography involves going to the research site, respecting the daily lives of individuals at the site, and collecting a wide variety of materials. Field issues of respect, reciprocity, deciding who owns the data, and others are central to ethnography. Ethnographers bring sensitivity to fieldwork issues (Hammersley & Atkinson, 1995), such as attending to how they gain access, giving back or reciprocating with the participants, and engaging in ethical research, such as presenting themselves

honestly and describing the purpose of the study. LeCompte and Schensul (1999) organize types of ethnographic data into observations, tests and measures, surveys, interviews, content analysis, elicitation methods, audiovisual methods, spatial mapping, and network research.

6. **Generate an overall cultural interpretation of the group from the analysis of patterns across many sources of data.** The researcher begins by compiling a detailed description of the culture-sharing group, focusing on a single event, on several activities, or on the group over a prolonged period of time. The ethnographer moves into a theme analysis of patterns or topics that signifies how the cultural group works and lives, and ends with an "overall picture of how a system works" (Fetterman, 2010, p. 10). Fetterman (2010) describes the function of thick description for the reader, stating "ideally the ethnographer shares the participant's understanding of the situation with the reader.

Thick description is a written record of cultural interpretation" (p. 125). This description includes verbatim quotes reflective of cultural concepts such as the social structure, kinship, political structure, and the social relations or function among members incorporating the views of the participants (emic) as well as the views of the researcher (etic).

7. **Present the patterns of the culture-sharing group in written or performance formats.** This is often accomplished by describing a working set of rules or generalizations as to how the culture-sharing group functions. This may also be referred to as a holistic cultural portrait. Writing ethnographies involves an interactive analysis and writing process often begins during fieldwork. A general reporting structure includes an introduction to familiarize the reader with the culture-sharing group, research procedures to provide a rationale for use of an ethnography, and details about data collection and analysis, providing a cultural interpretation using a variety of ways

describing the patterns that emerge from an analysis of cultural. The final product is a holistic cultural portrait of the group from both the participants and the interpretation of the researcher that might also advocate for the needs of the group or suggest changes in society. Other products may be more performance-based, such as theater productions, plays, or poems.

Figure 6: **Procedures for Conducting**

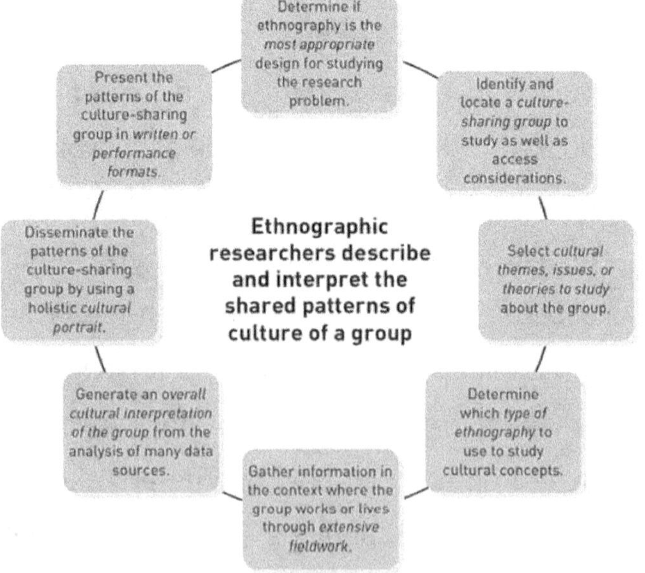

Ethnographic Research

Methods of Data Collection

1. Participants observation
2. Semi-structured or unstructured interviews with "informants"
3. Artifacts/document collection.
4. Survey and questionnaires.

Methods of Data Analysis

1. Identification of significant phenomenon and underlying structures and beliefs.
2. Organization of data into a logical whole (e.g., chronological, typical data).

Case Study

Case study is an in-depth examination of an individual, group of people, or an institution. Some of its purposes are to gain insight into a little–known problem, provide background data for broader studies, and explain socio-psychological and socio-cultural processes (Cristobal & Cristobal, 2017). A case study also involves a comprehensive and extensive examination of a particular individual, group, or situation over a period of time. It provides information on where to draw conclusions about the impact of a significant event in a person's life (Sanchez, 2002).

Procedures for Conducting a Case Study (Creswell, 2014).

1. **Determine if a case study approach is appropriate for studying the research problem.** A case study is a good approach when the inquirer has clearly identifiable cases with boundaries and seeks to provide an in-depth understanding of the cases or a comparison of several cases.

2. **Identify the intent of the study and select the case (or cases).** In conducting case study research, we recommend that investigators consider the intent and type of case study—single or collective, multisite or within-site, and focused on a case or on an issue (intrinsic, instrumental)—is most promising and useful. The case(s) selected may involve an individual, several individuals, a program, an event, or an activity (Stake, 1995; Yin, 2009) with an array

of possibilities for purposeful sampling is available. Often, we have found selecting cases that show different perspectives on the problem, process, or event preferable (called purposeful maximal sampling; see Creswell, 2012), but ordinary cases, accessible cases, or unusual cases are also desirable options.

3. **Develop procedures for conducting extensive data collection drawing on multiple data sources.** Among the common sources of information are observations, interviews, documents, and audiovisual materials. For example, Yin (2014) recommends six types of information to collect: documents, archival records, interviews, direct observations, participant observation, and physical artifacts.

4. **Specify the analysis approach on which the case description integrates analysis themes and contextual information**. The type of analysis of these data can be a holistic analysis of the entire case or an embedded analysis of a specific aspect of the case (Yin,

2009). Through data collecting and analysis, a detailed description of the case (Stake, 1995) emerges in which the researcher details such aspects as the history of the case, the chronology of events, or a day-by-day rendering of the activities of the case. Then the researcher might focus on a few key issues (or analysis of themes, or case themes), not for generalizing beyond the case but for understanding the complexity of the case. One analytic strategy would be to identify issues within each case and then look for common themes that transcend the cases (Yin, 2009). This analysis is rich in the context of the case or setting in which the case presents itself (Merriam, 1988). When multiple cases are chosen, a typical format is to provide first a detailed description of each case and themes within the case, called a within-case analysis, followed by a thematic analysis across the cases, called a cross-case analysis, as well as assertions or an interpretation of the meaning of the case. Whether that meaning comes from learning about the issue of the case (an instrumental case) or learning about an unusual situation (an intrinsic case). As Lincoln and Guba (1985) mention, this phase constitutes the lessons learned from the case, and Stake (1995) describes them as assertions. Stake (1995) focuses some of the assertions on lessons learned about the case stating, "Having presented a body of relatively uninterpreted observations, I will summarize what I feel I understand about the case and how my generalizations about the case have changed conceptually or in level of confidence" (Stake, 1995, p. 123).

5. **Report the case study and lessons learned by using case assertions in written form.** Writing case descriptions involves a reflective process, and the sooner you begin, our experiences tell us, the easier it is to finish. Certainly, the architecture for what works best for individual studies will emerge and be shaped differently by the study's assertions. We adopt the advice forwarded by Stake

(1995), "The report needs to be organized with readers in mind" (p. 122). A general reporting structure includes an entry vignette to provide the reader with an inviting introduction to the feel of the context in which the case takes place, an introduction to familiarize the reader with the central features including rationale and research procedures, an extensive narrative description of the case or cases and its or their context, which may include historical and organizational information important for understanding the case. Then the issue description draws from additional data sources and integrates with the researcher's own interpretations of the issues and both confirming and disproving evidence are presented followed by the presentation of overall case assertions. Finally, a closing vignette provides the reader with a final experience. Stake (1995) portrays the purpose of the closing vignette as way of cautioning the reader to the specific case context saying, "I like to close on an experiential note, reminding the reader that the report is just one person's encounter with a complex case" (p. 123).

Figure 7: Procedures for Conducting Case Study Research

Methods of Data Collection

1. Observation

2. Interviews

3. Appropriate written documents and/or audiovisual materials.

Methods of Data Analysis

1. Categorization and interpretation of data in terms of common themes.

2. Synthesis into an overall portrait of the case.

Illustrative Example of Grounded Theory Research Design

A qualitative study on the stigma experienced by people with mental health problems and epilepsy in the Philippines (Tanaka, et al., 2018).

The current research utilized the principles of constructivist grounded theory, which is deemed suitable for revealing the social phenomenon of people with mental health problems (PMHP's) experiences of stigma (Charmaz, 2014) in the Filipino context. The constructivist grounded theory assumes a relativist ontology (accepting that multiple realities exist) and a subjectivist epistemology (involving a co-construction of meaning through interaction between the researcher and participant) (Charmaz, 2014). It provides a means of studying power, inequality, and marginality (Charmaz, 2017).

Illustrative Example of Ethnographic Research

**Unveiling the Mystical Lucban Pahiyas Festival
(Rosaroso & Rosaroso, 2015)**

This is an ethnographic research investigating the Lucbanins' culture. According to Rossman and Rallis (2011), ethnography looks into the appreciation of people's culture and setting, geared towards face to face interactions and discovers how these interactions shape and construct meaning. Further, Fetterman (2010), defined ethnography as the key informants' way of narrating a true to life story which provides an avenue for hearing the natives' voices with their own meanings and interpretations.

Illustrative Example of Narrative Research

Political Dynasty in Public Governance: A Close Encounter with the Cebuanos (Guarde et al, 2016)

This is a qualitative research which utilized narrative inquiry as method of data analysis. Informants are engaged in narrating their stories while being interviewed. For Bell, narrative inquiry involves meaning making during data collection, interpretation and writing of the findings (Bell, 2005)

Data Collection Procedure in Qualitative Research

The data collection procedure is a section in the methodology that details the specific steps that the researcher took in order to gather the needed data. This section explains who collected the data and how he or she did it. This section also presents all the processes or activities the participants have engaged in and where these took place.

Characteristics of Qualitative Data Collection (Henson & Soriano, 2016).

1. Use of open-ended and less structural protocols, for example, researchers may change the data collection strategy by adding refining, or dropping techniques of questioning informants, generally thinking "outside the box".

2. Reliance on immersive (also referred to as iterative) interviews like informants may be interviewed several times to follow up on a particular issue, clarify concepts, or check the reliability of data.

3. Use of triangulation to increase the credibility of their findings (e.g., researchers rely on multiple data collection methods to check the authenticity

of their results).

4. Findings are not generalizable to any specific population, rather each case study produces a single piece of evidence that can be used to seek general patterns among different studies of the same issue.

Below are common data collection instruments and procedures in qualitative research (Clemente, Julaton, & Orleans, 2016).

1. **Documentary analysis.** This instrument may require the researcher to examine available resources or documents. Inspecting the primary and secondary sources is important when using the type of data collection.

2. **Interview.** It happens when the researcher personally asks the key informants about things or information he/she needs from the subjects. The interviewer must be trained to conduct an effective interview. There are different types of interviews:

    a. **Structural interview** happens when the researcher prepares and organized questions that the respondents will answer.

The researcher does not ask beyond what is written in the interview sheet but could ask the interviewee for the purpose of clarifying his/her answers.

b. **Unstructured interview** occurs when the researcher prepares an outline of the topics that he/she needs to personally ask the interviewee in a spontaneous and conversation-like manner. In this kind of interview, the researcher should be knowledgeable about the topic and skilled in asking probing questions.

c. **Semi-structured interview** is when the researcher prepares a specific set of questions but could ask follow-up questions to the respondents for them to elaborate their answers. It is easy for the researcher to gather additional information and to have an in-depth perspective on the response of the interview is used.

3. **Observation.** In these techniques, the researcher tracks the subjects' behavioral change over a specific period of time.

Observation may happen in the following manner:

a. **Naturalistic observation.** In this type of observation, the researcher observes the subjects in natural settings or their actual environment. The observation is done from outside of the environment.

b. **Participative observation.** The observer in this type of observation requires the researcher to be involved in the usual activities of the subjects. This gives the researchers direct and first–hand experience of what the respondents are experiencing.

c. **Non – naturalistic observation.** This is also called the "the ideal- situation" observation. Subjects are taken away from their actual environment and are subjected to ideal conditions determined by the researcher.

d. **Questionnaire.** This is one of the most commonly used data collection instruments. Questionnaires are easier to administer and could gather larger turnout at a single time. It requires respondents to answer a prepared set of questions regarding the information that the researcher wants to elicit from them. The following are some types of questions used:

a. **Yes or No.** Items in the questionnaire are answerable by yes or no.

b. **Recognition.** Respondents are made to choose from the choices given in the questionnaire.

c. **Completion.** Respondents are requested to supply the necessary information in the blank placed after each statement or question. This is also called an open-ended questionnaire.

d. **Coding.** The respondents are asked to rank or give numerical ratings for the information required of them.

e. **Subjective.** The respondents are free to give their opinions and answer the questions posed by the researcher.

f. **Combination.** This makes use of one or

more types of questions in a single questionnaire.

4. **Focus group discussion (FGD).** It is a good way to gather to agree or disagree with each other. In this case, it provides an insight into how the group thinks about issues, inconsistencies, and variations that exist in their community.

FGD can be used to explore the meanings of survey findings that cannot be explained statistically, determine the range of opinions and view about a topic of interest, and collect a wide variety of local terms. In bridging research and policy, FGD can be useful in providing insight about opinions among parties involved in the change process, thus enabling the process to be managed more smoothly. It is also a good method to employ prior to designing questionnaires.

Steps in Data Collection for Qualitative Research

The following are the steps for the qualitative data collection procedure (Jackson, 2013).

1. Perform a literature review of the topic to

discover what evidence is already available with a wide range of sources from trusted journals, books, and experts.

2. Use the findings of the literature review to refine the objectives of the study.

3. Investigate various approaches used in qualitative research and when they can be applied.

4. Choose a research approach while considering the subject, the amount of evidence already published to meet research objectives.

5. Create a data collection tool, such as an interview tool but prevent bias and extract as much useful information suitable for analysis using your chosen method.

6. Select the participants rich with experience, and should not just be selected randomly but purposively.

7. Record the interview or discussion data in an appropriate way.

8. Transcribe your data into written text, and convert ideas into themes using the appropriate method.

Illustrative Example of Research Instrument

Influence of Facebook to Voters' Political Practices (Salvador, et al., 2017)

The researchers used survey questionnaires and interview guide in gathering data. In terms of validation, the survey questionnaire was checked by three faculty experts in both the Department of Public Governance and the Social Sciences Department, was tried out among the millennials in the City and residents in one of the rural barangays in Northern Cebu, before it was used to target key informants. The researchers distributed the survey questionnaires to the different key informants. In the interview part, responses of the respondents were recorded using video tape, these were transcribed to support on the information gathered from the questionnaires.

Illustrative Example of Data Gathering Procedure

A qualitative study on the stigma experienced by people with mental health problems and epilepsy in the Philippines (Tanaka, et al., 2018).

Interview procedures

Data on the PMHP were collected through semi-structured in-depth interviews. Prior to the beginning of data collection, an interview guide was developed, referring to previous research [18, 50], and then modified based on six pilot interviews in the setting. The interview guide had a series of open questions on three major topics: onset of mental health problems and coping behaviours, experiences of being treated negatively owing to the problem and its consequences, and activities PMHP gave up because of how others might respond to their health problem. The interview guides for interviews with PMHP and for interviews with carers and community health volunteers can be accessed in Additional files 1 and 2, respectively. Consistent with the grounded theory methods, we used the interview guide as a flexible tool that could be revised as the analysis progressed.

The carers and community health volunteers were not asked about their own experiences of stigma as a carer or person working in mental health. Instead, we asked them about the PMHP's experiences regarding the same topics, based on their observations. Demographic data of the PMHP were also obtained at the beginning of the interview. The first author, CT (female, a Japanese public health nurse), conducted all of the data collection between January and March 2017. During the interview, Tagalog or English was used as preferred by the participants. When Tagalog was chosen, the interviews were interpreted by one of two health workers who had lived in the city for more than 30 years and were fluent in both Tagalog and English. After explaining the study and gaining informed consent, the interviews were conducted in their home, a health centre, or the city hospital, depending on the participants' preference. Wherever possible, we conducted interviews in a space where there was no one but the interviewee, interviewer, and interpreter around. However, five PMHP were not willing to be interviewed alone. In which case, a family member was in the same place and assisted the interview. All the interviews were digitally recorded with interviewees' permission and lasted between 19 and 53 min; the median length was 29 min. The participants received 100 Philippine pesos (1.9 US dollars) as acknowledgement for their participation.

Supplementary data collection

We included data of interviews with seven health workers into our analysis to gain a wider perspective on the stigma experienced by PMHP. CT conducted the interviews during her one-month participant observation at health services provided by the city government. During the observation, CT discussed the role of stigma and its impact on PMHP with more than 85 health and welfare workers. We analysed seven interviews with those who shared episodes on PMHP with whom they were in direct contact as a part of their duty at work. The interviewees were three community health volunteers, two nurses, one doctor, and one rehabilitation program officer. Notes were taken during the interviews and six out of seven interviews were audiotaped with their permission.

Sampling Techniques in Qualitative Research

In qualitative research, there are no hard and fast rules about the meaning of a population sample. To determine who and how many participants to include or what materials or artifacts to examine in qualitative research, the students must go back to the research question (s) and aims of its research.

1. **Purposive sampling** is a non – probabilistic sampling technique that intentionally selects the participants, sites, documents, and visual materials because it is believed that these sources of information provide or present the appropriate responses to the research questions (Creswell 2007, 2003). In here, student researchers seek what type of individuals, sites, documents, and visual materials could provide meaningful information. Students researchers should be wary that their selection should include details on the:

   a. **setting** (refers to the place where the researcher should take place) e.g., a specific village or certain group of people.

   b. **actors** (refers to the individuals to be observed or interviewed) e.g., an expert of a particular field, a specific age group (or other socio-demographic characteristics);

c. **events** (refers to the phenomenon /activity that will be observed the actors are doing) e.g., climate change mitigation age group (or other socio-demographic characteristics).

d. **process** (refers to the developing process of events undertaken by the actors within the situation) e.g., parts or elements of a ritual.

For example, if a student examines the spending behavior of children of seafarers in a particular private school, the researcher for sure would only interview participants who are both "children of seafarer" and who are enrolled in a "particular school."

If the study focuses primarily on non-human participants such as documents records, artifacts, or visual materials, the same principle applies to purposive sampling. That is, choosing the best and appropriate materials that will contribute to the researcher's understanding of the research problem and questions. For example, if a student intends to research on the policies of corporate social responsibility (CSR) of a company, the researcher could examine official records or documents of the organization that pertains to such issue.

2. **Snowball sampling or snowballing** is a method of enlarging one's sample by asking the pre-identified participants if they know someone else who could respond to the research questions or participate in the research (Abila & Fernandez, 2020). This method is usually used if the researcher has a very limited number of participants due to various reasons, such as unfamiliarly with the targeted participants or difficulty of accessing participants. For example, if a student conducts research on fellow students who are children of Overseas Filipino Workers (OFWs) snowballing would mean that the researcher intends to ask those whom he or she knows as children of OFWs and if they know other students who are children of OFWs.

Sample Size

There is no formula for sample size in determining the number of participants, sites, documents, and visual materials in qualitative research. Typically, the size depends on the types of qualitative research design. For example, in narrative studies, one or two participants are acceptable, phenomenology usually has three to ten while ethnography study generally has one group with numerous interviews or observations. In case of studies, two or more cases are needed to make meaningful comparisons.

Some qualitative researchers adopt the concepts of saturation in finding the sample size. Saturation means if adding new participants, sites, documents, and visual materials no longer reveal new insights or ideas, researchers may stop collection. The situation implies that the theme or key findings are already more or less similar, therefore, the key findings are saturated.

Illustrative Example of Sampling Technique

Political Dynasty in Public Governance: A Close Encounter with the Cebuanos (Guarde et al, 2016)

Purposive sampling was used in identifying the key informant politicians while random sampling for key informant voters was determined. There were two key informant" politicians who were members of political dynasty families. Both were prominent politicians that came and been rooting political clans in Cebu. Criteria include the number of relatives or family members presently positioned in public office.

The research setting is the physical place where you plan to conduct your research projects. It can be a school, a local community, a town, a church or mosque, a classroom, a prison or jail, a hospital or health clinic, a street, or any other place that fits best for your research study. It is very important to describe fully the research setting because it helps the readers to visualize it and decide on their own whether or not the findings of your study are applicable to them (Lune & Berg, 2017; Neuman, 2014). You are expected to thoroughly describe your research setting. You need mentally walk your reader through the research setting in your written description. You need to describe your research setting in such a way that your readers "can see better what the researcher saw, hear better what the researcher heard, and feel clearly what the researcher felt in that setting" (Wa-Mbaleka, 2017, p. 68). It is therefore important to spend quite some time writing important details about the research settings that will help people understand your research findings better.

Illustrative Example of Research Setting

A qualitative study on the stigma experienced by people with mental health problems and epilepsy in the Philippines (Tanaka, et al., 2018).

Our study was conducted in Muntinlupa, the southernmost city in the Philippines' National Capital Region. The city has a population of 481,461 as of 2016. The majority comprises Tagalog ethnic groups and professes Christian, primarily Roman Catholic, faith. Households below the food threshold, the minimum income required to meet basic food needs, account for 21.5% of the total in the city (City Government of Muntinlupa, 2017). The majority of citizens cannot afford private medical services, which cost five times more than the public medical services (PSA, 2013). With respect to public psychiatric service, the city has one outpatient and no in-patient facility. The nearest public in-patient psychiatric facility is located about 23 km away.

Methods of Analyzing Qualitative Data

Rebullida, et al. (1993), pointed out that there are different ways of analyzing qualitative data. Some of these methods are as follows:

1. **Comparative methods of analysis.** This method relies on comparison and contrast in the analysis of a phenomenon, object, or situation. In using this method, the researcher has to remember that the things to be compared or contrasted have to belong to the same category or class. Moreover, there has to be a basis for comparison and contrast.

2. **Institutional method of analysis.** This method examines the characteristics, behavior patterns, roles, structure, functions, and even development of established or observed institutions. Institutional method of analysis can be done using history, description, comparison, and contrast.

3. **Descriptive Methods of Analysis.** In this method of analysis, the researcher has to present in greater detail the nature or characteristics of the phenomena or situation

being described. Data analysis in this approach may take any of the following forms: establishing categories or typologies; and determining a sequence of events or patterns of behavior.

4. **Historical Analysis.** This can be utilized when the researcher is after explaining events or phenomena in the past so as to understand the present. In this method of analysis, the researcher needs to trace the events which had taken place and, at the same time, come up with a meaningful way of comprehending and interpreting these events. Generalizations in historical analysis are arrived at, based on the patterns of events that the researcher is able to discover.

5. **Inductive Analysis.** This method of analyzing qualitative data allows the pattern of thinking and reasoning that starts from specific to universal. The process starts from a particular observation and ends up with a generalization based on these specific observations.

6. **Deductive analysis.** This is the exact opposite

of the inductive method of analysis. Here, the researcher has to begin with a general statement about a phenomenon, situation, or object. He ends up by providing details, particular or specific facts to support the said general statement.

7. **Content analysis.** This method is appropriate to use when the researcher is concerned about explaining the status of some phenomenon at a particular time or its development over a period of time using available documents. Content analysis is also called documentary analysis. Sources of data for this method of analysis are as follows: records, reports, printed forms, letters, autobiographies, diaries, compositions, themes or other academic works, books, periodicals, bulletins or catalogues, syllabi, court decisions, pictures, films, and cartoons.

8. **Theory-Based Analysis**. In this particular method, the researcher analyzes a phenomenon or situation based on a specific theory. Hence, analysis and interpretation of

data are related to the presuppositions of the theory.

Guidelines in designing, conducting, and presenting qualitative data analysis procedure

The following are guidelines in designing, conducting, and presenting your qualitative data analysis procedure (Barrot, 2018).

1. Keep your research problem and research questions in mind as these will be the focus of your data analysis. Your qualitative data analysis also starts with the research problem and research questions.

2. Conduct a pilot test to get an idea of how to go about with your data collection and analysis. This will then help you better facilitate your actual data collection and analysis.

3. Transcribe the data you will obtain from interviews and focus group discussions. Ask another person to code the same data you will collect in order to ensure the reliability of your analysis. Results of interceding reliability refer to the consistency in the data analysis of two coders.

4. Conduct an initial tabulation and analysis of a few sets of data you have first gathered. Doing this will allow you to adjust in your interview questions, observation techniques, and collection of additional data. You do not want to be caught by surprise realizing that the data you have gathered does not allow you to make conclusions about the topic you are analyzing.

5. Decide on your level of analysis, e.g., word-level or sentence-level. Your level of analysis depends on the nature of data you have obtained and the focus of your study. If you want to analyze vocabulary use or the frequency of word usage, you may use word-level analysis. On the other hand, if you want to understand the meaning of a statement, sentence-level analysis may be more appropriate.

6. Decide on what to do with outliers and irrelevant information. You can either discard or reanalyze them.

7. Make sure to incorporate actual data in your presentation of your data analysis.

ASSESSMENT TASKS

I. **Directions:** identify the qualitative methodology that is probably most appropriate for each project.

1. In an effort to learn the nature and appeal of long-standing men's social group researcher plans to spend a 9-month period with a local chapter ("lodge") of the Benevolent and Protective Order of Elks. By observing and interacting with the Elks, discover the chapter's beliefs, values, goals, and interpersonal dynamics.

2. A researcher is intrigued by Asperger syndrome, a cognitive disability in which people have average or above intelligence and language skills but poor social skills and little or no ability to interpret other people's nonverbal social cues (e.g., body language). The researcher wants to find out what it is like to be an adolescent with this syndrome – how a teenager is apt to feel about having few or no friends, being regularly excluded from classmates' social

activities, and so on.

3. A researcher wants to determine how doctors, nurses, and other hospital staff members coordinate their actions when people with life-threatening traumatic injuries arrive at the emergency room. The researcher can find very little useful research on this topic in professional journals.

4. A researcher is interested in the life histories and professional trajectories of African American women in university leadership positions and how these experiences might provide insights into the nature of leadership and mentorship for African American women in academic institutions.

II. **Directions:** Identify the sampling methods in the given situations.

1. The researcher wishes to interview undocumented immigrants from Mexico, he or she might interview a few undocumented individuals that he or she knows or can

locate, gain their trust, then rely on those subjects to help locate more undocumented individuals.

2. The researchers determine the patterns of use of social media by global IT consulting companies based in the US. The researcher chooses IT companies whose availability and attitude are compatible with the study.

3. The researcher interested in studying how people with genital herpes cope with their medical condition would be unlikely to find many participants by posting an advertisement in the newspaper or by announcing the study at a social gathering. Instead, the researcher might know someone with the condition, interview that person, and ask the person to refer others they may know with genital herpes to contact you to participate in the study.

4. A researcher is studying environmental engineers but can only find five. She asks these engineers if they know any more.

They give her several further referrals, who in turn provide additional contacts. In this way, she manages to contact sufficient engineers.

5. TV reporters stopping certain individuals on the street in order to ask their opinions about certain political changes constitutes the most popular.

III. **Directions:** Identify what is being describe in the following statement.

1. This method relies on comparison and contrast in the analysis of a phenomenon, object, or situation.

2. It is the physical place where you plan to conduct your research projects.

3. In conducting the narrative inquiry how many participants are acceptable.

4. It is referring to the phenomenon /activity that will be observed the actors are doing.

5. A qualitative inquiry which the inquirer generates a general explanation (a theory) of a process, an action, or an interaction shaped by the views of a large number of

participants.

6. The researcher writes and records the experiences of another person's life.

7. This method is usually used if the researcher has a very limited number of participants due to various reasons, such as unfamiliarly with the targeted participants or difficulty of accessing participants.

8. It is occurring when the researcher prepares an outline of the topics that he/she needs to personally ask the interviewee in a spontaneous and conversation-like manner.

9. A qualitative inquiry that describes and interprets the shared and learned patterns of values, behaviors, beliefs, and language of a culture-sharing group.

10. It serves blueprint or a skeletal framework of the study.

PERFORMANCE TASKS

Design and Make a Research Methodology

Direction: Focusing on the research problem that you developed in previous chapters, design or formulate a plan for research Methodology to answer your questions. Make sure to include a description of each of the components of the research methodology.

1. **Research Design**
   a. Indicate the reason why you used qualitative as your research methods.
   b. Describe your chosen research design.

2. **Population and sample**
   a. Describe the population in the study (including size, if it can be determined, and how it will be identified).
   b. Identify whether sampling design for this population is purposive or snowball sampling.
   c. Identify how an individual will be selected.
   d. Describe in detail the sampling procedure (the sample size and how the size was determined; the procedure for selecting the sample; the sampling frame, etc.).

3. **Instrumentation/ Research Instrument (s).**

   a. Identify the instrument to be used in the study, whether it is a self-designed, a modified instrument, or an intact instrument developed by someone else.

   b. If you plan to use an existing instrument, describe the established validity and reliability, and scales of the instruments include sample items to inform the readers of the actual items used.

   c. Indicate the major contents sections in the instruments, such as the cover letter, items, and closing instructions.

   d. Discuss plans for pilot testing or field testing the instrument and provide a rationale for this procedure.

4. **Data Gathering Procedure.**

   a. Indicate the reasons why a survey is the preferred type of data collection method for the study. (quantitative research. Specify the form of data collection (mailed to the respondent in the sample, administered in a face-to-face interview, or gathered through telephone interviews). For a mailed survey, electronic survey, identify to be taken in administering and following up the survey to obtain a high response rate.

a. Identify the parameters for data collection (qualitative research)

- The actors – who will be observed or interviewed and how will they be sampled.
- The events – what the actors will be observed doing or interviewed about; and
- The process – (the evolving nature of events undertaken by the actors within the setting.

b. Provide a rationale for the data collection procedure (e.g., costs, availability/time, and convenience).

c. Discuss actions to be taken to gain entry to the setting and to secure permission to study the informants or situation. Include a justification why the site of study has been chosen, a description of what will be accomplished during the research study, the impact of the research-related activities, and how the results will be reported? (qualitative research)

d. Indicate potential or anticipated sensitive ethical difficulties or problems such as maintaining confidentially of data, preserving the anonymity of informants, and using research for intended purposes.

5. Data Recording Procedure (Qualitative Research)

Describe your plan for data recording. What is to be recorded? How will you have recorded it?

6. Data Analysis

a. Indicates that information about the number of returns and nonreturns of the survey will be reported.

b. Discuss the methods by which response bias will be determined.

    c. Describe the plan for making sense and interpreting data collected. Is there a coding procedure to be applied, and why?

Rubric for Writing the Research Methodology

Criteria	Excellent 15-20	Good 8-14	Poor 1-7
Research Design	Appropriate design was chosen; good definition of the design; demonstrates familiarity with the defining features of the design	Appropriate design chosen; good definition of the design but lacks a complete understanding of the key characteristics of the design chosen.	Inappropriate research design was chosen; lacks a clear articulation of the rationale for selecting the design; inaccurate characterization of the design.
Sampling and Sampling Procedure	Elaborate description of the sample and sampling procedure	Lacks detailed description of the sample and sampling procedure.	Shows no familiarity with sampling and sampling procedure.
Variables	Clear operational definitions of variables, clear and sufficient indicators for the variables.	Clear operational definitions of variables but insufficient indicators used for the variables	Lacks clear operational definitions of variables, inaccurate indicators for variables.
Instruments	Elaborate description of instruments used.	Instruments for the study not sufficiently described and justified.	Poor description of instruments for the study.
Data Collection Procedure	Four parameters for data collection are clearly described: clear description and justification for data collection procedures.	Four parameters for data collection are not sufficiently described and justified.	Four parameters for data collection are missing: no clear indication of data collection procedures.

Data analysis procedures	Clear plan for analyzing and interpreting data.	Insufficiently clear articulation of data analysis and interpretation procedures.	No clear indication of data analysis procedures.

Cited References and Suggested Readings

Abila, S. & Fernandez, C. J. (2020). *Practical Research 1: Introduction to Qualitative Research for Senior High School.* Anvil Publishing House.

Baraceros, E. L. *Practical Research 1 (2nd edition).* Rex Book Store.

Barrot, J. S. (2017). *Practical Research 1 for Senior High School.* C & E Publishing, Inc.

Birks, M., & Mills, J. (2015). Grounded theory: A practical guide (2nd ed.). Thousand Oaks, CA: Sage

Bueno, D. C. *Practical Qualitative Research Writing.* Great Books Trading.

Carter, K. (1993). *The place of a story in the study of teaching and teacher education.* Educational Researcher, 22, 5–12, 18. http://www.jstor.org/stable/1177300.

Casey, K. (1996). *The new narrative research in education.* Review of Research in Education, 21, 211–253. http://www.jstor.org/stable/1167282.

Charmaz, K. (2014). *Constructing grounded theory (2nd edition).* Thousand Oaks, CA: Sage.

Clandinin, D. J., & Connelly, F. M. (2000). *Narrative inquiry: Experience and story in qualitative research*. Jossey-Bass.

Clandinin, D. J. (2013). *Engaging in narrative inquiry*. Left Coast Press.

Corbin, J., & Strauss, A. (2015). *Basics of qualitative research: Techniques and procedures for developing grounded theory (4th edition)*. Sage Publications, Inc.

Cortazzi, M. (1993). *Narrative analysis*. Falmer Press.

Creswell, J. W., & Miller, D. L. (2000). *Determining validity in qualitative inquiry. Theory into Practice*, 39, 124–130. http://doi:10.1207/s15430421tip3903_2.

Creswell, J. W. (2007). *Qualitative Inquiry & Research Design: Choosing Among Five Approaches (2nd edition).* Sage Publications, Inc.

Creswell, J. W., & Plano Clark, V. L. (2011). *Designing and conducting mixed methods research (2nd edition).* Sage Publications, Inc.

Creswell, J. W. (2013). *Qualitative Inquiry & research design: Choosing among the five approaches (3rd edition).* Sage Publications, Inc.

Creswell, J. W. (2013). *Research Design: Qualitative, Quantitative, and Mixed Methods Approaches (4th edition).* Sage Publications, Inc.

Creswell, J. W. (2014). *Research Design: Qualitative, Quantitative, and Mixed Methods approaches (5th edition)*. Sage Publication, Inc.

Cristobal, A. P., & Cristobal, M. C. (2017). *Practical Research 1*. C & E Publishing, Inc.

Czarniawska, B. (2004). *Narratives in social science research*.

Sage Publications, Inc.

Denzin, N. K. (1989). *Interpretive biography*. Sage Publications, Inc.

Fetterman, D. M. (2010). *Ethnography: Step-by-step (3rd edition).* Sage Publications, Inc.

Gaddi, Z. A. (2019). *Practical Research: Discovering Meaning the Qualitative Way*. Golden Cronica Publishing Inc.

Gee, J. P. (1991). *A linguistic approach to narrative. Journal of Narrative and Life History/Narrative Inquiry*, 1, 15–39.http://www2.clarku.edu/~mbamberg/Pages_Journals/journal-narrative.html.

Guarde, E. A., Rosaroso, R. C., Rama, F., Batac, R., & Lasala, G. (2016). *Political Dynasty in Public Governance: A Close Encounter with the Cebuanos.* Asia Pacific Journal of Multidisciplinary Research, 4(2), 29-36.

Hammersley, M., & Atkinson, P. (1995*). Ethnography: Principles in practice (2nd edition).* Routledge.

Henson, R. M., & Soriano, R. F. (2016). *Qualitative Research: Word of Reality Dissections.* Mutya Publishing House Inc.

Huber, J., & Whelan, K. (1999). *A marginal story as a place of possibility: Negotiating self on the professional knowledge landscape*. Teaching and Teacher Education, 15, 381–396. http://doi:10.1016/S0742-051X(98)00048-1.

Janesick, V. J. (2013). *Oral history, life history, and biography. In A. A. Trainor & E. Graue (Eds.), Reviewing qualitative research in the social sciences* (pp. 151–165). Routledge.

Jackson, L. S. (2013). *Research Methods and Statistics: A Critical Thinking Approach (5th edition)*. Cengage Learning.

LeCompte, M. D., Millroy, W. L., & Preissle, J. (1992). *The handbook of qualitative research in education*. Academic Press.

LeCompte, M. D., & Schensul, J. J. (1999). *Designing and conducting ethnographic research (Ethnographer's toolkit, Vol. 1)*. AltaMira Press.

Lempert, L. B. (2007). *Asking questions of the data: Memo writing in the grounded theory tradition. In A. Bryant & K. Charmaz (Eds.), The SAGE handbook of grounded theory (pp. 245–264)*. Sage Publications, Inc.

Lincoln, Y. S., & Guba, E. G. (1985). *Naturalistic inquiry.* Sage Publications, Inc.

Marshall, C., & Rossman, G. B. (2015). *Designing qualitative research* (6th ed.). Sage Publications, Inc.

Merriam, S. B. (1998). *Qualitative research and case study applications in education*. Jossey-Bass.

Moustakas, C. (1994). *Phenomenological research methods.* Sage Publications, Inc.

Neuman, W. L. (2014). *Social research methods: Qualitative and Quantitative research approaches*. Pearson.

Ollerenshaw, J. A., & Creswell, J. W. (2002*). Narrative research: A comparison of two restorying data analysis approaches.* Qualitative Inquiry, 8, 329–347. https://doi:10.1177/10778004008003008.

Pinnegar, S., & Daynes, J. G. (2007). *Locating narrative inquiry historically: Thematics in the turn to narrative. In D. J. Clandinin (Ed.), Handbook of narrative inquiry: Mapping a methodology* (pp. 3–34). Sage Publications, Inc.

Plummer, K. (1983). *Documents of life: An introduction to the problems and literature of a humanistic method.*

George Allen & Unwin.

Polkinghorne, D. E. (1989). *Phenomenological research methods. In R. S. Valle & S. Halling (Edition.), Existential-phenomenological perspectives in psychology* (pp. 41–60). Plenum Press.

Posecion, O. T., Go, M. B., & Albano, H. P. (2011). *Language Research: Principles and Application*. Lorimar Publishing, Inc.

Rebullida, M. L. et al. (1993). *The Practice of Research*. UP Intructech.

Riessman, C. K. (2008). *Narrative methods for the human sciences.* Sage Publications, Inc.

Rosaroso, R. C., & Rosaroso, N. A. (2015). *Unveiling the Mystical Lucban Pahiyas Festival*. Asia Pacific Journal of Multidisciplinary Research, 3, (4).

Salvador, P., Vivar, P.C., de Vera III, E., Inocian, R. B., Rosaroso, R.C. (2017). *Influence of Facebook on Voters' Political Practices*. Asia Pacific Journal of Education, Arts, and Sciences, 4 (1).

Sanchez, C. A. (2002). *Methods and Techniques of Research, (Revised Edition)*. Rex Book Store, Inc.

Silverman, D. (2013). *Doing Qualitative Research (4th Edition)*. Sage Publications, Inc.

Stake, R. (1995). *The art of case study research*. Sage Publications, Inc.

Tanaka, C., Tuliao, M.T.R., Tanaka, E. *et al.* (2018). *A qualitative study on the stigma experienced by people with mental health problems and epilepsy in the Philippines*. BMC Psychiatry **18**, 325. https://doi.org/10.1186/s12888-018-1902-9.

van Manen, M. (1990). *Researching lived experience: Human*

science for an action sensitive pedagogy. Albany: State University of New York Press.

van Manen, M. (2014). *Phenomenology of practice: Meaning-giving methods in phenomenological research and writing.* Left Coast Press.

Wolcott, H. F. (1987). *On ethnographic intent. In G. Spindler & L. Spindler (Eds.), Interpretive ethnography of education: At home and abroad* (pp. 37–57). Lawrence Erlbaum.

Wolcott, H. F. (1994). *Transforming qualitative data: Description, analysis, and interpretation.* Sage Publications, Inc.

Wolcott, H. F. (2008a). *Ethnography: A way of seeing (2nd edition).* Walnut Creek, CA: AltaMira Press.

Wa-Mbaleka, S. (2017). *Fostering Quality in Qualitative Research: A List of Practical Strategies.* International Forum Journal, 20(1), 58-80. https://journals.aiias.edu/info/article/view/79.

Yin, R. K. (2009). *Case study research: Design and method (4th edition).* Sage Publications, Inc.

Yin, R. K. (2014). *Case study research: Design and method (5th edition).* Sage Publications, Inc.

MODULE 6:

FINDING ANSWERS THROUGH DATA COLLECTION

LEARNING OUTCOMES
At the end of this module, students should be able to collects data through observation and interviews

Interview

When researchers want to understand how people make meaning of their life experiences, they often go straight to the source and ask questions. Considered broadly, interview research includes a wide range of question and response strategies. This variety in strategies crosses multiple domains: variation in purpose (e.g., asking to better understand a range of responses or asking to gain a deep and complex understanding of a difficult-to-define concept), variation in organizing respondent opportunities (e.g., individual and group), variation in tools for data collection, variation in analytic perspectives, and variation in representation forms. Qualitative interviews provide opportunities for mutual discovery, understanding, reflection, and explanation via a path that is organic, adaptive, and oftentimes energizing. Interviews elucidate subjectively lived experiences and viewpoints from the respondents' perspective (Tracy, 2020).

During an interview, a researcher asks participants directly about their personal experiences related to the study's topic; their values, attitudes, and beliefs; their knowledge or understanding of various topics; or any other matters pertinent to the study. While researchers must continuously engage in analysis during and after an interview, the researcher's role changes because participants are able to answer questions explicitly. Of course, participants might not always answer questions directly or honestly, but during interviews, researchers need not rely entirely on inference making. On the other hand, because they are actively engaged in conversations with their participants, researchers must exercise different skill sets such as understanding appropriate interview protocols, maintaining the conversation, and constantly analyzing responses in order to determine what question would be most appropriate to ask next.

Qualitative Touchstones of Interview (Trainor & Graue, 2013).

1. The sample of participants generates a breadth and depth of interviews necessary to answer the research questions.
2. The individuals interviewed are in positions of

experience to respond to the types of interview questions that map to the research questions.

3. The researchers establish relationships with participants who are congruent with both the interview design and paradigmatic ties to relational inquiry.

4. The researchers present themselves and associated subjectivities (e.g., background, experience, and positionality) to supplement or aid the interpretation of the results and implications of interview data.

5. Interview questions map to research questions.

6. The researchers describe their approach to collecting and/or constructing interviews and related logistical decisions to the extent that these procedures fundamentally impact interpretation.

7. The method of analyzing interviews is identified and explicated.

8. The representation of the interview research project is an integration of interviews and their interpretation that results in new knowledge.

Level of structure in interviews (Braun and Clarke).

1. **Structured**. The questions and the response categories are predetermined by the researcher; this is the commonest type of interview in quantitative research.

2. **Semi-structured**. the researcher has a list of questions but there is scope for the participants to raise issues that the researcher has not anticipated; this is the commonest type of interview in qualitative research.

3. **Unstructured.** The researcher has, at most, a list of themes or topics to discuss with the participant, but the interview is strongly participant-led; this type of interview is used by some qualitative researchers.

Types of Interview

1. **Ethnographic interviews** (Spradley, 1979) are informal conversational interviews; they are emergent and spontaneous. They usually occur in the field and sound as though they are

a casual exchange of remarks. However, in contrast to other fieldwork conversations, the ethnographic interview is a conversation that is specifically instigated by the researcher and may not have occurred otherwise.

2. **Informant interviews** are another common type of interview. Despite the pejorative connotations of the word, "informants" are not always snitches or moles. Rather, the qualifier "informant" is used here to characterize participants who are veterans, experienced insiders, key connectors within the scene, and/or mavens who "hoard and dispense certain kinds of cultural capital in a scene" (Lindlof & Taylor, 2019, p. 227). Further, such people tend to be friendly and interested in talking to the researcher. Finding good informants usually requires a long-term relationship. Furthermore, for reasons of ethics and credibility, ethnographers should seek out insight from a variety of informants rather than relying on just a few to speak for the entire culture.

3. **Respondent interviews** are those that take place among social actors who all hold similar subject positions and have experiences that directly attend to the research goals. Respondents could be a group of volunteers, children, breastfeeding moms, or lawyers. In contrast to informants (described above), who have a unique depth and breadth of experience and feel articulate about a range of cultural issues, respondents are relied upon to speak primarily of and for themselves – about their own motivations, experiences, and behaviors. Respondent interviews may be particularly worthwhile when attempting to understand similarities and differences within a certain cultural group.

4. **Narrative interviews** are open-ended, relatively unstructured interviews that encourage participants to tell stories rather than just answer questions. Stories might relate to the participants, their experiences, or the events they have witnessed. One type of narrative interview is the **oral history**

(Brinkmann & Kvale, 2015), which queries those who witnessed past events for the purpose of (re)constructing history. Such interviews focus less on individual experiences and more on participants' standpoints and depth of knowledge on specific social and historical events. Oral histories often focus on the experiences and perspectives of marginalized group members, whose views may otherwise be hidden or written out of formal accounts.

5. **Life-story interviews** (Atkinson, 2012) or biographic interviews (Wengraf, 2001) also elicit narratives. In contrast to oral histories, which focus on a specific event, life-story interviewees discuss their life as a whole, their memories, and what they want others to know. Life-story interviews may be particularly interesting to conduct with members of your own family or with famous personalities who have caught the public imagination. They can also provide understanding – and perhaps even empathy – for people who may otherwise

be seen as socially aberrant or undesirable.

6. **A discursive interview** pays attention to large structures of power that construct and constrain knowledge and truth – and to how interviewees draw upon larger structural discourses in creating their answer. A discursive interview picks up on the fact that participants' compassion emerges from and intersects with larger discourses of race, class, and myth. In turn, the interviewer probes the meaning of this discourse, critically asking questions in light of societal structures and myths. Furthermore, in such interviews, researchers engage in practices by which participants are more likely to critically reflect upon and possibly transform viewpoints that uphold problematic power relations.

Interview Stances

1. **Deliberate naïveté** it asks interviewers to drop any presuppositions and judgment while maintaining openness to new and unexpected findings (Brinkmann & Kvale, 2015).

2. **Collaborative or interactive interviewing** interviews are jointly created so that the researcher and the participant are on an even plane and can ask questions of each other (Ellis & Berger, 2003).

3. **Pedagogical interviews**. It is an interview not only asks participants for their viewpoints but also encourages researchers to offer expertise in the form of knowledge or emotional support.

4. **Responsive interviewing.** The researchers have responsibilities for building a reciprocal relationship, honoring interviewees with unfailing respectful behavior, reflecting on their own biases and openly acknowledging their potential effect, and owning the emotional effect of interviews (Rubin & Rubin, 2011).

5. **Confrontational interviews** are marked by deliberate provocation (Brinkmann & Kvale, 2015). The interviewer may contradict or challenge the interviewee and, in doing so, highlight their differences of opinion. Confrontation is ethically questionable when you are interviewing participants who are

traumatized or hold relatively low power positions. However, such an approach may be warranted in situations where social justice is an issue – especially when the participant is powerful, confident, or otherwise belongs to an elite group. Indeed, relatively secure interviewees may welcome the intellectual and identity challenges that come with confrontation. One word of warning, though: if you choose to challenge, you should also prepare for a counterattack – and be able to deal with it good-naturedly, without defensiveness.

Illustrative Example of Interview Guide for a semi-structured interview

Effectiveness of Claim, Evidence and Reasoning as an Innovation to Develop Students' Scientific Argumentative Writing (Samosa, 2021)

Interview Questions

Did the use of the CER framework help you when writing scientific explanations? If so, what was most helpful?

Did you find the CER template helpful in organizing your thoughts before you wrote you explanations?

Did using the CER framework help you make connections between data in class and concepts that we learned in class?

Do you think the practice we did with CER will help you evaluate claims in other classes?

Advantages and Disadvantages of Interview

Research interviews of all kinds and types have inherent advantages and disadvantages these are following.

Advantages

1. Allow for in-depth data gathering and analysis through the use of systematic observation and probing inquiry.
2. Allow for the interaction of the researcher with the respondents and the environment.
3. Discover more information and data not found in surveys or questionnaires.
4. Reveals rich qualitative data that are not inherent in quantitative research.
5. Synchronous factors in FtF (same time and space) enrich data.
6. Useful to complement and understand deeper quantitative data.
7. Helpful in primary source of data.
8. Useful tool to validate or verify existing data.

Disadvantages

1. Availability of respondents.
2. Sampling limitations; the researcher can only

do so much interviews.

3. Asynchronous issues (different time and space) in telephone interviews, webcam interviews, online and email interviews can affect quality of data.

4. Can be annoying, especially in telephone interviews being employed in telemarketing research.

5. Can be expensive; a big number of interviewees need more interviewers.

6. Can be time-consuming, from the conduct of each interview up to the transcription or processing of interview results.

7. Data leakage; importance information and data are not recorded.

8. Data leakage; important information and data are not recorded.

9. Sensitivity in handling identity of interviewees; respondents do not want to reveal their identity in exchange for sensitive information.

10. Difficulty in establishing the reliability of the respondents' responses: how can one know if the interviewee is lying? Thus, interviews alone

have reduced reliability and validity; the research needs to have other methods and techniques to gather verified data.

Basic Skills that researchers and interviewers need to learn.

1. **Networking skills.** Identify and locate **an** eminent person for interview; chasing difficult but very important persons to interview.

2. **Administrative skills.** Preparing the necessary logistics, setting schedules for an interview, and preparing the conducive time and place for interview.

3. **Interpersonal skills:** making the respondents feel comfortable; being sensitive to the reactions and body movements of the respondents.

4. **Interview skills.** Preparing observation and interview guides; asking questions and probing deeper for answers, and managing time for the conduct of the interview.

5. **Facilitating skills.** Moderating group interviews or focused group discussion.

6. **Documentation skills.** Jotting down notes and recording of information.

7. **Analytical skills.** Making patterns, categories, and relationship from the interview results; processing and synthesizing various information and data from the interview.

8. **Integrity skills.** Safeguarding ethics in the conduct of interviews; employing meticulous on interview details ensuring thoroughness in the coverage of the interview.

To help the researchers in holding interviews, the following do's and dont's can be helpful. The researchers can add some more based on their experiences (Amorado & Talili, 2017).

Do's

1. Arrange for schedule and get prior permission to interview a respondent.

2. Orient the prospective respondent on the nature and purpose of the interview.

3. Inform the respondents if you will be alone or bring somebody else. This will affect the responses of the interviewee.

4. Make sure the interviewee approves of the time and place of the interview.

5. Before the interview, set the mood. Make the respondent relaxed. It is good to offer coffee or refreshment and have some chit chats before the actual interview.

6. During the interview, ask permission if the respondent allows for recording the interview by any recording device.

7. Be sensitive to the tones, gestures, facial expressions, or body movements of the respondents; this can indicate changes in the mood of the respondent.

8. After the interview, always express gratitude and thank the respondent. Broach the idea and get permission of holding a follow–up interview for additional information.

9. Sometimes, depending on prior arrangement, the researcher needs to pay the respondent or respondents a moderate amount of tokens. For long interviews, a respondent may have to be properly compensated as bother fee.

Don't's

1. Do not come unprepared for the interview.

2. Do not hold interviews in noisy areas; always ensure a conducive time and place for the interview.

3. Do not impose or insist on asking a question that makes the respondent uncomfortable.

4. Do not record the interview conversation without the permission of the interviewee.

5. Do not ask roundabout or confusing questions; ask one question at a time to avoid confusion.

6. Do not ask leading, suggestive or judgemental questions.

7. Do not get lost during the interview discussions; always be aware of the questions that need to be asked. Manage the time properly.

Types of Questions in the Interview

An interviewer can ask several types of questions to stimulate responses from an interviewee. Patton (2002) suggests six types of questions:

1. **Experience and behavior questions**. This

type of question gets at the things a person does or did, his or her behaviors, actions, and activities. For example, in a study of leadership exhibited by administrators, one could ask, "Tell me about a typical day at work; what are you likely to do first thing in the morning?"

2. **Opinion and values questions**. The researcher is interested in a person's beliefs or opinions, what he or she thinks about something. Following the example above of a study of administrators and leadership, one could ask, "What is your opinion as to whether administrators should also be leaders?"

3. **Feeling questions**. These questions " tap the affective dimension of human life. In asking feeling questions — 'how do you feel about that?' — the interviewer is looking for adjective responses: anxious, happy, afraid, intimidated, confident, and so on" (p. 350).

4. **Knowledge questions**. These questions elicit a participant's actual factual knowledge about a situation.

5. **Sensory questions.** These are similar to

experience and behavior questions but try to elicit more specific data about what is or was seen, heard, touched, and so forth.

6. **Background/demographic questions**. All interviews contain questions that refer to the particular demographics (age, income, education, number of years on the job, etc.) of the person being interviewed as relevant to the research study. For example, the age of the respondent may or may not be relevant.

Guidelines in Conducting an Interview

The following are guidelines in conducting an interview. These guidelines apply to any type of interview (Barrot, 2018).

Before the interview

1. Decide on how you will conduct the interview. Will you be interviewing your participant one – one or in group? Are you going to interview them personally, or through a different medium (e.g., email, video conferencing, or phone)?

2. If you are conducting a focus group discussion, it is deal to have two research assistants who

will take notes during the session. This way, you can focus on facilitation the discussion.

3. Choose a comfortable venue for the interview. Make sure that this venue has the least amount of distraction possible.

4. Decide on the length of your interview. Note that conducting the interview for a long period of time can affect your participants' responses to your questions.

5. Prepare an interview guide and master it. Ask expert or knowledge people to give comments on your interview guide, and make the necessary revisions based on their feedback.

6. Make your interview questions as specific as possible. Furthermore, do not limit your question to those that are answerable by yes or no. Dig deeper by asking open-ended questions.

7. Make your interview questions focused on and directly related to your specific research questions. Otherwise, the questions will be irrelevant.

8. Pilot -test your interview guide on a group of

people who have similar demographic characteristics to your actual respondents. Doing this will help you further improve your interview guide. However, make sure that the members of this group are not included in your actual respondents.

9. Make sure that you ask permission from your respondents before the interview. Obtain their consent by having them read and sign an informed consent form. The informed consent form states that the participants are willing to participate in the study and understand its purposes and the risks that may be encountered. The informed consent form also includes a confidentiality agreement, which guarantees that the information provided by the participants will not be disclosed to the public.

10. Determine what kind of recoded you will use in the interview. If nonverbal cues are important in your analysis, consider using a video recorder. Make sure that your recorder is functioning well.

During the Interview

1. Explain the purpose of the study and the interview to your respondents. Discuss also the format of the interview.

2. Remain as neutral as possible and refrain from telling your respondents about your hypothesis in order to avoid response bias. Response bias is the tendency of respondents to answer in a way that they think that interviewer wants, instead of giving their honest answers.

3. Establish rapport with your interviewees. Introduce yourself to them, smile, and maintain eye contact. In addition, avoid verbal mannerisms like using fillers such as "ahm" and "ah".

4. Observe good manners throughout the interview. Avoid arguing with your interviewees. Also, turn off your cellphone or set it in silent mode.

5. Help the interviewees participate as easily as possible. Begin the interview by asking easy questions, and asking one question at a time. Deliver each question clearly, and rephrase

your questions if you feel that the respondent did not understand it. Allow your interviewee to ask for clarification about the interview as well.

6. Make sure that the interviewee participates as much as possible in the interview. Let the interviewee speak more than you do. Also, ask your interviewee if there is any information that he or she was not asked about and would like to add.

7. Be firm but gentle throughout the interviewee. Be in control of the flow of the interview. In addition, prevent the interviewees from presenting ideas that may provoke arguments or misunderstanding. However, be patients with your interviewees if they are unable to respond immediately to your questions.

8. End the interview by thanking the interviewees for their participation.

After the Interview

1. Check if your audio or video recorder worked well throughout the interview.

2. Transcribe the interviewees' responses as they are. Avoid adding any information or comment

that was not given by the interviewees.

3. Write your observation about the interview.

Focus Group Discussion (FGD)

Focus group discussion is a kind of method wherein the researcher groups his/her respondents into clusters. It should be noted that the cluster or groups that must be formed should follows some criteria (Francisco, Francisco, & Arlos, 2016). You cannot group people randomly.

For example, you can group the respondents by age, gender, religion, etc., Essentially, you can group them based on their similarities. More so, you can group them into their age because you would like to gather their perception based on their age group. Another way grouping is to form a "rainbow" group. You can group the respondent based on their differences.

The researcher can do this so that he/she can gather more complex data. Thus, it still depends on how the study is framed. In some situations, the researcher can change the group to see some changes in the dynamics. The reason is that might help in relating the profile of the respondents to the way they respond to the discussion. After the grouping the respondents, FGD is usually done by asking questions. Hence, unlike interviews, the conversation focuses mainly on the respondents rather than the researcher and the respondent. However, the one employing this strategy should know how to frame questions well so that he/she can gather the necessary data. This methodology will allow more freedom for the respondents to discuss the topic. Thus, there will be more information and data flowing the respondents to answer the research questions. The problem, however, with this strategy is that it might yield too many irrelevant information or data since you are giving more liberty to the respondents. If this happens, it would be difficult for the researcher to get his/her needed data. Thus, the researcher should know how to facilitate the discussions within the groups so that he/she can get the answers for the study. Lastly, this strategy, it should be noted, must be implemented by more than one (1) researcher since each group must have its own facilitator. This is to lessen the chance of irrelevant data. Apparently, focus group discussion is a good strategy for getting data. But, just like the other methods, the researcher should know its disadvantages so that it can lessen the negative pay-offs of this research method.

Advantages and Disadvantages of Focus Groups in Research

The following are the main advantages of and disadvantages of focus group discussion in research.

Advantages

1. It is an inexpensive and fast method of acquiring valuable data.
2. Co-workers and friends are more comfortable in voicing views in each other's company than on their own with the researcher.
3. Participants are given a chance to reflect or react to the viewpoint of others with which they may disagree or of which they're unaware.
4. The dynamic discussion between participants stimulates their thoughts and reminds them of their own thoughts regarding the research subject.

5. All individuals along with the researcher have a chance to ask questions, and these will produce more information when compared with individual interviews.

6. Informants can build on the answers of others.

7. The researcher can clarify clashes among participants and ask about these diverse opinions.

Disadvantages

1. The researcher has trouble controlling discussion and managing the process in comparison to individual interviews.

2. A few individuals could possibly be introverts while others take control of the debate and impact the end result, or possibly even introduce bias.

3. The group climate can hinder or fail to energize the individual, or it can be livelier and produce more data.

4. Recording data can present difficulties; it is actually not possible to record when so many participants are speaking at the same time. Also, tape recorders may record just those who

are closer.

5. Data analysis could be a time-consuming and challenging task.

6. Focus group discussions usually are not replicable. The validity and dependability of the findings are tough to ascertain on their own.

Guidelines in Conducting a Focus Group Discussion

Take the following steps in order to successfully conduct a focus group discussion.

1. **Identify the number of participants in your group discussion.** In an FGD, there are usually six to twelve participants. Note that when you involve a large group in your FGD, some of your respondents may be unable to participate as much as others. On the other hand, having a very small group may not generate a rich discussion.

2. **Invite more than the number of participants you originally planned.** For example, add 10 to 20% of the number of participants you will originally invite. This is to anticipate the

possible failure of some of the selected participants to appear during the actual FGD.

3. **Select your participants based on the criteria that will fit your study.** As much as possible, select participants who do not know each other to maximize disclosure. However, this may not be applicable in all cases. These are instances that participants may know one another.

4. **Have the participants sign an informed consent form.** Inform them as well as the expected duration of the focus group discussion.

5. **You may offer tokens or incentives to your participants.** However, these should be reasonable so as not to influence the responses of your participants.

6. **Assign a moderator who can effectively facilitate the discussion.** You can also assign an assistant moderator who will help record of your participants.

7. **Prepare a set of predetermined questions to**

guide the discussion. Make sure to sequence these questions systematically. Ask engagement questions first to make the participants comfortable with the topic. Afterward, ask exploration questions, which address your research questions. Finally, ask exit questions to check whether there are items that were missed during the discussion.

8. **Prepare for the other aspects your focus group discussion.** Conduct your focus group discussion on a date when the participants are most available. Select a venue that is comfortable enough. Prepare food and drinks for the participants as well. Finally, if you are going to make a video or audio recording of the focus group discussion, make sure that your recording device works properly.

9. **During the focus group discussion, cover all of the predetermined questions.** However, make sure that the discussion will still be free-flowing. Also, make sure that your participants fully understand your questions. This is especially important since your

participants will not see your questions. Rephrase questions if you feel that the participants find it difficult to comprehend them.

10. **Demonstrate good manners as you conduct the focus group discussion.** Welcome the participants as they arrive, treat them tactually and do not debate with them, and thank them once the focus group discussion is over.

Observation

Observation involves may take place in natural settings and involves the researcher taking lengthy and descriptive notes of what is happening (Apolonio & Basilan, 2017).

Observations enable the researcher to gather data on:

1. The physical setting (e.g. the physical environment and its organization)
2. The human setting (e.g. the organization of people, the characteristics and make-up of the groups or individuals being observed, for instance, gender, class)
3. The interactional setting (e.g. the interactions

that are taking place, formal, informal, planned, unplanned, verbal, non-verbal, etc.)

4. The programme setting (e.g. the resources and their organization, pedagogic styles, curricula, and their organization).

The researcher can assume one of several stances while collecting information as an observer; stances range from being a full participant—the investigator is a member of the group being observed— to being a spectator. The following are the classic typology offers a spectrum of four possible stances.

1. **Complete participant.** The researcher is a member of the group being studied and conceals his or her observer role from the group so as not to disrupt the natural activity of the group. The inside information obtainable by using this method must be weighed against the possible disadvantages—loss of perspective on the group, being labeled a spy or traitor when research activities are revealed, and the questionable ethics of deceiving the other

participants.

2. **Participant as an observer.** The researcher's observer activities, which are known to the group, are subordinate to the researcher's role as a participant. Schensul and LeCompte (2013) refer to this as "a data-collection technique that requires the researcher to be present at, involved in, and actually recording the routine daily activities with people in the field setting" (p. 83) while maintaining an active participant role. The trade-off here is between the depth of the information revealed to the researcher and the level of confidentiality promised to the group in order to obtain this information.

3. **Observer as a participant.** The researcher's observer activities are known to the group; participation in the group is definitely secondary to the role of information gatherer. Using this method, the researcher may have access to many people and a wide range of information, but the level of the information revealed is controlled by the group members

being investigated. Adler and Adler (1998) refer to this as a "peripheral membership role," which is different from having an active membership role. Here researchers "observe and interact closely enough with members to establish an insider's identity without participating in those activities constituting the core of group membership" (p. 85).

4. **Complete observer**. The researcher is either hidden from the group (for example, behind a one-way mirror) or in a completely public setting such as an airport or library.

There are three techniques that you use in collecting data through observation. These are written descriptions, video recording, and using photographs or artifacts. Each of these techniques has its own advantages and disadvantages.

Written description

Advantages

1. flexible techniques as it does not require gadgets or technology.
2. Has little effect on the behavior of the

participants during observation.

Disadvantages

1. More prone to subjective interpretation.

2. May cause the researcher to miss out on other important aspects of events as he or she is focused on taking notes.

Video recording

Advantages

1. Allows researcher to take notes

2. Provide an accurate record of actual events.

3. Serves as a backup tool for recording data.

Disadvantages

1. Prone to technical glitches.

2. May increase the possibilities of Hawthorne effect (It is a phenomenon in which the participants of the study change their behavior due to their awareness of being observed).

Using photographs and artifacts

Advantage

1. Provides observable information about phenomenon.

Disadvantage

1. Provides limited information.

Guidelines in Conducting an Observation

Here are guidelines that can help you in conducting an observation.

Before the Observation

1. Plan the details of your observation. Decide on the following aspects:

   a. The type of observation you will conduct and the observational role you will take.

   b. The collection techniques you will use.

   c. The duration, date and time, and place of your observation.

   d. The behavior you want to observe.

2. Make sure that you focus on events or behaviors that will address your research questions or objectives.

3. Prepare an observation checklist or guide and master it. Ask help from experts and consult scholarly literature during the preparation of your guide.

4. If possible, make a preliminary visit to the site

before the actual data collection.

During the Observation

1. If applicable to your chosen type of observation and observational role, introduce yourself, explain the purpose of your study and observation, and obtain consent from the participants.

2. Begin writing your field notes or written comments and records of your observation. Start with writing the date, time, and place of your observation, as well as the type of behavior you are observing. Note that field notes can be written during or after the observation of a specific phenomenon being studied.

3. Include the following in your field notes:

    a. Description of the participants and the context are situated in

    b. The behavior reactions, and actual conversations among the participants

    c. The flow of people throughout the observation.

    d. Reflective comments during the

observation.

    e. The link between what you have observed and your research questions or objectives.

4. Report the actual accounts and your observations accurately and objectively. Avoid reporting your own interpretation.

5. Use codes to write your field notes more effectively. Also, use keywords and phrases instead of full sentences.

6. Write your notes as soon as you can. The fresher your notes are in your memory, the better.

7. Have multiple observers conduct the data collection with you in order to increase the reliability and validity of your data.

8. Observe good manners and be discreet during the observation.

After the Observation

1. Compile all your field notes and save them on your computer.

2. Review your notes and expand their discussion. Develop your keywords, codes, and phrases into full sentences and narratives.

3. Maintain the confidentially of your data.

Document Analysis

Document analysis is a form of qualitative research that uses a systematic procedure to analyze documentary evidence and answer specific research questions. Similar to other methods of analysis in qualitative research, document analysis requires repeated review, examination, and interpretation of the data in order to gain meaning and empirical knowledge of the construct being studied. Document analysis can be conducted as a stand-alone study or as a component of a larger qualitative or mixed methods study, where it is often used to triangulate findings gathered from another data source (e.g., interview or focus group transcripts, observation, surveys). When used in triangulation, documents can corroborate or refute, elucidate, or expand on findings across other data sources, which helps to guard against bias.

There are three primary types of documents (O'Leary, 2014):

1. Public Records. The official, ongoing records

of an organization's activities. Examples include student transcripts, mission statements, annual reports, policy manuals, student handbooks, strategic plans, and syllabi.

2. **Personal Documents.** First-person accounts of an individual's actions, experiences, and beliefs. Examples include calendars, e-mails, scrapbooks, blogs, Facebook posts, duty logs, incident reports, reflections/journals, and newspapers.

3. **Physical Evidence.** Physical objects found within the study setting (often called artifacts). Examples include flyers, posters, agendas, handbooks, and training materials.

Guidelines in Performing Document Analysis

1. Identify the documents to be analyzed using an inclusion criterion appropriate for your research questions.

2. Obtain a copy of the documents. Other documents are really available online with others require formal requests to be obtained.

Make sure to assess the authenticity of the documents.

3. Make your analysis focused. You may use a guide (e.g., checklist) when analyzing the document.

4. Explore the content of the document and note basic information about it, including the author, date of publication, the publisher, and the type of data it contains.

5. Make annotations during the analysis. These annotations will help you better understand your documents.

6. Observe utmost objectivity during your analysis.

Ethical Consideration in Data Collection

1. **Respect the site, and disrupt as little as possible. Researchers need to respect research sites so that they are left undisturbed after a research study.** This requires that inquirers, especially in qualitative studies involving prolonged observation or interviewing at a site, be cognizant of their

impact and minimize their disruption of the physical setting. For example, they might time visits so that they intrude little on the flow of activities of participants. Also, organizations often have guidelines that provide guidance for conducting research without disturbing their settings.

2. **Make sure that all participants receive the benefits.** Both the researcher and the participants should benefit from the research. In some situations, power can easily be abused and participants can be coerced into a project. Involving individuals collaboratively in the research may provide reciprocity. Highly collaborative studies, popular in qualitative research, may engage participants as co-researchers throughout the research process, such as the design, data collection and analysis, report writing, and dissemination of the findings (Patton, 2002).

3. **Avoid deceiving participants.** Participants need to know that they are actively participating in a research study. To counteract

this problem, provide instructions that remind the participants about the purpose of the study.

4. **Respect potential power imbalances.** Interviewing in qualitative research is increasingly being seen as a moral inquiry (Kvale, 2007). It could equally be seen as such for quantitative and mixed methods research. As such, interviewers need to consider how the interview will improve the human situation (as well as enhance scientific knowledge), how a sensitive interview interaction may be stressful for the participants, whether participants have a say in how their statements are interpreted, how critically the interviewees might be questioned, and what the consequences of the interview for the interviewees and the groups to which they belong might be. Interviews (and observations) should begin from the premise that a power imbalance exists between the data collector and the participants.

5. **Avoid exploitation of participants. There needs to be some reciprocity back to the participants for their involvement in your**

study. This might be a small reward for participating, sharing the final research report, or involving them as collaborators. Traditionally, some researchers have "used" the participants for data collection and then abruptly left the scene. This results in exploitation of the participants and rewards and appreciation can provide respect and reciprocity for those who provide valuable data in a study.

6. **Avoid collecting harmful information.** Researchers also need to anticipate the possibility of harmful, intimate information being disclosed during the data collection process. It is difficult to anticipate and try to plan for the impact of this information during or after an interview (Patton, 2002). For example, a student may discuss parental abuse or prisoners may talk about an escape. Typically, in these situations, the ethical code for researchers (which may be different for schools and prisons) is to protect the privacy of the participants and to convey this protection to

all individuals involved in a study.

Reliability and Validity: Trustworthiness

Can you trust the findings of a qualitative study? Do the concepts offered make sense, given the data collection, analysis, and interpretation? Are the arguments compelling? Are they supported with sound reasoning and ample evidence? Is the whole process, from research question to implications, truly transparent and open to critical thinking by the reader? Many qualitative researchers agree that data trustworthiness, whether collected from direct observations, focus groups, or interviews, is evidenced by the following (Lincoln & Guba, 1985):

1. **Transferability** refers to evidence supporting the generalization of findings to other contexts—across different participants, groups, situations, and so forth. This is akin to the notion of external validity used by quantitative researchers. Transferability is enhanced by detailed descriptions (as is typical in qualitative research) that enable judgments about a "fit" with other contexts. Comparisons across cases ("cross-

case comparisons") or other units of analysis (classrooms, schools, etc.) that yield similar findings also increase transferability. At the theoretical level, transferability can be achieved by evidence of theoretical transference; that is, the same ideas apply more widely and are shown to be applicable in other fields.

2. **Dependability** is akin to the concept of reliability in quantitative research paradigms. In this case, the qualitative researcher gathers evidence to support the claim that similar findings would be obtained if the study were repeated. Naturally, even if the study were repeated in the same context with the same participants, it would become a "new" study, given the ever-changing social world and perceptual shifts (including news events that may change our thinking overnight). Dependability is enhanced by common qualitative strategies (audit trails, rich documentation, triangulation, etc.) but also by traditional methods such as intercoder or interobserver agreement (two coders or observers are consistent) and code-recode

consistency (the same coding or observation occurs more than once using the same "human instrument")

3. Confirmability refers to objectivity (neutrality) and the control of researcher bias. Bias in qualitative research is an ever-present concern, but unbiased interpretations are more likely once researcher self-reflection recognizes them overtly and factors them into the design by, for example, intentionally seeking potentially contradictory evidence predicted by alternatives (essentially different biases or worldviews). Confirmability is also enhanced by consistency with quantitative research findings that reach similar conclusions. Other evidence includes the consensus reached by peer review.

4. **Credibility** refers to the believability of the findings and is enhanced by evidence such as confirming evaluation of conclusions by research participants, convergence of multiple sources of evidence, control of unwanted influences, and theoretical fit. Maximum confidence in the believability of conclusions comes from support

provided by participants' agreement, analysis of multiple sources of data, others' interpretations, and prediction based on relevant theoretical models (i.e., a predicted pattern matches an actual pattern). As such, credibility is related to construct validity, uncovered by evidence revealing that the construct being studied is the same one theory presumes exists. The concept of credibility is also close to the idea of internal validity as used in quantitative designs (ruling out alternative hypotheses while controlling extraneous influences and artifacts that distort findings).

Many researchers argue that the most important criterion for judging a qualitative study is its credibility. To assess credibility, one would focus on the data quality, its analysis, and resultant conclusions. Any weak link here would threaten the usefulness of the study. According to Miles and Huberman (1994), qualitative analysis includes three streams of activity, each deserving sharp focus to evaluate credibility.

   a. data reduction (simplifying complex data

by, for example, extracting recurring themes via coding);

b. **data display** (e.g., matrices, charts, graphs, even stories); and,

c. **drawing conclusions and verifying them as a means of testing the validity of findings.**

Qualitative researchers agree on strategies that promote trustworthiness in a study. These procedures are described well by Merriam (2009) and include:

1. Triangulation, or multiple sources of data as evidence
2. Member checks, or arranging for those who provided data to evaluate the conclusions
3. Saturation, or continuous data collection to the point where more data add little to regularities that have already surfaced
4. Peer review, or consultation with expert
5. Audit trail, or the detailed record of data collection and rationale for important decisions
6. Thick description, or providing rich detail of

the context of the study

7. Plausible alternatives, or the rationale for ruling out alternative explanations and accounting for discrepant (negative) cases

ASSESSMENT TASKS

I. **Directions:** Identify the what is being describes in the following statement.

1. It is an informal conversational interview; it is emergent, spontaneous, and usually occurs in the field.

2. It involves may take place in natural settings and involves the researcher taking lengthy and descriptive notes of what is happening.

3. Type of interviewing that encourages researchers to build a reciprocal relationship between themselves and their participants.

4. An interview that is flexible and organic in nature and uses questions or topics of dialogue that vary from one participant to

the next.

5. An interview that takes place across a range of social actors who hold similar positions and have the appropriate experiences, attending to the research goals.

6. The researcher's stance is either hidden from the group or in a completely public setting.

7. This type of interview encourages the researcher to share his/her expertise with participants who may be appreciated as supportive.

8. This type of question gets at the things a person does or did, his or her behaviors, actions, and activities.

9. It uses a systematic procedure to analyze documentary evidence and answer specific research questions.

10. The researcher is interested in a person's s beliefs or opinions, what he or she thinks about something.

II.   **Directions:** Consider each of the following scenario, and answer the accompanying questions.

5. Imagine that you want to conduct a documentary analysis to study the nature of students' interaction in an inclusionary classroom – that is, one in which students with disabilities are educated along with their nondisabled peers. Qualitative researchers who use documentary analysis as a research collection design sometimes use documents and artifacts as data. Give one concrete example of each of these types of records, and explain how you could use it to address the nature of student interactions in an inclusionary classroom.

6. Ms. Jatme Meñoza is an undergraduate college student who is interested in conducting fieldwork for an ethnographic study of social interaction among high school girls. Give at least three specific examples of the types of data Ms. Meñoza might collect for this type of study.

7. Should Ms. Jatme Meñoza approach her study as participant observer? Explain your answer,

paying attention to the benefits and pitfalls of this method.

PERFORMANCE TASKS

TASK 1: Planning for Observation

In an observational study, the results are a rich description of the events, people, and interactions around the topic of interest as you observe them. Try to create a guide on what you need to observe. Then based on the guide visualize what you can observe in your data collection. Write them down here as a draft. Try to apply the lessons learned in this module.

TASK 2: Interviewing Planning

Consider your own research questions and the type of interview that you have chosen to conduct; an unstructured, semi-structured, or structured interview. Prepare some questions as guide. Begin with your opening questions and consider how you will start your interview. It may be that your interviewees answer all your research questions based upon the opening questions. A more likely scenario is that you will need to use a range of questioning techniques from these above in order to gain the information that you want. It is a good idea to plan some of these questions in advance as far you can. Whether you use them all and whether you ask more "on the spot questions" is dependent upon your skills as an interviewer.

Creating an interview plan is a crucial step in the qualitative interview process. The wording of your questions is key in that it is important to develop questions that are open-ended and not leading. You do not want to use suggestive language, you instead want the participant is be able to share their experiences or ideas with you without feeling as though you want to hear a specific answer. Questions should be succinct, straightforward, and free of jargon. Make the questions easy for the participant to understand so that they feel comfortable throughout the interview process.

Conduct a pilot study to practice asking the questions and having someone answer them. Pilot testing allows you a chance to see what questions work and which do not. Don't be afraid to throw a question away when pilot testing your interview questions. This will also provide an opportunity to see if you have enough questions prepared to gain an in-depth insight into the topic being researched. You may be surprised at how many questions you will need to create in order to conduct a thorough and substantial interview.

Cited References and Suggested Readings

Adler, P. A., & Adler, P. (1998). *Observational techniques*. In N. K. Denzin & Y. S. Lincoln (Edition), *Collecting and interpreting qualitative materials* (pp. 79–109). Sage Publications, Inc.

Amarado, R. D. & Talili, I. N. (2017). *Qualitative Research: A Practical Approach*. Mutya Publication House. Inc.

Apolonio, J. A., & Basilan, MLJ. C. (2017). *Practical Research 1.* Unlimited Books Library Services & Publishing Inc.

Atkinson, R. (2012). *The life story interview as a mutually equitable relationship*. Sage Publications, Inc.

Barrot, J. S. (2017). *Practical Research 1 for Senior High School*. C & E Publishing, Inc.

Braun, V., & Clarke, V. (2013). *Successful Qualitative Research: A Practical Guide for Beginners*. Sage Publications, Inc.

Brinkmann, S., & Kvale, S. (2015). *Interviews: An introduction to qualitative research interviewing (3rd edition)*. Sage Publications, Inc.

Ellis, C., & Berger, L. (2003). *Their story/my story/our story:*

Including the researcher's experience in interview research. Sage Publications, Inc.

Francisco, P M. S., Francisco, V. S., & Arlos, A.P. (2016). ***Practical Research 1: Qualitative Research.*** Mindshapers Co., Inc.

Kvale, S. (2007). ***Doing interviews. In U. Flick (Edition), The Sage qualitative research kit***. Sage Publications, Inc.

Lincoln, Y. S., & Guba, E. G. (1985). ***Naturalistic observation.*** Sage Publications, Inc.

Lindlof, T. R., & Taylor, B. C. (2019). ***Qualitative communication research methods (4th edition)***. Sage Publications, Inc.

Merriam, S. B. (2009). ***Qualitative research: A guide to design and implementation.*** Jossey-Bass.

O'Leary, Z. (2014). ***The essential guide to doing your research project (2nd edition).*** Sage Publications, Inc.

Patton , M. Q.(2002). ***Qualitative research and evaluation methods (3rd edition)***. Sage Publications, Inc.

Rubin, H. J., & Rubin, I. S. (2011). ***Qualitative interviewing: The art of hearing data (3rd edition).*** Sage Publications, Inc.

Samosa, R. C. (2021). ***Effectiveness of Claim, Evidence, and Reasoning as an Innovation to Develop Students' Scientific Argumentative Writing***. European Journal of Research Development and Sustainability, 2(5), 25-35. https://doi.org/10.17605/OSF.IO/76CG5.

Schensul, J. J., & LeCompte, M. D. (2013). ***Essential ethnographic methods: A mixed-methods approach. Ethnographer's toolkit, book 3 (2nd edition).*** AltaMira Press.

Spradley, J. (1979). ***The ethnographic interview***. Harcourt

Brace

Wengraf, T. (2001). *Qualitative research interviewing*. Sage Publications, Inc.

Tracy, S. J. (2020). *Qualitative Research Methods: Collecting Evidence, Crafting Analysis, Communicating Impact (2nd edition).* John Wiley & Son

Trainor, A. A., & Graue, E. (2013). *Reviewing Qualitative Research in the Social Sciences*. Taylor & Francis.

MODULE 7:

ANALYZING THE MEANING OF THE DATA AND DRAWING CONCLUSIONS

LEARNING OUTCOMES

At the end of this module, students should be able to:

1. infers and explain patterns and themes from data.

2. relates the findings with pertinent literature

Qualitative Data Analysis

After the data have been collected, the romance of fieldwork is over, and the researcher must concentrate solely on the task of data analysis. The researcher must fully examine each piece of information and, building on insights and hunches gained during data collection, attempt to make sense of the data as a whole. Qualitative data analysis is based on induction. The researcher starts with a large set of data representing many things and seeks to narrow them progressively into small and important groups of key data. No predefined variables help to focus analysis, as in quantitative research. The qualitative researcher constructs meaning by identifying patterns and themes that emerge during the data analysis.

Broadly, qualitative research is generally employed to support a researcher in generating a deep and nuanced understanding of a given phenomenon. The outcomes of such research range from generating findings that can inform practice to providing detailed descriptions of a given problem of practice to offering insights about professional practices within a given context and tackling issues related to the subjective nature of qualitative research among others. The potentiality of conducting qualitative research is notable and yet dependent upon researchers being able to conduct grounded, rigorous analyses, and more generally, understanding what it means to do qualitative analysis.

Broadly conceived, qualitative data analyses bring meaning to a data set (Anfara et al., 2002), with qualitative data including a wide range of materials (e.g., conversational data, images, observations, and unstructured, semi-structured, or structured interviews, among others). Indeed, qualitative data analysis means various things, as it is often aligned with a particular methodology, theoretical perspective, research tradition, and/or field (Lochmiller & Lester, 2017). Coffey and Atkinson (1996) remind us that "there is no single right way to analyze qualitative data; equally, it is essential to find ways of using the data to think with" (p. 2).

Miles and Huberman (1994) argued that there are several common practices that often (but not always) persist across qualitative approaches to analysis, including the following:

1. Affixing codes to a set of field notes drawn from observations or interviews;
2. Noting reflections or other remarks in the margins;
3. Sorting and sifting through these materials to identify similar phrases, relationships between variables, patterns, themes, distinct differences between subgroups, and common sequences;
4. Isolating these patterns and processes, commonalities and differences, and taking them out to the field in the next wave of data collection;
5. Gradually elaborating a small set of generalizations that cover the consistencies discerned in the data;
6. Confronting those generalizations with a formalized body of knowledge in the form of constructs or theories (p. 9).

Bueno (2016), enumerated some classification of qualitative analysis.

1. **Descriptive Analysis**. Researcher gives an

account of a place or process helping to visualize the situation as a means of understanding.

2. **Interpretative Analysis.** The researcher explains or creates generalizations to help develop new concepts or elaborate on existing ones with a goal to provide insights.

3. **Verification Analysis**. The researcher verifies assumptions, theories, and generalizations.

4. **Evaluative Analysis**. The researcher provides judgments about policies, practices, and attempts to answers such as "how was a process implemented?", "What was the process like?", How has it worked, for whom, and are there exceptions?"

Twelve Tips for Ensuring a Strong Foundation for Qualitative Analysis (Patton,2015).

1. **Begin analysis during fieldwork.** Note and record emergent patterns and possible themes while still in the field. Add confirming cases to deepen analysis and possible disconfirming

cases to test thematic ideas while still in the field.

2. **Inventory and organize the data.** Make sure you have all the interviews, observations, and documents that constitute the raw data of your qualitative inquiry. Check that the data elements and sources are labeled, dated, and complete.

3. **Fill in gaps in the data**. As soon as possible, fill in the gaps in the data while connections in the field are fresh. If later interviews turn up issues that need to be checked out with earlier interviewees, do so quickly. If documents are missing, take steps to get them.

4. **Protect the data.** Back them up. Make sure the data are secure.

5. **Express appreciation**. Thank those who have provided you with data. Fieldwork creates relationships. Once out of the field, analysis and writing can take a lot of time. Don't wait until it's all done to show your appreciation to those who have provided you with data. Follow up with appropriate expressions of appreciation

sooner rather than later. Procrastination can too easily lead to never getting it done. Do it!

6. **Reaffirm the purpose of your inquiry.** Restate the purpose of your inquiry, and therefore the purpose of your analysis. Purpose drives the analysis. Design frames and sets the stage for analysis. Be clear about why you're doing this work, revisit and reengage with the questions and the purposeful sampling strategy that have guided your inquiry, and get clear about the primary product that you are producing that will fulfill your study's purpose and answer priority questions in accordance with your design.

7. **Review exemplars for inspiration and guidance**. Reexamining classic works in your field can be a source of inspiration. They are classics for a reason. Keep those exemplars nearby to reinvigorate and motivate you when the drudgery of analysis sets in or doubts about what you're finding emerge. Those who wrote the classics experienced analysis fatigue and doubts as well. They persevered. So, will

you.

8. **Make qualitative analysis software decisions**. If you're using qualitative data management software, learn how to use it effectively. Locate technical support. Practice data entry and some simple analysis. All qualitative analysis software has a steep learning curve. Leave time and mental space to learn if you're new to the software. If you're an old hand, check out new versions and features that might be useful.

9. **Schedule intense, dedicated time for analysis.** Qualitative analysis requires immersion in the data. It takes time. Make time. Set a realistic schedule. Enlist the support of family, friends, and colleagues to help you stay focused, and give the analysis the dedicated time it deserves.

10. **Clarify and determine your initial analysis strategy.** Inductive qualitative analysis can follow a number of pathways. Various theoretical traditions (ethnography, phenomenology, constructivism, realism, etc.)

provide frameworks and guidance. Data can be organized and reported in different ways: case studies, question-by-question interview analysis, storytelling, elucidating sensitizing concepts or principles, and thematic analysis, among others. Grounded theory provides a highly prescriptive framework for analysis. Decide what strategy fits your purpose, write it down with your rationale, and get started analyzing. This process involves reconnecting with the theoretical and strategic framework that presumably guided design decisions and the formulation of your inquiry questions.

11. **Be reflective and reflexive**. Monitor your thought processes and decision-making criteria. Be in touch with predispositions, biases, fears, hopes, constraints, blinders, and pressures you're under. Qualitative analysis is ultimately highly personal and judgmental. You are the analyst. Observe yourself. Learn about yourself and your analysis processes, both cognitively and emotionally.

12. **Start and keep an analysis journal.** Document analysis decisions, emergent ideas, forks in the road, false starts, dead ends, breakthroughs, eureka moments, what you learn about analysis, what you learn about the focus of the inquiry, and what you learn about yourself. You may think you'll remember these things. You won't. Document the analytical process—in-depth, systematically, and regularly. That documentation is the foundation of rigor. Qualitative analysis is a new stage of fieldwork in which you must observe and document your own processes even as you are doing the analysis.

Coding

Coding is an almost universal process in qualitative research; it is a fundamental aspect of the analytical process and the ways in which researchers break down their data to make something new. Coding is the process of analyzing qualitative text data by taking them apart to see what they yield before putting the data back together in a meaningful way (Creswell, 2015). More so, it is a process of assigning meaning to different parts of the data (Miles et .al, 2014). We have to go through the whole set of our data to code it. It is true that some parts of our data may be irrelevant to our topic. In that case, we can't code the part. For instance, in the middle of your interview, something may come up that is off-topic. You cannot include that off-topic data in your coding.

The following are the cycle or levels of coding (Wa-Mbaleka & Gladtone, 2018)
Level 1 Coding: Assigning the Codes.

You read every single sentence, listen to every recorded interview (if you recorded), and you start assigning meaning to some chunks of your data. The label you assigning to the smallest meaningful unit of qualitative research data is called code. Each code has only one meaning. A code can be a word or a group of a few that represent one meaning.

Level 2 Coding: Classifying Codes into Categories

You classify the codes into broader concepts. These concepts are called categories. A category can therefore be defined as a concept that summarizes a set of codes that are related in meaning. Each category can be made of two to five codes. When you get more than five codes together, it may be a better idea to divide them into two separate categories to be able to visualize your data more easily.

Level 3 Coding: Classifying Categories into Themes

You now classify the categories into the biggest ideas of your data, which we call themes.

Illustrative Example of Coding

Getting Parents More Involved in School Activities in Cavite, Philippines: A Case Study

Level 1 Coding: Assigning Codes	
Text	**Code**
I wish I could participate more in my children's academic activities (1), but I can't. I work from 6am to 9pm every day (2) to be able to meet the needs of my children (3) I should have a better – paying job (4) That could certainly allow me to work fewer hours and spend more time helping my children.	(1) willing to help children (2) cause 1: time limit (3) cause 2: prioritizing other needs of the children. (4) solution 1: better – paying jobs

Level 2 Coding: Classifying Codes into Categories	
Codes	**Category**
• Unstable job • Long working hours • Walking long time	Low income

Level 3 Coding: Classifying Categories		
Codes	**Categories**	**Themes**
• Unstable job • Long working hours • Walking long time	Low income	
• Have too many children • Sickly children • Limited food	Inability to meet children's basic needs	Cause 1: Poverty
• Walking to work • Too much time in household chores	Loss of time	

Coding Strategies

1. **Description-focused coding.**

   Describing relevant excerpt selected. Then create a code that reflects the description of the excerpt (with the research question in mind).

   Features

   - Tell what it is
   - No passing judgment
   - No implying
   - No interpretation

2. **Interpretation–focused coding.**

   Making sense of the relevant excerpt selected. Then, create a code that reflects the interpretation of the excerpt (with the research question in mind

   Features

   - Tell what it is
   - Reflect possible
   - Consider the context.

3. **Presumption-focused coding**

   Making claims based on the evidence in the data. Then, creating codes that reflect the claims.

Thematic Analysis

Thematic analysis is the most commonly used method in Qualitative research. To help you with the most practical model that combines components from many different models, let' use the one introduced by Wa-Mbaleka (2018). It is based on the 10 steps, presented systematically below. Although they are presented in some kind of consecutive order, in practice, these steps may overlap and may even change in order of implementation. Qualitative research data analysis is reiterative process.

1. **Prepare and organize your data.**
   a. Select needed data (from different sources).
   b. Chose the data that truly fits for your study
   c. Remove any data that does not seem to have any clear connection to your research study.
   d. Transcribe your interview (if needed or if required).
   e. Create folder for different types of data; for example, interviews, focus group discussion, videos, and photos.
   f. Within each folder, create sub-folders as the

need arises. For instance, within the folder for participants, you can have one sub-folder per participant and make sure everything related to that participant is placed in that sub-folder.

g. Develop an identification system. For instance, P1 may be used for the first participant, P2 for the second participant, S1 for the first school, I2 for the second interview, C3 for the third company, Ch4 for the fourth church, and B5 for the fifth bank, and so on. Such an identification system helps organize and retrieve data more effectively. It saves you a lot of time.

h. For each identification code, you need to develop your own interpretation. For instance, you can have a table. In the rows, you can have P1, P2, P3, P4, etc. for the participants.

i. You can then have a different column that provides specific important information for each participant such as a row for gender, educational attainment, number of years of experience, socio-economic status, profession, region, marital status, etc.

j. You can use Microsoft word or excel to work on this first.

2. **Read your transcript (or go over your data) once or twice.**

   a. This helps you to get a general idea about your data.

   b. You may read all your transcript or just a few of them at this point.

   c. You can already start writing down the big ideas that came to your mind as you read your transcripts or listen to the interviews. These are what we referred to earlier as analytic notes.

3. **Develop your coding manual.**

   a. Code one or two transcripts /interviews.

   b. Develop your coding manual, also known as codebook or coding scheme or list of codes, as you code the first one or two sets of data.

   c. Continue to improve it as you code more data until no additional code merges.

4. **Code all your data.**

   a. Code more transcripts.

   b. Refine your coding scheme.

   c. Code all your data.

   d. Have an illustration or definition for each code. Such an illustration can be added to your report as an appendix.

5. **Find recurring or repeating ideas.**

   a. Find recurring or repeating ideas.

   b. Group them together in the second level of coding.

   c. Assign the group a specific name which is the category.

   d. Remove codes that did not recur, if they don't seem to be relevant to the study.

6. **Abstract your ideas.**

   a. Put the codes together in different groups called categories.

   b. For each category, make sure you have some illustrations as evidenced in the direct quotes from your data (e.g., direct quotes from the interviews or a statement from a document that you collected).

    c. Put categories together in a different group called themes.

7. **Write the interpretation of all your data.**

    a. Organize your themes logically in relation to your research study.

    b. Create tables, charts, figures, or other types of graphics to display the synthesis of your data.

    c. For each section, discuss the different categories.

    d. Use some direct quotes from your transcripts or other data as illustrations of each category.

    e. End the discussion of each theme with a short synthesis and some connection to the research problem or research questions. Such short syntheses will help you later when it comes to your conclusion chapter where you synthesize all your findings.

8. **Write your report.**

    a. Have a logical order of presenting your results.

    b. Start with the demographic information of

your participants. This helps people to know information such as age group, socio-economic status, completed education, marital status, and profession of each participant. Of course, you need to request and report only the information that is important to understand better the research study. For instance, it would be meaningless to report the marital status of high school students, if you had some of them in your research study because, by default, we know that high school students are supposed to be single.

c. Indicate what kind of data analysis you did and why you did and why you did it that way. It's preferable to follow a specific established model that is relevant to your research design.

d. You can have major sections of your results chapter divided by themes, by case (if it's multiple case study, for instance), by research question, or by phases (if your study is about process). Presenting your result by themes, however, is a lot more practical for new qualitative researchers.

e. Make sure to cite some of the direct quotes from your data to support your points.

f. Do not put more direct quotes in your results chapter than your own analysis and discussion.

g. Present your ideas clearly and logically so that it is easy for everyone to read and understand what you wrote.

h. Decide what writing style you will use and be consistent with it. It can be more artistic and more personal as suggested by Van Manen (2014) or much more structured as proposed by other scholars. Whichever style you use, it should effectively guide your readers to understand what you did, why and how you did it, and how you reached your conclusion.

i. Keep your audience in mind as you write your final report. By default, the first people who read your report will be teachers/professors. They, therefore, expect a more formal and technical than informal writing style.

  j. Present your finding logically, convincingly, and with clear evidence.

9. **Verify your finding and conclude.**

  a. Send your major findings to your participants for their final input. This is known as member check.

  b. Ask for peer review from your classmates, friends, or other qualitative research experts. This is known as peer review.

  c. Synthesize your findings and explain what they mean. Address the research questions, if you haven't done so.

  d. In your conclusion chapter (usually the last chapter), cite some of the existing literature. This helps you to compare and contrast your findings with what you have read during your review of the literature.

  e. Add recommendation for practical application: give specific recommendations on how people can apply what you found in your research study.

f. Add recommendation for additional research. if someone likes your research report and wishes to do another research study on the same topic, he/she should find these recommendations and follow up with them.

10. Make final revisions.

a. Review your manuscript and make it has a clear alignment with your research questions.

b. Make sure your research problem and research questions are addressed.

c. Check your tables, charts, and figures to make sure they are logically introduced, presented, and discussed.

d. Proofread your work.

e. Make sure all the chapters are well aligned.

f. If you used the future tense in your methodology section, now it's time to go back to that chapter and change the tense to the past. Be careful in this process because you may change the verb tense that wasn't supposed to be changed.

    g. Make sure all the headings fit well for the different sections where they are placed.

    h. Make sure to implement the criteria of a good qualitative research manuscript.

Discovering the Patterns

These are the six ways of looking for patterns in a particular research topic. The following make sense out of the data gathered.

1. **Frequencies** refer to how often a situation occurred.

   Illustrative Example:

   > How often does bullying occurs among selected public schools under study?

2. **Magnitude** provides the level of the situation.

   Illustrative Example:

   > What are the levels of bullying? How severe are they in the research locale?

3. **Structures** give information on whether types and relationships exist in the given situation.

   Illustrative Example:

> What are the different types of bullying? Are they related in any particular manner?

4. **Processes** denote if there are order and variation in the given research interest.

   Illustrative Example:

   > Is there any order among the elements of structure? Do bullies begins with verbal, move to social, then to physical and cyberbullying? Does the order of the elements differ?

5. **Causes** refer to how common and how the causes are.

   Illustrative Example:

   > What are the causes of bullying? It is common in public schools or private schools? Does it occur more often during break time or after class?

6. **Consequences** mean the effect, if there is in both short – term and long–term periods and the changes that the situation caused.

   Illustrative Example:

   > How does bullying affect the students in both short-term and log-term periods? What change did it cause to the bullied student?

Qualitative Data Process and Presentation

Data processes are any operation done on the data such as gathering and managing it. Data gathered may be processed by using a computer program and presented in textual, tabular, and graphical formats.

In the context of research, data presentation refers to the process of arranging data in a logical, sequential, and meaningful manner to make them acceptable for analysis and interpretation.

1. Textual Presentation

In the textual presentation, most cases use statements with numerals or numbers to describe data. This also includes reporting key findings under each main theme or category and by using applicable verbatim quotes to describe those findings.

Qualitative researchers often use figures and pictures to display their findings and argument the textual discussion. Below are some suggestions to report qualitative findings.

a. Construct a hierarchical tree diagram.

From broad themes, interconnection of

subthemes can be represented visually using a tree diagram

b. Capture ideas in figures

Illustrations with boxes themes showing connections best describe a figure. Hierarchy of themes may not be obvious in this illustration.

c. Draw a map.

Maps can depict the location of the research settings easily and clearly. They can also provide visuals for the researchers of the location of various activities or events.

2. Tabular Presentation

By definition, a table is a systematic arrangement of related data in which a row is designed for each group of numerical data and a column for each subgroup. This procedure is suggested to present the relationship of a given set of numerical information. If they exist, in definite and understandable forms.

3. Graphical Presentation

In qualitative research, graphs may represent individual categories and descriptive statistics, if needed. The commonly used descriptive statistics in qualitative research are percentage, frequency, measure of centrality (mean, median, and mode), and measure of variation (standard deviation). Qualitative data does not come with a pre-established ordering necessary for some statistical measures.

Interpretation of Qualitative Data

Interpretation of qualitative findings is a process of intellectualizing beyond the emerging themes to broader perspectives of the data. In simple terms, interpretation of findings is making sense of the data collected, and an act to identify the lessons learned from the study. In interpreting results, it is helpful to group similar responses into categories then identify usual patterns to derive meaning from what may seem unrelated and wordy responses. This strategy is very important in making sense of the outcomes of focus group discussions and interviews. It must also be remembered that interpretation depends on the point of view of the researcher. The researcher can interpret qualitative findings by the following:

1. **Extend the analysis by asking questions.** This strategy involves asking questions about the investigation and taking note of the possible results that can be drawn without actually making one. It may also include findings suggested by the data gathered, which are not part of the initial plan but can be considered for future research.

2. **Link results to personal experiences**. Interpreting and sharing data can be based on the researcher has a sole point of the view from becoming an expert on his/her data.

3. **Ask for advice from colleagues.** Colleagues in the same field can provide insights. However, the disadvantage of having much advice may give concurring or conflicting opinions.

4. **Contextualize findings in the literature.** Using other sources can be helpful in drawing out connections or supporting results and emphasize contributions of the research to the body of research.

5. **Direct to theory.** The attempt to develop a

theory from the data collected will connect the present study to larger issues and help in the abstraction and applications of localized findings. This may also include further meanings to the data of the study.

Relating the Finding with Pertinent Literature

No study in qualitative research is so novel or possesses such a restricted that it has absolutely no relation to previously published research. In a research study, the researcher will have to present an argument, or rather a set of arguments, about the significance of his results, about any limitations or problems of his research design or implementation, and consequent proposals for future work. This calls on his skills as a researcher to interpret the results he has obtained and to locate them in the context of existing research. Reference to the research literature usually occurs in the discussion section of a research study.

The discussion section should relate to those found in other studies, particularly if questions raised from prior studies served as the motivation for your research. This is important because comparing and contrasting the findings of other studies helps to support the overall importance of the results and it highlights how and in what ways the study differs from other research about the topic. There are two reasons for referring to the research literature. First, a researcher needs to compare his results with those reported previously. This allows him to show how his findings reflect, contradict or extend previous research. Second, when he is generalizing from his findings, he can use the existing literature to support the deductions arising from his research.

Illustrative Example of Relating the Finding with Pertinent Literature

Political Dynasty in Public Governance: A Close Encounter with the Cebuanos (Guarde et al., 2016)

Facebook Remained Exclusive for Politically Motivated Netizens Only

Since the key informants revealed that they were non-participative online because of the restraint sanctioned by their jobs of being government servants; and the limitations brought by varying motivations or predispositions, Facebook as a political tool remained an online site to perform political interactions more especially to the motivated netizens who represented mostly in the private sectors. As Ellison (2007) stated, "A politically motivated person whether offline or online would remain the same; otherwise he or she would be included regular participants in daily conversations like: sharing and liking to any political issues.

"There was a difference to being politically active online; Facebook was only for the netizens who were really politically active. I was not into politics and whether on a regular basis, I refused to talk about politics that much (KI-2)."

ASSESSMENT TASKS

I. **Directions:** Identify what is being described in the following statement.

1. It is coding strategies that make sense of the relevant excerpt selected. Then, create a code that reflects the interpretation of the excerpt.

2. It is a systematic arrangement of related data in which a row is designed for each group of numerical data and a column for each subgroup.

3. It is the process of analyzing qualitative text data by taking them apart to see what they yield before putting the data back together in a meaningful way.

4. A type of textual presentation of data that shows Illustrations with boxes themes showing connections best describes a figure.

5. Researcher gives an account of a place or process helping to visualize the situation as a means of understanding.

6. It is a process of intellectualizing beyond

the emerging themes to broader perspectives of the data.

7. It denotes if there are order and variation in the given research interest.

8. It is any operation done on the data such as gathering and managing it.

9. A type of textual presentation of data provide from broad themes, interconnection of subthemes can be represented visually using a tree diagram

10. It is referring to the process of arranging data in logical, sequential, and meaningful manner to make them acceptable for analysis and interpretation

II. **Directions:** Answer the following questions briefly.

1. Ms. Stefhany Balasta is a college student who is conducting a qualitative research study of mentoring among high school choir students. Ms. Balasta received permission to sit in the back of the choir room, and she took extensive field notes on social interactions between choir members during

practices. She also videotaped interviews with each choir member, as well as choir performances.

a. Describe the first steps Ms. Balasta must take before she can begin the analysis of her data.

b. Describe useful strategies that would help Ms. Balasta to organize her data in a preliminary way that will enable her to locate them more easily as she proceeds.

c. Explain how Ms. Balasta might identify preliminary categories that likely to be helpful in coding the data.

2. In a qualitative study, the interpretation of data is influenced by the researcher's biases and values to some extent, reflecting by the researcher – as – instrument. Qualitative research requires the researcher to make significant decisions and judgments throughout the data analysis process, not only about what strategies to use in general but also about which data are most likely to be noteworthy and how to

evaluate and code specific pieces of data. Consider the following questions about the researcher can use to minimum bias in the final analysis of data. Image that a political science researcher decided to conduct a qualitative case study of the political campaign of candidate for statewide office whom he believed to be running an unusually honest and ethical campaign. In the 6 months between the primary and the general election, the researcher observed the weekly community organizing meetings of the campaign staff, collected all of the press releases distributed to members of the media, videotaped all of the public statements made by campaign spokespeople, and conducted structured interviews with each member of the paid campaign staff as well as with the candidate.

    a. As an alternative to maintaining complete objectivity – a goal that is probably impossible – describe at least three strategies this researcher can use to strive for balance and fairness in his data analysis.

b. Describe how the participants in this qualitative study might themselves introduce bias in response to the researcher.

c. Explain how and why this researcher should deal with his potential biases when the time comes to write up his final research paper.

PERFORMANCE TASKS

Design and Make Results and Discussion

Directions: Looking your collected data from the survey questionnaire or interview, tally each of the responses of your participants/respondents by following the basic principles of qualitative procedure for thematic analysis. Show your findings in tables and interpret each of the findings with supported literature and studies.

Rubric for Writing the Results and Discussion

Criteria	Excellent 15-20	Good 8-14	Poor 1-7
Introduction	Use all of the titles of the subsection in the introduction as sign posts for the reader to know what is coming.	Preview the contents of the chapter. Explain what organization of the data and analysis using themes provided from design, instrument, or analysis and align with the research question.	Identify the problem & restate the research question (do not repeat your whole chapter 1).
Data Presentation	The findings are detailed and flow easily.	Visual representations (form of tables, figures, quotes, or photos) are properly identified, self-descriptive, informative, directly related to and referred to within the narrative of text, and immediately adjacent comments are provided.	Describe the findings within the context of the setting, questions, and field of education.
Data Analysis	Sufficient evidence is provided. Sophisticated explanation and integration of research in the field.	Iterative use a systematic review, make sure nothing is left out of analysis.	Appropriately analyze and explain your analysis.

Interpretation	Articulate how the author's insider/outsider impacted the findings and interpretations. Articulate insight gained from the study in reference to data analysis	Intelligently interpret using layman approach to explain contextualized data – so that anyone can understand findings and their value to the field. Include inconsistent findings and discuss possible alternative interpretations.	Interpret how you made sense of the findings outcomes are logically and systematically summarized and interpret in relation to their importance to the research questions.
Summary	Provide a transition to chapter 5	Re-articulate research question	Summarize key concepts in chapter 4

Cited References and Suggested Readings

Anderson, V. (2017). *Criteria for evaluating qualitative research*. Human Resource Development Quarterly, 28(2), 125–133. https://doi.org/10.1002/hrdq.21282.

Bueno, D. C. (2016). *Practical Qualitative Research Writing*. Great Books Trading.

Coffey, A., & Atkinson, P. (1996). *Making sense of qualitative data: Complementary research strategies*. Sage Publications, Inc.

Creswell, J. (2015). *30 Essential Skills for the Qualitative*

Researcher. Sage Publications, Inc.

Guarde, E. A., Rosaroso, R. C., Rama, F., Batac, R., & Lasala, G. (2016). ***Political Dynasty in Public Governance: A Close Encounter with the Cebuanos.*** Asia Pacific Journal of Multidisciplinary Research, 4(2), 29-36.

Lochmiller, C. R., & Lester, J. N. (2017). ***An introduction to educational research: Connecting methods to practice***. Sage Publications, Inc.

Miles, M. B., & Huberman, A. M. (1994). ***An expanded sourcebook: Qualitative data analysis (2nd edition).*** Sage Publications, Inc.

Patton, M. Q. (2015). ***Qualitative Research & Evaluation Methods: Integrating Theory and Practice (4th edition)***. Sage Publications, Inc.

Van Manen, M. (2014). ***Phenomenology of Practice: Meaning–giving method in phenomenological research and writing.*** Left Coast Press.

Wa – Mbaleka, S., & Gladstone, R. K. (2018). ***Qualitative Research for Senior High School.*** Oikos Biblios Publishing House.

Wa – Mbaleka, S., & Gladstone, R. K. (2018). ***Writing your thesis and dissertation qualitatively: Fear no more.*** Oikos Biblios Publishing House.

MODULE 8:

REPORTING AND SHARING THE FINDINGS

LEARNING OUTCOMES
At the end of this module, students should be able to:

1. draws conclusions from patterns and themes.

2. formulates recommendations based on conclusions.

3. lists references.

Conclusion

Conclusion is not simply a summary of the findings and the research conducted. Importantly, the conclusion provides a significant and vital opportunity to explain to the reader exactly what the research means to the various audiences who have an interest in the research. The conclusion provides the potential to explore the depth and details of the broader implications of the findings while stating the limitations of the research and clearly delineating the parameters. In qualitative research, the conclusion of a research is not expected to generalize its findings. Rather, what the conclusion should report clearly are its significant findings and how these expand the understanding of the phenomenon that was studied. This means asking questions such as: "Does my research findings expand the existing literature?" Do my research findings affirm what the literature says? If so, does, it proposes something new?

Types of conclusions for research papers (Samosa, et al. 2021).

1. **Summarizing conclusion.** A summarizing Conclusion is typically used for giving a clear summary of the main points of your topic and thesis. This is considered the most common form of conclusion, though some research papers may require a different style of conclusion. Common type of research papers calls for this kind of conclusion includes a persuasive essay, problem and solution research, argumentative papers, and scientific and historical topics.

2. **Externalizing conclusion.** An externalizing conclusion presents points or ideas that may not have been directly stated or relevant to the way you presented your research and thesis. However, these types of conclusions can be effective because they present new ideas that build off of the topic you initially presented in your research. Externalizing conclusions get readers thinking in new directions about the impact of your topic.

3. **Editorial conclusion.** In an editorial conclusion, you are presenting your own concluding ideas or commentary. This type of conclusion connects your thought to the research you present. You might state how you feel about outcomes, results, or the topic in general. The editorial conclusion can work especially well in research papers that present opinions, take a humanistic approach to a topic, or present controversial information.

Characteristics of Conclusions

1. Conclusions are inferences, deductions, abstractions, implications, interpretations, general statements, and/or generalization based upon the findings.
2. Conclusion should appropriately answer the specific questions raised at the beginning of the investigation in the order they have given under the statement of the problem.
3. Conclusions should point out what was factually learned from the inquiry.

4. Conclusion should be formulated concisely that is, brief and short, yet they convey all the necessary information resulting from the investigation.

Purposes of a Conclusion

1. Stress the importance of the thesis statement
2. Give the written work a sense of completeness.
3. Leave a final impression on the reader.
4. Demonstrates good organization.

Importance of a Good Conclusion (Prieto, et al. 2017)

A well-written conclusion provides you with important opportunities to demonstrate to the reader your understanding of the research problem. These includes:

1. **Presenting the last word on the issues you raised in your paper.** Just as the introduction gives the first impression to your reader, the conclusion offers a chance to leave a lasting impression. Do this, for example, by

highlighting key points in your analysis or results or by noting important or unexpected implications applied to practice.

2. **Summarizing your thoughts and conveying the larger significance of your study.** The conclusion is an opportunity to succinctly answer the "So what?" question placing the study within the context of past research about the topic you've investigated.

3. **Identifying how a gap in the literature has been addressed.** The conclusion can be where you described how previously identified a gap in the literature (described in your literature review section) has been filled by your research.

4. **Demonstrating the importance of your ideas**. Don't be shy. The conclusion offers you the opportunity to elaborate on the impact and significance of your findings.

5. **Introducing possible new or expanded ways of thinking about the research problem.** This does not refer to new information (which should be avoided), but to

other new insight and creative approaches for framing or contextualizing the research problem based on the results of your study.

Guidelines in Writing the Conclusions subsection of your study (Barrot, 2018).

1. **The conclusions drawn do not correspond to one item in the findings alone**. Each conclusion should instead be applicable to all of the findings in the study.

2. **At least one conclusion should directly address your general questions or objective.** For example, if your general research questions are "how does traffic impact the well-being of senior high school students in Marilao, Bulacan?" your conclusion can be "heavy traffic adversely affects the well-being of senior high school students in Mario, Bulacan."

3. **Each conclusion should be supported by sufficient evidence obtained during the study.** If there are very limited data to support a particular conclusion, consider replacing or

excluding this conclusion.

4. **In this subsection, avoid merely repeating the findings you stated in the summary.** Instead, make inferences regarding these findings.

5. **Limits the conclusion to the subject of the study, and avoid extending it to other populations or subjects from different contexts.** For example, when making a conclusion regarding school A, do not extend this conclusion B or school C.

6. **Observe other conventions in writing the conclusion subsections.** For example, avoid using numerals and figures since you are no longer reporting findings. In addition, avoid using terms that signify doubt as *may be, perhaps,* and *possibly*.

In drawing and verifying conclusions from qualitative data among the most useful in the analysis are:

1. **Noticing patterns and theme.** These are recurring themes that put together many separate pieces of data. The data may be

grouped according to a theme. It may however happen that evidence may be applicable to one or more themes.

2. **Making contrast and comparisons.** Comparison is a classic way to test a conclusion. The responses gathered from parents, students, teachers, and other groups can be compared and contrasted so that differences can be noted. When conflicting information comes up can refer to the sources of the different data.

3. **Clustering.** This process refers to the grouping of data then, conceptualizing information that has similar patterns or characteristics. it called "categorizing" because steps must be taken to ensure that other information is considered or included.

4. **Counting.** Qualitative research, as discussed is basically descriptive and goes beyond how much of something to describe the subject or topic under investigation. However, the number of times something occurs or is reported tells something about

important or how significant an item is.

Common Errors in making Qualitative Conclusions

1. When a concluding statement that the researchers think is correct and important is not supported by the study.

2. When a generalization is made beyond the questions, contexts, population, and interventions that were not actually studied.

3. When there is no caution on important limitations in methods and/or their execution in the study.

4. When there is false interpretation of statistical significance lacking in the study. When selective focus on some results while ignoring others and the pattern of results; and

5. When there is veering away from inference to values and speculation, with subjective wordings clearly the researchers' point of view.

Illustrative Example of Conclusion

Campus Bullying in the Senior High School: A Qualitative Case Study 9Galabo, 2019)

This study implies the strict implementation of Republic Act No. 10627 otherwise known as the Anti-Bullying Act of 2013 in secondary schools. A re-orientation of the implementing rules and guidelines may be needed in order that the students, parents, teachers and the entire community would be aware of their important role in addressing the problem on campus bullying. Besides, a school may have a peer counselor's organization or club that would help victims cope with their emotional distress caused by bullying. Future research about campus bullying may have better results when the participants may be escalated into a bigger number to generate substantive patterns, similarities and differences.

More in-depth and longitudinal study is recommended to enrich the body of knowledge and for the development of theoretical models of campus bullying. Moreover, the researcher may include not only the victims of bullying but also those bullies in the school of basic education, junior high school and senior high school. Campus bullying is prevalent in every school, specifically, inside the classroom. Teachers and students can be both victims and bullies; hence, it is a serious problem to address on. Classroom as a learning environment is not exempted from bullying, in fact, simple cases of it happen in the classroom. Bullying, if ignored, may create emotional and psychological effects on the part of the students. Hence, there is a big challenge on making a concrete intervention program which may help address problems on campus bullying.

Recommendations

Based on the findings and conclusions of the study, recommendations serve as practical suggestions for future research in similar fields. They are envisioned to further improve the pertinent variables that were the subject of the investigation undertaken.

The recommendations of your paper have two functions. While the implications identify the areas of concern that can be addressed based on the findings, the recommendations provided may be in terms of theoretical, practical, or methodological aspects. The second functions relate to how future studies can address the limitations of your research. For instance, if the sample size is one of the limitations of your study, you may state that future studies can increase the number of participants involved.

Here are the guidelines in writing the recommendations of your paper:

1. Write recommendations that match your conclusion.

2. Provide no more than two recommendations for future research. Your recommendation can

focus on specific agenda based on the findings of study.

3. Provide recommendation for the limitations of your study. However, avoid making recommendations for concerns that could have been easily addressed in the conduct of the study.

4. Make your recommendation as specific as possible for them to become practical and workable.

In writing a research report, the recommendations should be written in the future tense generally. The stylistic reason for the use of this tense suggests that the researcher is offering something that could be done in the near future.

Illustrative Example of Recommendation

> **Political Dynasty in Public Governance: A Close Encounter with the Cebuanos (Guarde et al., 2016)**
>
> The recommendations of the study will be limited to (1) social institutions to provide proper guidance on the use of proper discernment in making the right decisions on whom to vote, by not just relying on unprocessed opinions; (2) the university to conduct studies on the millennials' system of beliefs and practices in the use of Facebook in supporting their political candidate; and (3) the social media entrepreneurs that they may provide user-friendly programs for adults, the elderly, and persons with disabilities to have access on the use of political advertisements, political campaigns, and other platforms to increase a number of users.

Lists references

The reference list compiles all the bibliographic information for the materials you used in preparing your research. Providing a reference list aids your readers in tracing the works that guided you in conducting your study, thus making your research more reliable. It also helps you avoid committing intellectual dishonesty since a reference list is proof that you acknowledge other studies that shape your own.

Below are some guidelines you can follow in

listing your references (Barrot, 2017).

1. **Make sure that your reference list contains all of the works and publications you used for your research**. All the references that you cited in the text itself must be included in your reference list.

2. **Cite your sources completely**. Aside from providing the name of the references itself, you need to cite the author of the work; the publisher of the material (if it is printed); the date of its publication or release; and the date that you retrieved it (if it is an online reference).

3. **Exercise consistency in the format of your bibliographical entries**. Strictly follow the format for citing your references according to the citation style you are using in your research (APA, MLA, or Chicago). The citation style you are using will also determine the title or heading of your reference list. Paper written in the APA style uses heading "Reference", the MLA Style uses the heading "Works Cited," and the Chicago style uses the heading "Bibliography."

4. **Take note of other consideration in citing your references.** For instance, make sure to arrange your references alphabetically. In addition, use en dash (–) instead of a hyphen (-) when presenting range (e.g., 5 – 13)

Referencing with APA 7th Style – Brief Guide

All the materials referred to in the text and only those listed alphabetically in the references section of the manuscript should be written. Some examples are shown below.

For Reference Type

1. **Book & ebook with DOI**

    Illustrative Example:

    Ewert, E. W., Mitten, D. S., & Overholt, J. R. (2014). *Natural environments and human health.* CAB International. https://doi.org/10.1079/9781845939199.0000.

    Include the DOI using the format https://doi.org/10.xxxx/xxxx

2. **Book & ebook without DOI, ebook without DOI from research databases**

Illustrative Example:

> Foxall, G. R. (2018). *Context and cognition in consumer psychology: How perception and emotion guide action.* Routledge.

Use the copyright date. For more than one publisher, list all publishers in the order that they appear, separated by a semicolon. Do not include the database name or URL.

3. **Article with DOI from research databases.**

   Illustrative Example:

> Washington, E. T. (2014). An overview of cyberbully in higher education. *Adult Learning, 26*(1), 21–27. https://doi.org/10.1177/1045159514558412

4. **Article without DOI: From research databases, or From a Print journal**

   Illustrative Example:

> Moody, M. S. (2019). If instructional coaching really works, why isn't it working? *Educational Leadership, 77*(3), 30–35

articles from most academic research databases.

5. **Open access journal article without DOI**

   Illustrative Example:

   > Dayton, K. J. (2019). Tangled arms: Modernizing and unifying the arm-of-the-state doctrine. *The University of Chicago Law Review, 86*(6), 1497–1737. https://bit.ly/2SkWwc.

   Include the URL for articles without a DOI and with a non-database URL, e.g. free online journal articles

6. **Webpage, no date**

   Illustrative Example:

   > Athletics New Zealand. (n.d.). *Form a new club.* http://www.athletics.org.nz/Clubs/Starting-a-New-Club.

   When the author and site name is the same, omit the site name.

7. **Webpage, with a date**

   Illustrative Example:

   > Monaghan, E. (2019, December 10). *5 reasons modern slavery at sea is still possible in 2019.* Greenpeace. https://bit.ly/2PIXjqc.

   If the page you are citing includes a last updated date, use that date. Include the name of the website in the reference.

8. YouTube video or other streaming video.

Illustrative Example:

> MSNBC. (2020, January 7). *Julián Castro endorses Elizabeth Warren* [Video]. YouTube. https://www.youtube.com/watch?v=Uk2Tzc8H5po.

9. Conference paper

Illustrative Example:

> Mason, I., & Missingham, R. (2019, October 21–25). *Research libraries, data curation, and workflows* [Paper presentation]. eResearch Australasia Conference, Brisbane, QLD, Australia. https://bit.ly/2RGcFdn.

After the title, include a label in square brackets that matches the description of the presentation e.g. [paper presentation]. Create a short URL using https://bitly.com

By Author

1. One author

Illustrative Example:

> Pilger, J. (2006). *Freedom next time*. Bantam.

2. Two authors

Illustrative Example:

> Shaw, R., & Eichbaum, C. (2008). *Public policy in New Zealand: Institutions, processes and outcomes.* Pearson Education.

3. 3 or more authors, up to 20 authors

Illustrative Example:

> Watson, S., Gunasekaran, G., Gedye, M., van Roy, Y., Ross, M., Longdin, L., & Brown, L. (2003). *Law of business organizations* (4th ed.). Palatine Press.

List all authors up to and including 20. The last author's surname is preceded by an ampersand (&).

4. 21 or more authors

Illustrative Example:

> Loannidis, N. M., Rothstein, J. H., Pejaver, V., Middha, S., McDonnell, S., Baheti, S. Musolf, A., Li, Q., Holzinger, E., Karyadi, D., Cannon-Albright, L., Teerlink, C. C., Stanford, J. L., Isaacs, W. B., Xu, J.,Cooney, K., Lange, E., Schleutker, J., Carpten, J. D., ... Weiver, S. (2016). Revel: An ensemble method for predicting the pathogenicity of rare missense variants. *American Journal of Human Genetics,* 99(4), 877–885. https://doi.org/10.1016/j.ajhg.2016.08.016.

List the first 19 authors, then insert three dots (ellipsis …) and add the last author's name.

5. Group (corporate) author with abbreviation.

Illustrative Example:

> New Zealand Health Information Service. (2003). *Report on maternity: Maternal and new-born inequalities in Aotearoa New Zealand*. Otago University Press.

Do not include an abbreviation for a group author in a reference list entry.

6. Author in secondary citations.

Illustrative Example:

> Coltheart, M., Curtis, B. Atkins, P., & Haller, M. (1993). Models of reading aloud: Dual-route and parallel-distributed-processing approaches. *Psychological Review*, 100, 589–608.

Enter the reference list for the source you have read (secondary source).

7. Author of a chapter in an edited book.

Illustrative Example:

> Easton, B. (2008). Does poverty affect health? In K. Dew & A. Matheson (Eds.), Understanding health inequalities in Aotearoa New Zealand (pp. 97–106). Otago University Press.

ASSESSMENT TASKS

I.   **Direction:** Identify what is being describe in the following statement.

1. It provides the potential to explore the depth and details of the broader implications of the findings while stating the limitations of the research and clearly delineating the parameters.

2. It serves as practical suggestions for future research in similar fields.

3. These are recurring themes that put together many separate pieces of data.

4. It is typically used for giving a clear summary of the main points of your topic and thesis.

5. This process refers to the grouping of data then, conceptualizing information that has similar patterns or characteristics.

6. It presents points or ideas that may not have been directly stated or relevant to the way you presented your research and thesis.

7. It complies all the bibliographic information for the materials you used in preparing your research.

II. **Directions;** Write an APA Style reference list entry for the published work using the source information provided.

1. **Source Information**

   Document type: Journal article (Section 10.1)

   Authors: Kenneth Nowack and Paul Zak

   Publication year: 2020

   Article title: Empathy enhancing antidotes for interpersonally toxic leaders

   Journal information: Consulting Psychology Journal: Practice and Research, Volume 72, Issue 2, pages 119–133.

   DOI: https://doi.org/10.1037/cpb0000164

2. **Source Information**

   Document type: Journal article (Section 10.1) **Authors: Katharina** Bernecker and Jule Kramer **Publication year:** 2020

   Article title: Implicit theories about willpower are associated with exercise levels during the academic examination period

Journal information: Sport, Exercise, and Performance Psychology, Volume 9, Issue 2, pages 216–231

DOI: https://doi.org/10.1037/spy0000182

3. **Source Information**

Document type: Edited book chapter (Section 10.3)

Chapter authors: T. Lindsey Burrell, William Sharp, Cristina Whitehouse, and Cynthia R. Johnson

Publication year: 2019

Chapter title: Parent training for food selectivity in autism spectrum disorder

Book editors: Cynthia R. Johnson, Eric M. Butter, and Lawrence Scahill

Book title: Parent training for autism spectrum disorder: Improving the quality of life for children and their families

Chapter page range: 173–202

Publisher: American Psychological Association

DOI: https://doi.org/10.1037/0000111-008

PERFORMANCE TASKS

Design and Make Summary of Finding, Conclusion, Recommendation, and Reference List

1. Write your summary of finding based on the sequences from your research question or research objectives.

2. Write the conclusion of your study based on the sequences from your research question or research objectives.

3. Write the recommendation of your study Use the following guide questions.

   a. What can you recommend to future researchers to prevent the occurrence of negative results in the study?

   b. What can you recommend as new or additional courses of action to improve or to make a more effective program or policies?

   c. What possible areas of research within the topic can be studied further by future researchers who are interested to study the same topic?

4. Make the reference list for your research paper.

follow the correct format and citation style.

Rubric for Writing the Conclusions and Recommendations

Criteria	Excellent 15-20	Good 8-14	Poor 1-7
Conclusions	Explains the research problem very clearly and how the study adds new understanding or fills up an important gap in the literature; explains very clearly how the research contributes to new knowledge or how it provides a new understanding or interpretation of the research problem.	Explains the research problem fairly well and how the study adds new understanding or fills up an important gap in the literature; explains fairly well how the research contributes to new knowledge or how it provides a new understanding or interpretation of the research problem.	Does not explain the research problem clearly and how the study adds new understanding or fills up an important gap in the literature; does not explain clearly how the research contributes to new knowledge or how it provides a new understanding or interpretation of the research problem.
Recommendations of the study	Explain the weaknesses and shortfalls of the research very clearly; clearly provide new or additional courses of action to improve the research or to make it more effective.	Explain the weakness and shortfalls of the research fairly well; provide some new or additional courses of action to improve the research or to make it more effective.	Do not explain the weaknesses and shortfalls of the research clearly. Do not provide any new or additional course of action to improve the research or to make it more effective.

Reference	Done in the correct format with no errors.	Done in the correct format with few errors.	Done in the correct format with some errors.

Course Requirements in Qualitative Research

Oral Presentation & Research Report

Direction: Write and submit the draft of your research report and present orally. Your Output will be assessed using the following rubrics below.

Rubric for Writing the Research Report

Criteria	Excellent 16-20	Very Good 11-15	Good 6-10	Needs Improvement 1-5
Introduction/ Thesis	exceptional introduction that grabs the interest of the reader and states the topic. **thesis is exceptionally clear, arguable, well-developed, and a definitive statement	*proficient introduction that is interesting and states topic. **thesis is a clear and arguable statement of position.	*basic introduction that states topic but lacks interest. **thesis is somewhat clear and arguable.	*weak or no introduction of topic. **paper's purpose is unclear/thesis is weak or missing.
Quality of Information/ Evidence	*paper is exceptionally researched, extremely detailed, and historically accurate. **information clearly relates to the thesis.	*information relates to the main topic. **paper is well-researched in detail and from a variety of sources.	*information relates to the main topic, few details and/or examples are given. **shows a limited variety of sources.	*information has little or nothing to do with the thesis. **information has weak or no connection to the thesis.

Support of Thesis/Analysis	*exceptionally critical, relevant, and consistent connections made between evidence and thesis. **excellent analysis.	*consistent connections made between evidence and thesis **good analysis.	*some connections made between evidence and thesis. **some analysis.	*Limited or no connections made between evidence and thesis. **lack of analysis.
Organization/ Development of Thesis	*exceptionally clear, logical, mature, and thorough development of the thesis with excellent transitions between and within paragraphs.	*clear and logical order that supports thesis with good transitions between and within paragraphs.	*somewhat clear and logical development with basic transitions between and within paragraphs.	*lacks development of ideas with weak or no transitions between and within paragraphs.
Conclusion	*excellent summary of a topic with concluding ideas that impact the reader. **introduces no new information.	*good summary of topic with clear concluding ideas. **introduces no new information.	*basic summary of topic with some final concluding ideas. **introduces no new information.	*lack of summary of topic.
Style/Voice	*style and voice are not only appropriate to the given audience and purpose, but also show originality and creativity. **word choice is specific, purposeful, dynamic, and varied. ***sentences are clear, active (subject-verb-object), and to the point.	*style and voice appropriate to the given audience and purpose. **word choice is specific and purposeful, and somewhat varied throughout. ***sentences are mostly clear, active (SVO), and to the point.	*style and voice somewhat appropriate to given audience and purpose. **word choice is often unspecific, generic, redundant, and clichéd. ***sentences are somewhat unclear; excessive use of passive voice.	*style and voice inappropriate or do not address given audience, purpose, etc. **word choice is excessively redundant, clichéd, and unspecific. ***sentences are very unclear.

Grammar/Usage/ Mechanics	*control of grammar, usage, and mechanics. **almost entirely free of spelling, punctuation, and grammatical errors.	*may contain few spelling, punctuation, and grammar errors.	*contains several spelling, punctuation, and grammar errors that detract from the paper's readability.	*so many spelling, punctuation, and grammar errors that the paper cannot be understood.

Rubric for Presentation and Oral Defense

Criteria	Excellent presentation 15-20	Good presentation 8-14	Poor presentation 1-7
Introduction	contains a complete and well-organized overview statement.	Contains a complete but somewhat disorganized overview statement.	Provides no overview. statement or statement is so short as to be useless.
Completeness	addresses all required research guideline elements very well.	addresses most of the required research guidelines. elements fairly well.	addresses a few of the research guideline elements or does so poorly.
Organization	is well organized, moving from general topics to specific details; provides a good explanation of the work.	is somewhat disorganized and provides too much detail without giving a good explanation of the work.	is disorganized and deals completely with details without providing a broad explanation of the work.

Findings	a student has made significant findings that are evidence base, accurate, and clearly expressed.	student has made few significant findings or finding is inconclusive.	student has made no significant findings and has not met objectives.
Technology	makes effective use of technology to find answer(s) to leading question(s).	makes improper use of technology to find answer(s) to leading question(s).	makes no use of technology to find answer(s) to leading question(s).
Speaking Skills	uses presentation resources as a guide, gives detailed explanations, is easily understandable, and keeps eye contact with the audience.	relies heavily on presentation to make report; somewhat comfortable with the topic.	essentially reads the material from a presentation to make the report; clearly uncomfortable with the topic.
Visual Aids	contains visual aides that help audience understand work; visuals have a neat and professional look, easily understood; used well to make points.	contains few or inadequate visual aids or visual aids have a neat and professional appearance, but poorly used in making points.	contains no visual aids or visual aids are so poorly constructed as to be worthless.

Cited References and Suggested Readings

Barrot, J. S. (2017). ***Practical Research 1 for Senior High School***. C & E Publishing, Inc.

Galabo, N. R. (2019). ***Campus Bullying In The Senior High School: A Qualitative Case Study***. International Journal of Scientific & Technology Research, 8 (4).

Guarde, E. A., Rosaroso, R. C., Rama, F., Batac, R., & Lasala, G. (2016). ***Political Dynasty in Public Governance: A Close Encounter with the Cebuanos.*** Asia Pacific Journal of Multidisciplinary Research, 4(2), 29-36.

Prieto, N. G., Naval, V. C., & Carey, T. G. (2017). ***Practical Research for Senior High School: Qualitative.*** Lorimar Publishing Inc.

Samosa, R.C., Magulod, G.C., Capulso, L.B., Delos Reyes, R.J., Luna, AR. F., Maglente, S.S., Orte, CJ.S., Olitres, BJ.D., Pentang, J.P. Vidal, CJ. E. (2021). ***How to Write and Publish Your Thesis***. Beyond Books Publication

ABOUT THE AUTHOR

PROF. RESTY CALO. SAMOSA

He is currently a full-time Senior High School Teacher, Research and Testing Coordinator of Graceville National High School, and Professorial Lecturer in Colegio de San Gabriel Arcangel. He has taught courses in almost all facets of Natural Science and Research at Secondary and Tertiary Levels. He obtained his license as an educator in 2015.

He continues to contribute to academe as a resource speaker, lecturer, thesis adviser, statistician, evaluator, demonstration teacher, and paper presenter at various seminars, conferences, and science fairs. Prof. Samosa fosters his professional growth by attending international, national, and regional conferences and seminar-workshop, and by being an active member of the Philippine Association for the Career Advancement of Educators (PACAE), Philippine Educational Measurement and Evaluation Association, Inc. (PAMEA) Biology Teachers Association of the Philippines (BIOTA), Philippine Association of Physics and Science Instructors (PAPSI) and

Leadership in Education Academy & Development (LEAD) - Philippines.

He also published several textbooks includes the following Understanding the End- to End Praxis of Quantitative Research: From Proposal to Paper Presentation, Exploring the Essence & Meaning from the Sound of Experiences: Qualitative Research Fundamentals Earth Science, General Biology 1, General Biology 2, General Chemistry 1, General Chemistry 2, Practical Research 2: Quantitative Research, Inquiries, Investigation, and Immersion, How to Write and Publish Your Thesis? and Publish Your Dissertation.

Interconnectedly, Prof. Samosa is a registered author and writer from National Book Development Board. In addition, he published research on high indexes international Journals; He also one of the Peer-Reviewers of the International Journal of Discoveries and Innovation in Applied Sciences, International Journal of Innovative Analyses and Emerging Technology, European Journal of Agricultural and Rural Education, International Review of Social Sciences Research and International Journal of Development and Public Policy.

He was the 2019 Action Research Champion in the 5th Division Research Congress for Teachers Category in the DepEd, City of San Jose del Monte, Bulacan. He also bagged the 2021 Global Outstanding Teacher (Leadership in Education Academy & Development- Philippines), 2021 Global Leader Award in Excellence Leadership & Global Educators Award in Research (Beyond Books Publication), 2021 Outstanding Teacher (World Educators Leaders' Summit & Awards), 2021 Outstanding Teacher in Research (Educacio World), 2021 Best Speaker in the Research Intellectual Discussions (Institute of Industry and Academic Research Incorporated in partnership with Universiti Teknologi Mara in Thailand), 2021 Outstanding Educator of Philippine Association of Physics and Science Instructors and 2020 Outstanding Teacher in Research (DepEd CSJM, Bulacan)